Lacan's Medievalism

Lacan's Medievalism

Erin Felicia Labbie

University of Minnesota Press
Minneapolis · London

Published by the University of Minnesota Press
111 Third Avenue South, Suite 290
Minneapolis, MN 55401-2520
http://www.upress.umn.edu

Library of Congress Cataloging-in-Publication Data

Labbie, Erin Felicia.
    Lacan's medievalism / Erin Felicia Labbie.
        p.   cm.
    Includes bibliographical references and index.
    ISBN-13: 978-0-8166-4515-2 (hc : alk. paper)
    ISBN-10: 0-8166-4515-9 (hc : alk. paper)
    ISBN-13: 978-0-8166-4516-9 (pb : alk. paper)
    ISBN-10: 0-8166-4516-7 (pb : alk. paper)
    1. Lacan, Jacques, 1901–1981.   2. Psychoanalysis and philosophy.
3. Medievalism.   4. Desire.   I. Title.
    B2430.L1464L33   2006
    150.19'5092—dc22   200617387

Printed in the United States of America on acid-free paper

The University of Minnesota is an equal-opportunity educator and employer.

12 11 10 09 08 07   10 9 8 7 6 5 4 3 2

In memory of my grandparents

Desire must be taken literally.
—Jacques Lacan, *Écrits*

Contents

Acknowledgments   xi

Introduction: The Unconscious Is Real   1

ONE
Singularity, Sovereignty, and the One   35

TWO
Duality, Ambivalence, and the Animality of Desire   66

THREE
Dialectics, Courtly Love, and the Trinity   107

FOUR
The Quadrangle, the Hard Sciences, and Nonclassical Thinking   146

FIVE
The Pentangle and the Resistant Knot   190

Notes   223

Index   255

Acknowledgments

The title of Jacques Derrida's essay "For the Love of Lacan" has never had so many meanings to me as it does upon completion of this book. As I began work on Jacques Lacan's medievalism several years ago, I drafted a line saying that it is not easy to dwell with desire. Over the past few years those who have had the patience to dwell with me in various ways have certainly learned how true this is, because knowing me has meant also to know the traces of all that I read. I am deeply indebted to my former teachers, my friends, my family, and my students, as they have supported my engagement with Lacan's work so that I could produce this "first book."

Offering critical advice, friendship, and care with constant grace throughout the various stages of my process toward completing this book is John Mowitt. I cannot thank him enough for all he has done to help me develop as a thinker, reader, writer, teacher, and friend. He showed me that not all rapports are impossible and reminded me that intellectual detours are fruitful, but sometimes the direct route is more effective in getting to where one wants to arrive.

L. O. Aranye Fradenburg taught me about the pleasures of visual and sartorial aesthetics as well as how to integrate those pleasures with my love of theory and the sacrifices necessary within writing. I thank her for the lessons that I continue to learn every day. I am grateful to Thomas Pepper for his engagement with my work and his helpful suggestion that I consider the role of ambivalence in courtly love.

My work is partly a bricolage of the methodological approaches I gained from my outstanding former professors F. R. Akehurst, Greg Clingham, Tom Conley, Rita Copeland, Andrew Elfenbein, Bill Gracie, Lee Horvitz, Catherine Liu, Marilyn Mumford, Michael Payne, Paula Rabinowitz, David Wallace, and John Watkins. Since completing my "formal" education, Ann Astell, Andrew Cole, John Ganim, Bruce Holsinger, Arkady Plotnitsky, Elizabeth Scala, and Peter Travis have, in their own individual ways, been supportive colleagues in the fields of medieval studies and critical theory.

I could not have made the revisions to this manuscript in the form it has taken without Alexandre Leupin's crucial suggestion that I focus the book on Lacan's view of the real as it is in dialogue with the scholastic debates about the existence of universals. His suggestions and his faith in my readings of Lacan are foundational to my work. I thank him and the anonymous readers from the University of Minnesota Press for their helpful suggestions with revisions.

I am grateful to my colleagues at Bowling Green State University in the Department of English, in the American Culture Studies Program, and in the Institute for the Study of Culture and Society. Each of my colleagues has assisted my development and the writing of this book at different stages. I thank Bill Albertini, Khani Begum, Ellen Berry, Kris Blair, Bill Coggin, Phil Dickinson, Allan Emery, Julie Haught, Gary Heba, Piya Pal Lapinski, Dan Madigan, Don McQuarie, Robert Meyers, Simon Morgan-Russell, Vicki Patraka, Timothy Pogačar, Phil Terrie, Sue Carter Wood, and Tom Wymer. My students in my seminars often provide moments of creation and insight, and I thank them for their engaged reading and dedication. Jay Clevenger's earnest and incisive questions throughout my seminars have helped me to discipline my own thinking. Eric Anderson, Tim Cable, and Kelly Watson provided assistance with research at important final stages of the project. I also thank Tristan Blease for completing the graphs.

Richard Morrison, Heather Burns, and Nancy Sauro at the University of Minnesota Press as well as Deborah Oosterhouse have been enormously supportive and encouraging throughout the process of developing and preparing this manuscript. My gratitude to them is immeasurable.

I thank my friends and family for their patience, fortitude, and love as we have dwelled together through proximity and distance, as well as several hurricanes. My friends Cecily Marcus, Tommy Kim, Erica Messenger, Hannah Rule, and Britt Holland Ellice have helped me through various stages of this text and the production of my ideas. My family helped to teach me to sublimate and have been interested in and supportive of my work throughout my education and my early career. And thank you to Jeremy Skiles, who has made me reconsider my understanding of the *Che vuoi?* I offer this book to them with love and with the hope that next time it will be easier to dwell with desire.

INTRODUCTION

The Unconscious Is Real

Lacan's Medievalism

What does it mean to call the French psychoanalyst Jacques Lacan (1901–1981) a medievalist? What are the implications at stake in speaking of his medievalism? Although these questions seem similar, they articulate two different ideological and taxonomical systems by which we consider the differences among disciplinary lines and among epochal distinctions.

The assertion behind the first question presumes that Lacan may be described in the category known as those scholars who study the Middle Ages. Lacan is not a medievalist in the sense that some other psychoanalytic theorists like Julia Kristeva, who wrote her dissertation on Antoine de la Sale's late medieval text *Jehan de Saintré* (1456), might be called a medievalist;[1] nor is he a medievalist in the sense that Hannah Arendt, Martin Heidegger, or Georges Bataille, all of whom also wrote their theses and later worked (to varying degrees) on medieval texts, may be called medievalists as they establish the relationship between their general theories and the study of the Middle Ages throughout their work.[2] Nor is Lacan a medievalist in the sense that Giorgio Agamben, Roland Barthes, Mikhail Bhaktin, Jacques Derrida, Michel Foucault, Emmanuel Levinas, or Slavoj Žižek, all of whom study medieval texts and concepts, are potentially medievalists.[3] Nonetheless, Jacques Lacan is a medievalist, and not merely because he cites courtly love poetics as a means of developing and articulating his theory of desire (although that focus remains a crucial point in support of his medievalism). Perhaps, even more so than any of the above scholars (with the possible exception of Kristeva),

Lacan is a medievalist because his methodologies follow those established by the medieval scholastic scholars who sought to determine the potential for the human subject to know and to represent real universal categories.

Put most broadly, a medievalist is any scholar who pays attention to texts and cultural objects as well as ideas that were produced during what is known as the Middle Ages. John Simons's definition of medievalism as "a process by which the Middle Ages is experienced as an historical entity capable of offering meaningful and even satisfying intellectual, aesthetic, political, and religious images to subsequent societies" is useful in identifying the vast range of possible understandings of medievalism.[4] This distinction poses immediate difficulties since the lines determining the Middle Ages can fluctuate with given trends in academic discourse.[5] For the purposes of the present inquiry, the beginning of the Middle Ages is marked by the work of St. Augustine (354–430), but it comes to fruition with the intervention made by Boethius in the establishment of the quarrel about the universals (ca. 480–524/5). If we mark Teresa of Avila's conversion that began in 1555 as the end point for Lacan's view of the Middle Ages, we risk offending some early modernists; however, this date also coincides with what has been known as the epistemological cut of the Copernican revolution (1543) that leads to modernity. Since one of the main theses of this book is that we, in some sense, are still living with the epistemological and cultural determinations predominant in the Middle Ages, and since another thesis of this book is that epistemological cuts, viewed temporally and historically, do not carry the weight that they are attributed by many scholars in various fields, this long Middle Ages is appropriate to a discussion of Lacan's medievalism. Marking an end is always necessarily false, as is the simultaneous designation of beginnings.[6] It is perhaps more accurate to say, as Josef Pieper has, that we still are living with the Middle Ages. Pieper observes in his *Scholasticism,*

A new segment of man's history began concurrently with the Middle Ages, but has not ended with the end of the medieval era. The Middle Ages constitute an initial and completed period of this new segment of history; but that segment itself has continued into postmedieval times and into the present "postmodern" era, and will doubtless continue on beyond. Hence the difficulty we have in clearly stating wherein lies the distinguishing "medievalism" of the Middle Ages. For as might be expected, while all of antiquity is definitely over and done with, many "typically medieval" phenomena continue to mark the postmedieval centuries.[7]

The persistence of specific modes of epistemological inquiry such as the trivium and the quadrivium in contemporary thought have assisted in the shifting of the beginnings of "modernity" to the premodern, linking the understanding of the subject to a process of education, specifically scholastic education. Richard Glejzer asserts this connection in "Lacan with Scholasticism: Agencies of the Letter."[8] As Glejzer rightly points out, "both scholasticism and psychoanalysis are founded on an imperative to consider a knowledge that resists signification, to bare the signifiers that ground ontology within an epistemology" ("Lacan with Scholasticism," 105). The foundational structures of both scholasticism and psychoanalysis seek to investigate the limits of knowledge based on linguistic representation. Eugene Vance forges a connection between narrative and universal abstract patterns by way of logic and dialectics with reference to the structure of poetic narrative. In his *From Topic to Tale*[9] Vance illustrates the way in which forms of epistemological inquiry that we consider "modern," and that signal an awareness of the unconscious, are already at play in medieval romance precisely because that romance is engaged with the scholastic quarrel over universals.

The second question that opens this inquiry and intervention is the question of discipline. Throughout the various histories of the discipline of medieval studies, medievalists have adhered to the notion that the field is multidisciplinary and crosses boundaries marked as distinct in some other scholarly fields.[10] As such, a medievalist might be said, broadly, to focus on any type of text, whether that is philosophical, poetic, architectural, musical, visual, or otherwise phenomenologically known (including the psyche), that was produced during the period defined as the Middle Ages.[11]

As a psychoanalyst who develops his theories of desire, the unconscious, language, the processes of and possibilities of treatment partly in response to his readings and analyses of philosophical and poetic texts from the Middle Ages, Lacan is a medievalist. Of course, he is not *only* a medievalist; he is also a Freudian, a Kantian, a Sassurian, a Heideggerian, a Kojèvean, and even a Marxist (among others). These elements of

Lacan's theory will be addressed throughout this book. My main focus, however, is to address the question of Lacan's medievalism; one aspect of this is to respond to Kristeva's question and assertion, "Lacan a Thomist?"[12] The question of Thomism is always one of a balance between faith and reason. This is precisely what is at stake in believing that the unconscious exists. Whether we speak of what came before Freud or what happens after Freud makes little difference to the necessity of a certain degree of faith in the understanding of the unconscious. In fact, with an approach to the unconscious as a categorical real we arrive at a view of that which cannot be said to have been "discovered" or "coined." Either the unconscious exists, and it has always existed, or it does not exist and it has never existed.

The question "What does it mean to speak of Lacan's medievalism?" is a methodological rather than an epochal question. In addition to the temporal field of inquiry, medievalism typically is characterized by an approach to texts and ideas that plays with the balance between alterity (otherness) and identification (sameness).[13] A concern with philology and wordplay that is central to psychoanalysis is also dominant in much medieval criticism. On a more profound level, however, Lacan follows the inductive and Socratic methods of the medieval scholastics throughout his seminars.[14] His tone, which is often seen as didactic, is also evidence of an epistemophilia and, it must be confessed from the outset, a theological investment in the potential for knowing the unknowable that pervades the work of Boethius who struggles to articulate and translate the arguments about the potential existence of universals. As Paul Vincent Spade has shown, Boethius's *Commentary on Porphyry* reveals a certain element of nominalism that leads scholars to label him a "moderate realist."[15] In this groundbreaking moment for the inauguration of the quarrel of universals, Boethius calls attention to the problems of homonyms and wordplay that Aristotle marks as significant to an understanding of the difference between things as particulars and general universal categories. Boethius seeks to clarify what Aristotle meant when in the *Categories* he said that homonyms (or equivocals) share in common a name but have different definitions.

The definitional difference between the name and the thing itself inaugurates the discourse and debates surrounding the problem of universals. This problem is a taxonomical one, and it reflects the potential for categories to determine reality. Boethius focuses on Porphyry's distinction between the genera and the species in his commentary. He says, "Genera and species either exist and subsist or are formed by the understanding and by thought alone" [Genera et species aut sunt atque subsistent aut /intellectu et sola cogitatione formantur].[16] The problem becomes quite complex and unfolds with reference to metaphysical and physical questions that will be addressed throughout the following chapters.

What is significant to an understanding of this aspect of Lacan's medievalism is (1) the methodology that is developed as a textual commentary tradition by Boethius and the scholastics after him, and (2) the focus on wordplay and homonyms that are crucial to psychoanalysis in general and to Lacan's attempt to be as specific as he possibly can while revealing the inadequacies of language. Medievalists Roger Dragonetti and Jean-Charles Hûchet have both called attention to the way in which this wordplay is crucial to an understanding of the psyche and the text. Within a psychoanalytical framework, wordplay, including the use of homonyms, neologisms, metaphor, metonymy, and anagrams, is important because the unconscious does not filter out the differences among definitions. All potential meanings exist side-by-side in the reservoir of the unconscious, and this multiplicity affects conscious will and decisions. This means that at any given moment, although one might say that there is a difference between the two (or three, or more) definitions of homonyms, the potential for the multiplicity of the thing to open, unfold, or confuse the reader or auditor on an unconscious level problematizes any attempt to be clear.

In 1972 Paul Zumthor explained his use of the terms "medieval" and "poetics" as he introduced his foundational text, *Toward a Medieval Poetics (Essai de poétique médiévale).*[17] In so doing he set forth criteria for recognizing the categories of the "medieval" and the "poetic." Defining Lacan's medievalism calls for a similar redefinition of "Lacan" and "medievalism."[18]

Whereas Lacan's "father" Sigmund Freud focused on the classical epoch to find source material by which he could explain some of his most elementary and far-reaching concepts, such as the tale of Oedipus in order to develop the Oedipus complex, Lacan looks to the Middle Ages for various concepts, texts, and examples that enable him to develop his theories. A further crucial element by which we might distinguish Lacan as a medievalist is his own declaration that the psychoanalyst is a saint, and that he has been excommunicated.[19] Placing himself in the realm of the "Real" Lacan toys with the understanding of the role of the analyst and asserts unknowability into the scene of reading the psyche and the text.

The question of Jacques Lacan's medievalism has been limited to his reading of courtly love as an instance of desire. Indeed, Lacan's investment in locating courtly love as an instantiation of desire is a crucial element of his medievalism, not merely because it provides a direct example of a psychoanalytical reliance on medieval literature for the development and understanding of its theories, but also because within the framework of desire as articulated by the troubadours, we find a poetic contribution to the scholastic debates over the possibility for the existence of universals.

Put very briefly, this quarrel is characterized by a belief that language refers only to itself (nominalism) and creates the world of things, or that language signifies a greater category outside of itself (realism). For a realist, $A = A$ is true and valid; both signs are A and both are equivalent. For a nominalist, it is impossible to claim that $A = A$ due to variations in particular representations of the sign and, by extension, the thing. In the case of the troubadours, we find contributions to this debate at the level of the signifier itself, as well as subjectivity, the problem of desire, the object of love, and poetic expression as symptomatic of the existence of the unconscious.[20]

Lacan's medievalism exceeds his work on courtly love and exhibits a broadly philosophical intervention in a debate associated with medieval studies and that continues to be evident in critical theory, literary criticism, and philosophy today. If Lacan's theory of desire is based on his citation of courtly love, it is precisely because his epistemological system is founded on his participation in the scholastic quarrel about the universals.

Application/Implication

If we limit an understanding of Lacan's medievalism to the moments when he refers to courtly love and we then approach troubadour texts by using psychoanalysis as a "tool" for reading, then we are in the realm of application. If, instead, we find that the text and the psyche are equally significant to an understanding of the mode of analysis and the possibility of understanding the linguistic knot of the unconscious, then we enter the realm of implication.

Psychoanalysis is premised partly on the ability to locate moments of practical application for theoretical hypotheses. Two voices, one "theoretical" and one "medievalist," speaking about the subject of the applicative intersection between medieval literature and psychoanalysis help to make this point clear. The "theorist" Dominick LaCapra, addresses the problem of applicability in his *Representing the Holocaust: History, Theory, Trauma*.[21] Aware of the potential arguments against the applicability of psychoanalysis to cultural and historical subjects outside of Freud's own era, LaCapra shows that continuity across time and space is dependent on difference in repetition and not pure, identical sameness.[22] What emerges from his analysis of Freud is an understanding of application as that which occurs from within the text, rather than that which is imposed on the text from the outside. Similarly, the "medievalist" Jean-Charles Hûchet shows throughout his work that the structures of analysis are bound to the structures of the unconscious as it is symptomatically rendered poetic. In *Littérature Médiévale et Psychanalyse* Hûchet demonstrates how poetic structures are precisely symptoms of the subject's engagement with language. This internal evidence of what might appear to be a systematic and disciplinary distinction paves the way for an understanding of the transhistorical nature of the unconscious. Again, this is not to say that the unconscious is always structured in precisely the same manner; it is, however, to say that language determines subjective knowledge and this, in turn, affects our understanding of the knowable and articulable elements in the world.

If application of psychoanalysis is performed in a manner consistent with *analysis* it has the potential to lead to implication.[23] However, this procedure must actively take into account the mutual implications of texts and ideological systems.[24] If application, the imposition of a model, code, or map onto a text or ideology, prefers the model being applied to the text, then the results of analysis are limited. Roland Barthes's notion of textual analysis and Jacques Derrida's location of resistance in analysis both reflect, along with Freudian and Lacanian approaches to texts, a model by which the text and the psyche are structured in a similar manner and must be allowed to convey significance openly and with multiplicity.[25] Shoshana Felman's call for *implication* rather than *application* is echoed by Paul Zumthor.[26] Felman's introduction to *Literature and Psychoanalysis,* a short essay entitled "To Open the Question," urged her audience to find and create a relationship between the disciplines and discourses of literature and psychoanalysis that exists outside of a master-slave relationship. In this essay Felman succinctly states what she also argues and performs in her more extensive work, that literature and psychoanalysis need to find a discourse or discourses that enable them to exist as disciplines that inform each other. Her insistence on the notion that *implication* between two texts or ideas supplement *application,* the imposition of one text or idea onto another, begins the process of dynamic and dialectical reading necessary to a useful interaction between literature and psychoanalysis.

> What the literary critic might thus wish, is to initiate a real exchange, to engage in a real *dialogue* between literature and psychoanalysis, as between two different bodies of language and between two different modes of knowledge. Such a dialogue has to take place outside of the master-slave pattern, which does not allow for true dialogue, being, under the banner of competence, a unilateral monologue of psychoanalysis *about* literature. ("To Open the Question," 6)

Following Felman's lead, Zumthor calls for a methodology of *implication* rather than application.

> If the "thing" is a text, the method consists of what I could call a *discourse-on,* whose relation to the text is one of application. Now the practice that constituted, in the past, the same text, was a *discourse-in* (a relation of localization) and a *discourse-by* (a relation of cause and of instrument).
>   Whence a double opposition, of which at least one (on/by) is never resolved, because *on* tends to establish taxonomies, while *by,* referring to production itself, tends to annul rational clarifications. (*Speaking,* 15)

In this passage the focus on specific prepositional difference "on," "in," or "by" highlights the spatial quality of theoretical discourse as engaged in a mode of *extimacy* with the text at hand.[27]

Despite these urgings, scholarship continues to resist a consideration of the literary text as a model by which to read theory, rendering rare any analysis wherein mutual implication works.

As Lacan took it upon himself to draw out the literary and linguistic aspects of Freud's work, this project seeks to further extend the manner in which Lacan's theories, specifically of desire in relation to the real of the unconscious, are replete with a consideration of medieval literature and philosophy. As such, each chapter in this book attempts to locate the manner in which Lacan's theories engage ideas prominent in medieval literature such that our understanding of psychoanalysis and the Middle Ages is reconceived.

In part, this book seeks to engage those medievalists who continue to resist psychoanalysis because it is seen as ahistorical or transhistorical. L. O. Aranye Fradenburg has effectively characterized this resistance among historicists and has responded with her own resistance to resistance, claiming that "psychoanalysis is simply *in* medieval studies now, in a variety of acknowledged and unacknowledged ways."[28] And Elizabeth Scala has successfully taken up the task of uncovering and analyzing those many "unacknowledged ways," revealing the symptomatic power of resistance within criticism.[29]

Psychoanalysis is integrally tethered to a consideration of the way that the subject is formed in relation to culture and language. The speaking subject is always materially bound by way of language to a given historical context. This means that it cannot be ahistorical in any case; the subject is always situated historically and culturally. The unconscious, structured as it is, *like a language* is also, therefore, bound to and created by culture. Independent unconscious systems, each subject's different psyche, are unique and located in particularities of temporality and geography (as well as the race, class, sex trio). The unconscious understood as an abstract, conceptual entity, however, *is* precisely transhistorical in that it exists in each speaking subject throughout time, whether there is a name for it, the unconscious, or not. It does not matter if we say that Epicurus discovered the unconscious, that Teresa of Avila discovered the unconscious, or that Freud discovered the unconscious. No one, single discovery marks a historical moment or an epistemological break where, suddenly, an unconscious appears.[30] The unconscious is always already within the speaking subject. As an aspect of being, then, the unconscious is a real universal. The only way that we can know this is through symptoms that emerge within experience, and so the unconscious as a universal reasserts itself into particular modes and moments of being. My focus on the texts that relate most specifically to Lacan's theories, those by the scholastics and the troubadours, illustrates how his work is grounded within medieval poetics. My extension of the relationship between Lacan's theories and the poetics of Chaucer, the Gawain poet, and Marie de France both limits the intervention to the Old French and Provençal articulations of desire and the scholastic quarrel over universals, and extends that intervention into the field of Anglo-Norman studies.

Mutual implication will lead to an inversion of Fradenburg's statement, "psychoanalysis is in medieval studies," to say as well that *medieval studies is in psychoanalysis.* This mutual implication of the processes of reading and analyzing texts depends largely on an understanding of language in relation to things in themselves. The scholastic debates about the existence of universals are not over; they are evident actively in even the most apparently "postmodern" theories. For instance, Jean Baudrillard's notion of the real as fiction throughout his work, and his development of the hyperreal, takes us back to a consideration of the way in which the real is linguistically constructed or determined. He is an avid nominalist who nonetheless expresses nostalgia for the potential offered by a belief in the real of universals.[31] Baudrillard and Lacan share a belief in the fictional character of things in the world; as language creates and dominates our understanding and ways of knowing, the "real" whether it is *surreal* (as it is for Lacan) or *hyperreal* (as it is for Baudrillard) is that which is intangible, textual, and bound to unconscious resistance.

The Literal, the Real, and Realism

In a system of language that perceives the signifier (or the word) to always stand in as a mediator, a distanced metaphor for the signified (or the thing), what might it mean to "take desire literally" as Lacan suggests when he articulates a proposal for analytical treatment?[32] When Lacan suggests that we take desire "literally" in "The Direction of Treatment and Its Principles of Power," he calls attention to the paradox of analysis that attempts to take the subject at her *word,* even while accounting for the multiple layers of significance within that word.[33] The signifier is never simple and it always has the potential to untie the knot of the unconscious and of desire. As often as desire is defined and explained with reference to the various elements of the signifier, the subject, the cause, the referent, the other, and time, here in Lacan's articulation of the very process of treatment, he seeks to be direct and clear about desire as potentially "literal."[34] The property of the sign as a literal or real object and subject within desire contributes to the establishment of desire as a sign of the real of the unconscious. As it is always bound to another signifier, the sign rarely stands in solitude, and it participates in the signifying chain that marks the relationship between language and desire. Within this system, the subject attempts to articulate desire, which, properly speaking, is always out of reach. In relation to the self as fragmented subject, the speaking subject has a split desire; it is both the desire of the other *within* the self and the desire that is *imagined* as the desire of the Other external to the self. The manifold quality of desire makes it impossible to represent fully and renders its cause out of the reach of knowledge. This unattainability and unrepresentablity leads desire to appear ex nihilo, as if out of nothing.[35] Any attempt to locate proper causality improperly designates an object, which is always then a prosthetic for the imagined origin. As such, the empty center of desire circulates within language and within the subject as she exists in language. In "The Direction of Treatment and Its Principles of Power" Lacan writes:

> Desire is that which is manifested in the interval that demand hollows within itself, in as much as the subject, in articulating the signifying chain, brings to light the want-to-be, together with the appeal to receive the complement from the Other, if the Other, the locus of speech, is also the locus of this want, or lack.
>
> That which is thus given to the Other to fill, and which is strictly that which it does not have, since it, too, lacks being, is what is called love, but it is also hate and ignorance.
>
> It is also what is evoked by any demand beyond the need that is articulated in it, and it is certainly that of which the subject remains all the more deprived to the extent that the need articulated in the demand is satisfied.
>
> Furthermore, the satisfaction of need appears only as the lure in which the demand for love is crushed, by sending the subject back to sleep, where he haunts the limbo regions of being, by letting it speak in him. For the being of language is the non-being of objects, and the fact that desire was discovered by Freud in its place in the dream, which has always been the stumbling-block of any attempt on the part of thought to situate itself in reality, should be a sufficient lesson for us. (*Écrits*, 263)

If the being of language is distinct from the being of objects, then the problem of taking desire literally must exist within the lacunae between desire and its articulation. The troubadour poets are central in having produced a repertoire of texts about the impossibility of articulating desire. This erotic desire, however, is only one mode of understanding desire, which is also epistemological, spiritual, and signifies as well as provides evidence for the unconscious drives.

The attempt to find the real of desire is known by way of language but is not limited to the precise manner in which language conveys that which is found in the unconscious. A split between the literal quality of desire and the literal quality of the real of the signifier becomes obvious in this enigmatic approach to the desire of the subject. To take desire literally is not to take it "at its word" but, rather, to dig beneath the word itself to find the real that is beneath the metaphorical, metonymical, and metalinguistic structure of speech.[36]

In "The Direction of Treatment and Its Principles of Power," however, Lacan does not get to that point yet. Rather, he emphasizes the extent to which, in order to understand the literal quality of desire, we must become "literate" and we must focus on the "literary" quality of Freud's work, therefore repressing the connections to the real that will become evident throughout his work (*Écrits*, 276). The literal is not the same thing as believing in the possibility for direct speech or language. Like Jacques Derrida (despite arguments to the contrary) Lacan believes that there is no possible "literal" quality of language since all language is always already metaphorical and a mediator for the difference between the thing and its representation.[37]

There is a precise difference between the realist and nominalist elements of the scholastic debate. Universality or universalism is predicated on the ability to create universal categories. The quarrel of the universals finds at its core the determination and articulation of these categories. Without the potential for categorization a concept, thing, or word cannot potentially achieve a level of universality. The quarrel of the universals, then, is at the core of the way we might understand the distinctions among singularity, multiplicity, and universality.

It is also important here to note the various ways that the words "real," "realist," "realism," "the Real," and "reality" are employed in the quarrel of the universals, in literary criticism, and in Lacanian psychoanalysis.

1. *The "real"* is the most confusing signifier in this group because it can refer to "reality" as in things that exist in the world, or it can refer to Lacan's concept of the "Real" as that which is impossible to represent.

The context for each iteration must be carefully noted so that the distinction remains clear.

2. *"Realism"* or *"realist"* are to be understood here as adjectives defining one who believes in the possibility for the existence of universals.
3. *The Real* (or *the real*) refers to the element of the unconscious desire and fantasy that exceeds articulation and knowability.
4. *"Reality"* is always experiential and phenomenological.

These variations on the concept of realism should be distinguished from a general understanding of literary realism. As a mode of engagement with the impossible of the unconscious, the category of the "Real" in Lacan's tripartite scheme of Imaginary, Symbolic, and Real represents that which is beyond proper representation. It is separate from the "reality" of things in the world, but it exists as an abstract or incorporeal reality. Realist or realism does not refer to the genre of literary realism; rather, it should be understood here as referring to the elements of ideas that apply to those who believe in the potential for the category of the real. The real, according to Lacan, is then an element of the unconscious that cannot be accessed by consciousness. Belief in the potential for the real presumes a cognitive awareness of the real as a category, but it does not necessarily mean that one can know what form or shape or definition that real takes. It is in this sense that the belief in the potential for the real and the real as inaccessible are coexistent. The real's potentiality and inaccessibility are mutually defining rather than mutually exclusive, as one's lay intuition might lead one to think. The real is then that which is both universal, always at stake, and as obvious and evident as the real of a table or desk. Yet, the real remains intangible and dependent upon language.[38]

The ability or refusal to perceive self-identity in the formula $A = A$ is a simple example of the potential for, or impossibility of, universal categorization. If $A = A$ completely, then we are in the realm of realism. If A cannot equal A because the two are taken in their singular and discrete entities, then we are in the realm of nominalism. A nominalist does not hold that there is the potential for universal categories of distinctions; rather, the individual or particular instance is always necessarily different from any other instance that might resemble it, such that A does not equal A because the two As are different temporally, spatially. Further, our conception of the A as resembling itself is merely a construct of our mind as it seeks to impose categories on things in the world. In purely reductive form, this is the quarrel of the universals. Therefore, to say that Chaucer is a realist (for instance) is not to say that he accurately represents time and space in *The Canterbury Tales*, nor is it to say that the sound of the wind in his poetics is onomatopoetic to the point that one can feel the wind in her hair as she reads. Rather, it is to say that he believes in the possibility for a singular term to predicate many things. Those who perceive Chaucer to be a nominalist defend their position by considering the focus on the attention he pays to language, the disruption of categories (such as the estates system), and the modes of epistemological awareness presented and critiqued in his work to provide evidence for a search for singularity.

Most medieval poets, philosophers, theologians, and rhetoricians are somewhere on the fence in the quarrel of the universals, suggesting that their involvement in the debate over categorization (as a realist or a nominalist) already places them somewhere along the lines of realism. A pure nominalist would simply not engage in the debate once his point has been made about the way that language works particularly in the world and the split between our knowledge as humans and a form of divine knowledge. Since most medieval authors, and not merely the scholastics, engage in this debate, they reveal their concern to display the potentialities and limits of human knowledge in relation to the unknowable (which must always be redefined as systems approach new ways of articulating seemingly ineffable truths). As they do not fit nicely into a single category of realism or nominalism, medieval philosophers, poets, and theologians suggest that the significance of the debate is in the struggle itself and that the role of language in relation to things and ideas is ultimately the point of contention. How one articulates this struggle, then, is crucial to a reading of medieval poetry, philosophy, and theology.

The level upon which desire must be understood "literally" is that wherein we find ourselves discursively and ideologically in the realm of the real. As it takes a student of Freud (e.g., Lacan) to perceive the importance of language and the literary element of the psyche in articulating the complexity of the unconscious, similarly, Lacan's disciples point out his investment in defining and understanding the category of the real. If language is not the level at which we may discover the "literal" then how does the unconscious make its way into the real, and why focus on the "literary" aspects of the psyche to understand desire? Serge

Leclaire addresses this problem in "The Real in the Text"[39] when he perceives the way in which the text presents the lack of the unconscious and further complicates the discovery of the real of the unconscious. Leclaire says that "The work of the psychoanalyst is defined by one imperative: *to unmask the real*" ("Real in the Text," 320). As such, the project of psychoanalysis certainly contributes to the realism/nominalism debate that was at the center of the quarrel of the universals. Presently, I will show how Lacan's work fits precisely into the medieval search for the real. First, however, we must define Lacan's approach to the real. In order to do this we must turn to Leclaire's view of the real as that which underlies the unconscious and the text. For Leclaire, the literal is no more real than the metaphorical, and the language of literature is fraught with "defects" and "lack" such that

> the letter written on paper insidiously tends to substitute itself for the object and to reintegrate the absolutely other, or the real (lack, anxiety, *jouissance*), in a literary order in which the quasi-fetishized materiality of the text takes the place and function assumed by the real-object (the object as unnameable index of the real) in the reference text constituted by the unconscious corpus. ("Real in the Text," 322)

Literature or textuality does not, in this case, explicate the unconscious any more than the speaking subject can, and so we cannot appear to take desire "literally." The real lies beyond the language of literature and the subject, and is located in the unconscious itself. Understanding the real as a category in this manner, however, marks it as a site of impossible articulation and contradicts the ability to take desire "literally." Leclaire solves this conundrum by stating that "perhaps it is in the very impossibility of what he attempts that the writer truly discovers the real" ("Real in the Text," 323). This is a very common understanding of the relationship between language and the real in Lacanian psychoanalysis. Its inherent romanticism reflects another common understanding of Lacan's use of courtly love to explicate the process of desire: the real, the unconscious, and desire appear in this display to be idealized, impossible, even transcendent subjects that exceed our understanding as auditors or readers. In this view, we might understand Lacan to be a nominalist because the categories of knowledge upon which psychoanalysis is based are utterly dependent on the way that language constructs reality. By romanticizing that which is unknowable, the limits of our knowledge of the unconscious, the perception that we can remain separate or protected from the real by prohibiting access to it through unconscious defenses, and by limiting our understanding to the process of literal analysis (even when that analysis takes into account the metaphorical), reading Lacan as a nominalist limits an understanding of his work with the process of psychoanalytical treatment as well as his work with medieval literature and philosophy.

If the unconscious is subject to bracketing as that which is real and unknowable, it can be forgotten as that element that is simply at play in language and the subject. If, instead, the real is that which is determined by a Thomistic combination of reason and faith, if it is representative of the potential for universal categories, then the unconscious is not at play; it is, instead, always at *work*, and it cannot be cordoned off into a temporal or spatial moment. Further, by proposing a theory of the real by way of his reading and citation of medieval literature and philosophy, Lacan marks psychoanalysis as a subject that is always bound to a pursuit of the sovereign good.

When Julia Kristeva asks in *Tales of Love*, "Lacan, a Thomist?"[40] she is both ironic and earnest in her positioning of Lacan with and against Aquinas. As she discusses Aquinas's reading of the doctrine to "Love your neighbor as yourself," Kristeva shows how Aquinas's view in the *Commentary on Sentences* is aimed toward unification.[41] According to Aquinas, "Because love unites, as it were, the one who loves with the loved one, the former behaves toward the latter as toward himself, or toward that which concerns his own perfection" (III, 29:2.1, in Kristeva, *Tales of Love*, 180). And, as Kristeva observes, "the Thomist logic of love amounts to positing that because there is Unity and love for that Unity (of Self), there is also Union of the two (the loved one being identified with oneself)" (*Tales of Love*, 181). Clearly, this notion of love as the means toward Unity and Oneness is in direct contradiction to Lacan's belief that there is no possibility of achieving a proper connection with the other by way of love or desire. What does it mean then, when Kristeva posits Lacan as a Thomist? To answer this question, we must examine the paragraph preceding her pronouncement. She writes:

> If we reread Aquinas we shall again discover that the thinking subject is a subject thinking the other, and as such it is analogous to the subject loving the other. *Ratio diligendi* and *Ego cogito*: both bear the scar of a narcissism that aspires to tear itself away from—or unite itself with—the other, as from or with its own good. Aquinas, however, reveals the

delight of alienation at the very moment that he posits its impossibility in the citadel of *one's own:* of the *good.* The splitting between lovers, as the one within each lover, is immediately erased by the machinery of judgment pertaining to meaning and to one's own good. "Because the relation (of charitable work) to its effect is the good established in the other. From that standpoint, and to the extent that we consider the other's good as our own, because of the union in love, we take delight in the good that, for our sake, befalls to others, mainly to our friends, as we do in our own good." Would *amor sui* as a kernel of Thomistic love be the angelical treatment of alienation—a recommended paranoia, deemed necessary, and thus necessarily successful?

Lacan must have known something about this, since drives, for him were already signifying. Lacan a Thomist? As Marx was a Hegelian? The one without God, the other without absolute Spirit? (*Tales of Love,* 182–83)

If belief in the unconscious requires a certain amount of faith, it also depends largely on reason and leads to an understanding of the balance between faith and reason central to Aquinas. If Lacan is a Thomist like Marx is a Hegelian then he both follows Aquinas and simultaneously turns him on his head.

Attempting to secularize the problem of faith as that which exists at the limits of reason, but is still crucial to a complete understanding of universals and to a foundational realism, Lacan supplements the God of Christian faith with the unconscious. As Christ was proof of God's existence, desire is proof of the existence of the unconscious. Both rely on a belief in the potential for the literal in language even while the recognition of that impossibility disrupts clear understanding. Although the contributing texts often focus on the signifier and the signified to determine the potential for realism and universals or the extent to which we are limited to nominalist understandings, the core of the debate rests on the relationship (or distinction) between human law and divine law and the conception of God as singular or multiple. As a limit case, God represents the aporia in logical and rational comprehension and points to the necessity of faith; as the limit case in the understanding of the human subject, the unconscious, represented by desire, calls for faith in the potential for reason to untie the knot of language. Both circumstances depend upon an understanding of creation ex nihilo (out of nothing), but which is found as a precise cause that does exist in Aquinas. As the "Thomist" and medievalist Étienne Gilson claims, in order to understand the medieval view of causality, we must "return to a realism which may seem a little naïve, and which St. Thomas has put into a perfectly clear formula: *causa importat influxum quondam ad esse causati"* [but this name cause imports a certain influx into the being of the thing caused].[42] The notion of cause, then, immediately alters the object, thus creating an "effect." Gilson continues to state that in order to have causality we must have two distinct beings wherein a first acts upon or is affected by a second. This notion of two distinct beings can also apply to "nothing" as an entity, such that creation arises out of nothing (ex nihilo).[43] Additionally, if we consider the inherent fragmentation of a single thing in itself, then the difference between internal and external, as well as between one and two, is broken down resulting in the potential for a one to arise out of apparent nothingness and to be at once two.[44]

Familiar as he was with Gilson's work, directly and by way of his academic progress under the direction of the rationalist Catholic thinker Jean Baruzi, Lacan struggled to articulate a form of Thomistic inquiry that also accounted for his own lack of faith in God. Lacan's Thomism is clearly a perverted form of belief in the combination of faith and reason, in love and being, that exists without God as the primary cause that is so central to Aquinas. Absent causality, which has been addressed by Slavoj Žižek in his *Metastases of Enjoyment*,[45] and will be discussed extensively in chapter 3, leads desire to appear as if from nothing, and this ex nihilo quality renders it perplexing. I would suggest here (and I will elaborate later) that this absent causality is no more perplexing than the foundation of a causality like God; indeed, the lack of causality foundational to Lacan's theory of desire resembles the Thomistic identification of God as causality more than one might think, since in the scene of desire the presence (corporeal or incorporeal) of two beings is not only necessary but fundamental. As such, Lacan is a Thomist in the strictest sense *and* in the sense that he turns Aquinas on his head to formulate a realism wherein the unconscious substitutes for the absent-presence of God.

The overwhelming number of his citations of medieval theologians, philosophers, scientists, and poets combines to render Lacan's theories of the unconscious and language (and what may be called his exegesis of Freud) a complex theory or (anti)philosophy, by which we may locate evidence of the real existence and performance of the unconscious in the Middle Ages. This recognition of the unconscious as a real undoes the fiction of our modernity.[46] Modernity itself is premised on the adherence to major epistemological cuts, as Alexandre Leupin suggests, which also then displace ideas from each other.[47] Lacan's work struggles against this epochal definition of the human subject and the psyche, and often risks being perceived as universalizing or ahistorical because of its precise effort to analyze the subject in light of history (world history, the subject's history). In fact, Lacan's view of the universals and the historicity of the subject, the unconscious, and desire are quite sensitive to the dangers of universalization and idealization. This is not to say, however, that the epistemological cuts distinguishing premodernity, modernity, and postmodernity stand up to the force of the real of the unconscious. Rather, the unconscious as a real category is subject to these external epistemological changes, but it survives these alterations as it exceeds and evades the process of conscious registering. The narcissist will, for instance, claim that he knows, scientifically and consciously, that the earth revolves around the sun but that he continues to *feel* as if the sun rises when he opens his eyes. The distinction between the thought and the feeling of an apparent fact is one evidentiary model for the split between conscious knowledge and unconscious knowledge. Epistemological cuts and defining historical moments (such as the Copernican revolution) alter the way that we relate to the world, but they seem to affect the unconscious on a different level. As Sigmund Freud says in his "Notes upon a Case of Obsessional Neurosis," "everything conscious was subject to a process of wearing-away, while what was unconscious was relatively unchangeable."[48] The unconscious requires a different level of attention in order to be altered than that form of intervention, like the knowledge of epistemological cuts, that affects conscious understanding of the world.[49]

While the medieval scholastic debates were primarily concerned with the pursuit of proper knowledge so as to understand the limitations of knowing God, this Christian, religious motivation is translated in the language of psychoanalysis with an aim toward comprehending and articulating the unconscious. As scholastic inquiries into the universals reformulate the non-Christian theories of Socrates, Plato, Epicurus, Parmenides, Aristotle, Porphyry, and other classical philosophers and poets into Christian speculations about the precise way in which the existence or nonexistence of universals properly allows us to know the world and to know God, so too does psychoanalysis extend the language and methods of scholasticism to get at the core of the unconscious. Like the image of the monotheistic God, the unconscious is ineffable, though it speaks consistently in every word and action the subject performs. Like the voice of God as it is heard according to the apostles and the saints, the voice of the unconscious is often misinterpreted and ignored.

Similarly, the goal of psychoanalysis mirrors the goal of scholastic philosophy and theology when it seeks to understand the Sovereign Good and the potential for happiness in the world. As we find in *Seminar VII, The Ethics of Psychoanalysis* and *Seminar XX, Encore*, the articulation of the Sovereign Good is an ethical question that responds to Aristotle's *Nichomachean Ethics* (as well as Boethius's *The Consolation of Philosophy*) by reconfiguring the ethical question in light of the process of desire. As the primary means of knowing the unconscious, desire is foundational to the epistemological map of the subject. Although it has been obscured (or repressed) in the history of philosophy, desire should not be thought of as separate from the pursuit of knowledge or ethics. This means that when Lacan looks to the poetics of the troubadour poets for his articulation of desire, he is no less investigating the core of knowledge than when he cites Thomas Aquinas or Augustine; in fact, because courtly love poetics instantiate the process of desire and reflect the unconscious at play in its Fort/Da (presence and absence, or appearance and disappearance) game, it is *more* direct as an inquiry and point of analysis than the mediating and mediated language of the philosophers and theologians.[50]

Boethius's understanding of this power of poetic language is evident in his shift from the translation and commentary of Aristotle, which was so central to the medieval knowledge of the classical philosophers, to the poetic/prose structure of *The Consolation of Philosophy*. Both approaches to knowledge, the direct philosophical and the poetic, appeal to different modes of thinking about being. Underlying these various approaches to knowledge is a belief in the potential for the category of the "real." As he coins the term "universals," Boethius also determines the means by which we can know real categories. In the *Second Commentary on Porphyry's Isagoge*, a text that he translates as a way of introducing Aristotle's *Categories*, Boethius does not make his own position regarding their potential clear. He sets forth the arguments of others and works through, systematically, the potential for knowledge of particular elements of being. Similarly, Lacan often obfuscates his position regarding the potential for real categories and seems to occlude his meaning even when he is direct. Nonetheless, both Lacan and Boethius follow the order of the ten possible substantive and accidental attributes put forth by Boethius in his later work on the trinity:

> Decem omniino praedicamenta traduntur quae de rebus omnibus universaliter praedicantur, id est substantia, qualitas, quantitas, ad aliquid, ubi, quando, habere, situm esse, facere, pati. Haec igitur talia sunt qualia subiecta permiserint; name pars eorum in reliquarum rerum praedicatione substantia est, pars in accidentium numero est.

> [There are in all ten categories which can be universally predicated of all things, namely, Substance, Quality, Quantity, Relation, Place, Time, Condition, Situation, Activity, Passivity. Now these are such as their subjects allow; for some of them denote real substantive attributes of other things, others belong to the class of accidental attributes.] (*De Trinitate*, IV.1–7)[51]

Considered to be a moderate realist, Boethius forwards the problem of being and predication in relation to things in the world and to God. When one considers things in the world, the real categories are applicable in their various combinations of substantive and accidental attributes. Put simply, substantive attributes are those that are inherent to a being or entity, and accidental attributes are those qualities that do not necessarily determine the being or entity and may exist or may merely be located in a particular being.

As Boethius explains in his epistolary *Contra Eutychen et Nestorium (A Treatise against Eutyches and Nestorius)*, substantive attributes are corporeal or incorporeal things existing in nature. Only those substances predicated of individuals that are categorizable by genre or species, such as man and animal, are said to be universal, such that "person," a category that can only be reflected in particulars and individuals, is not a universal. Explaining the difference between "man" and "person" Boethius verges on representing the concept of universals as a psychoanalytical problem:

> Sed de persona maxime dubitari potest, quaena, ei definitio posit aptari. Si enim omnis habet natura personam, indissolubilis nodus est, quaenam inter naturam personamque posit esse discretio; aut si non aequatur persona naturae, sed infra terminum spatiumque naturae persona susistit, difficule dictu est ad quas uswue naturas persona perveniat, id est quas naturas conceniat habere personam, quas a personae vocabulo segregari. Nam illud quidem manifestum est personae subiectam esse naturam nec praeter naturam personam posse praedicari.

[But the proper definition of person is a matter of very great perplexity. For if every nature has person, the difference between nature and person is *a hard knot to unravel;* or if person is not taken as the equivalent of nature but is a term of less scope and range, it is difficult to say to what natures it may be extended, that is, to what natures the term person may be applied and what natures are dissociate from it. For one thing is clear, namely that nature is a substrate of person, and that person cannot be predicated apart from nature.] (*Contra Eutychen,* II.1–11, emphasis added)

The tethering of person to nature problematizes the ability to categorize person as a universal since person is also bound to particular instances. Since the category of person is predicated of corporeal and incorporeal substances, some of which are rational and some of which are not rational, "person can never be predicated of universals, but only of particulars and individuals" [Sed in his omnibus nusquam in universalibus persona dici potest, sed in singularibus tantum atque in individuis] (*Contra Eutychen,* II.48–50). This leads Boethius to claim that the person is the "individual substance of a rational nature" [naturae rationabilis individual substantia] (*Contra Eutychen,* III.4–5). According to this definition, a person, as individual and rational, would be a whole being, singular, subject to interaction on the level of language and the multiple forms that the signifier takes in the world. For this reason, it is crucial that Boethius distinguishes between "man" as a universal category and "person" as a singular structure. We can say that the category of "man" exists, but the category of "person" does not exist. This would seem to be in direct conflict with Lacan's view of universals in which Lacan erases the category not of "man" but of "woman," fragmenting and gendering the universal form and apparently displaying skepticism regarding the possibility of universals.

The psychoanalytical aspects of the category of universals are evident in the decision to mark the person as a rational individual. Free will and voluntarism seem to be undone by the power of the unconscious, but, according to William of Ockham, knowing is willing and even if that knowledge is unconscious (as it is for Lacan) it is still bound to a rational power. What does it mean to call the person a rational individual in light of our awareness of the unconscious? If the unconscious is anything, it is certainly not rational, and to claim that the subject is (at least) partially driven by the unconscious presumes that reason or logic are not always dominant in the subject who enacts being in the world. Indeed, Boethius is aware of this limitation of rationality, and it leads him, in *The Consolation of Philosophy*, to tether the question of happiness to the concept of free will.

The primary question driving both psychoanalysis and *The Consolation of Philosophy* is "How do we end human suffering?" What Lady Philosophy teaches is that philosophy is not limited to the realm of reason, but extends to the field of emotion, thus signaling the interaction among the various drives and wills of the unconscious and the conscious. As "man" is a universal but "person" is singular, the unconscious is a real universal, but the "unconscious of a subject" is particular. The significance of the category of the unconscious as a real contributes to an understanding of the way in which Lacan's medievalism, his realism, engages philosophical ideas that appear in logical and poetic form in premodern and postmodern approaches to the epistemology of desire.

Like Boethius (and Aristotle before him) Lacan foregrounds language as a determining foundation for a discussion of the human subject. Prior to Boethius, Isidore of Seville's *Etymologies* present an instance of the potential for designating the relationship between words and things.[52] The categorizing of the definitions and genealogical history in the etymologies sets forth the multiple layers of significance found in each utterance.

Language is never simple, and least so when it is set forth in apparently clean categories. And, like his predecessors the scholastics, Lacan's position in the quarrel of the universals is neither clean nor simple. His views on language and the construction of the world appear to make him a nominalist. When he claims "It is the world of words that creates the world of things" he sounds precisely nominalist and constructivist. But when he follows that statement by claiming, "the things originally confused in the *hic et nunc* (here and now) of the all in the process of coming-into-being—by giving its concrete being to their essence, and its ubiquity to what has always been: κτημα εζ αει (lasting possession)." To make matters more confusing he then says, "Man speaks, then, but it is because the symbol has made him man" (*Écrits*, 65), which again sounds thoroughly nominalist and constructivist. This confusion led his astute disciples to push him to articulate his precise stance regarding language, the real, and universals.

In *Seminar II, The Ego in Freud's Theory and in the Technique of Psychoanalysis*,[53] two members of his seminar, Guy Durandin[54] and

Jean-Bertrand Lefèbvre-Pontalis, interrogate Lacan about his position with regard to realism, reality, and the real. Durandin initiates the line of thinking by seeking to understand what Lacan means when he says "deverbalization," a term that Lacan employs to describe ideas that must be taken out of their linguistic moment and analyzed so that the unconscious and proper signification might be located within the subject's speech. In the encounter, Durandin implicitly exposes the extent to which Lacan struggles to articulate realism within an awareness of nominalism. Language is revealed to be inadequate to the expression of emotion; this is nothing new for Lacan, or for others working in a postclassical world. However, the explanation in which Lacan struggles to show how what one feels "in one's gut" cannot be properly expressed in language leads immediately and logically to Lefèbvre-Pontalis's concern with realism.

If there is a prearticulate, or preverbal, sensation that must be "deverbalized" in order to uncover what is at the heart of the feeling, then emotion is excessive and beyond the world of words that creates the world of things. In a nominalist view, this would mean that the emotion does not exist in the world until or unless it is properly articulated. In a realist view, however, the emotion exists but cannot be known to us through the fragility that results from our linguistic dependence. This paradox results in Lacan's return to the discourse of the obsessional, which Lefèbvre-Pontalis identifies in Lacan when he opens his question by stating, "I sense a certain unease" (*Seminar II,* 218). Lefèbvre-Pontalis may be referring to the unease among the participants, as he then says, "A lot is said here about the symbolic and the imaginary, but not much is said about the real. And the questions just asked show that we've somehow lost the real" (*Seminar II,* 218). Astutely, he perceives the actual difficulty in defining the "real" (since it is always already lost), locating the definition of reality in the obliqueness of the recognition of desire as a concomitant impossibility: "the recognition of desire must somehow pass through a certain number of mediations, of avatars, of imaginary formations, of states of being ignorant or of misunderstanding of a symbolic order. Finally, is that what you would call reality?" Lacan says, "That's what everybody calls reality" (*Seminar II,* 218). That the unease of the seminar is shared by Lacan is evident by his desire to evade the question and place it in the realm of the mundane by universalizing its understanding as well as his subsequent turn to the material given in his responses to the question of the real.

The discourse illustrates Lacan's ambivalence toward his own realism. As Lefèbvre-Pontalis provokes Lacan to choose between his belief that a universal real exists and his awareness that language constructs the world, he leads Lacan, and so shifts the master's discourse into one that must, by its determined trajectory, become grounded in "reality." He states, "Still, in reality there's something, which isn't like a thing, but like a category, like a norm, something more than there is in other orders. Reality isn't the totality of the symbol" (*Seminar II*, 218). Lacan resists this reading at first, and even later, when he turns to his example of the "table of presence," he converts that categorical model into a thing. First, Lacan's resistance is evident in his response to the question with a question: "I am going to ask you a question. Are you aware how rare it is for love to come to grief on the real qualities or faults of the loved one?" By shifting the issue to one of desire (as if we have ever left, or ever can leave, desire's domain), Lacan also invokes the problems of historical narrative. The dialogue is telling of Lacan's own struggle with his relationship to realism.

> M. Lefèbvre-Pontalis: *I'm not sure I can answer no. I'm not sure whether that might not be a retrospective illusion.*
>
> I said it was rare. And in fact, when it comes down to it, they appear to be much more like pretexts. One wants to believe that this reality has been touched on.
>
> M. Lefèbvre-Pontalis: *But that has very great consequences. It amounts to saying that there is no true conception, that one only moves from one corrective to the next, from one mirage to the next.*
>
> In fact, I do believe that to be the case in the register of intersubjectivity within which our entire experience is to be located. Do we ever reach as simple a real as those limitations of individual capacities which the various psychologies aim to attain? . . . I am therefore not trying to render the approach to the real through intersubjectivity fundamentally null and void. But in the end, the human drama as such is located outside the domain of such appraisals. Each person's drama, what each of us has to deal with, which produces certain effects, sometimes pathological, sometimes simply alienating, is of an entirely different order from these appraisals of the real, though they have their utility.
>
> So I don't question the existence of the real. There are all kinds of real limitations. It is undoubtedly true that I can't lift this table with one hand, there are all kinds of things that can be measured. (*Seminar II*, 218–19)

Within this apparently nominalist rejection of universals, Lacan manifests his utter belief in the real. He wants to shift the force of the real into elements that are measurable, calculable, and potentially reveal certainty, and in so doing, fails to see his own notion of the "real" as the instinct felt in the gut that exceeds linguistic articulability. Lefèbvre-Pontalis perceives Lacan's struggle and comments, "You only see the real under its aspect of adversity, as what resists, what is troublesome" (*Seminar II*, 219); to which comment Lacan responds by returning to a primary, empirical realism that foregrounds his engagement with the quarrel of the universals.

> It doesn't trouble me that I can't lift this table, it forces me to take a detour, that's obvious, but it doesn't trouble me to take a detour—I don't think that is the meaning of what I teach you when I distinguish the symbolic, the imaginary and the real.
>   . . . I am presenting the idea I'm putting forward here in a perceivable form, since I'm replying to someone who's putting the question of realism to me, someone who is a long way from being an idealist. There's no question of saying that the real didn't exist beforehand. But nothing that is effective in the domain of the subject emerges out of it. In so far as the subject exists, in so far as he sustains his existence, in so far as he raises the question of his existence, this subject with whom you are in dialogue in analysis and whom you cure through the art of speech, his essential reality consists in the junction of reality and the appearance of tables of presence. That doesn't mean that it's him who creates them all. What I'm going blue in the face telling you is precisely that they are already made. The game is already played, the die already cast. It is already cast, with the following proviso, that we can pick it up again, and throw it anew. The game has been going on a long time. Everything I'm showing you is already part of a story concerning which one can pronounce every possible and imaginable oracle. (*Seminar II*, 219)

To this long detour Lefèbvre-Pontalis says, "That doesn't answer my question," a quick, clear statement showing that Lacan's detour is symptomatic of his inability to articulate precisely what he believes with regard to reality and the limitations or potentialities within language. The exposure of this fragility leads Lacan to foreground the fullness in the lack of his precision and his simultaneous refusal (or inability) to be precise, and it forces him to put his cards on the table.

> We are reconsidering it. But what is striking is the extent to which a vacillation—quite apparent, because on the contrary it allows things to conserve a remarkable stability, somewhere other than where you are

accustomed to find it—a certain vacillation in the usual relations of the symbol and the real can throw you into considerable disarray. To be quite candid, if I had to sum you up—I'm not talking about you personally, but about people of your generation—I'd say what strikes me is the number of things they believe in.

I have found a very odd ordinance from 1277 for you to use. In those days of faith and darkness, there were forces to curb those who, on the forms at school, in the Sorbonne and elsewhere, openly blasphemed the name of Jesus or Mary during mass. That's not done any more—it would not occur to you to blaspheme against Jesus and Mary. But I've known highly surrealist people who would rather be hung than publish a poem, blaspheming the Virgin, because they thought that, after all, something just might happen to them.

The most severe punishments were decreed for those who played dice at the altar during the Holy Sacrament. Such things seem to me to indicate the existence of a working dimension which is singularly lacking in our time.

It is not for nothing that I am telling you about dice and making you play the game of even and odd. Without the shadow of a doubt, there's something rather scandalous about playing a game of dice on the altar, and all the more so during the Holy Sacrament. But I think that the fact that it is possible should restore to you the sense of a capacity which has been far more obliterated than one thinks in the circles we frequent. It is simply what is called the possibility of criticism. (*Seminar II*, 220)

In addition to the complicated display of a simultaneous belief in and resistance to the real, this interaction reflects a crucial pattern in Lacan's work: when he is pushed to the limits of his ability to articulate an idea, he relies on, appeals to, or falls back on the medieval text as an authority. At the end of his rope, Lacan defends his own thought by referring to a text or an idea from the Middle Ages, demonstrating his own belief in the power of medieval thought and relying on the idealization of the past in his students as an appeal to truth. When challenged, Lacan says, "if you don't believe me, consider the ordinance I found from 1277," gesturing toward the medieval as a proper source of truth-value, evidence of the logical formation of ideas, and thus revealing, symptomatically, the profundity of his own belief in the real of universals. Lacan's symptomatic display of his belief in the real of universals clarifies his argument about the real where his language fails. Such a performance also reflects the way he may be categorized as a realist. Additionally, the offhanded gesture toward the "odd ordinance from 1277" is a significant moment in the history of knowledge. After the condemnation of 1277 discussions of realism and nominalism and the limitations of human knowledge by way of reality and in the face of divine knowledge flourished.[55] This suggests that what seems like a random, antisystematic comment on Lacan's part is a citation of a significant moment in the debates over universals that is dropped to leave his students to the background work necessary to determine his own position. If one already knows the significance of the 1277 ordinance, then one will immediately understand that Lacan is locating his discussion in that medieval context, and he is extending the debate so that he can assert his own theory of the potential for real categories.

An additional factor at stake in this debate about the relationship between knowledge, language, and things is the indeterminable quality of the extent to which some thinkers are categorized as realists or nominalists. Most thinkers, including William of Ockham, who is often seen as the most extreme nominalist among the participants in the quarrel, exist in the middle on the spectrum of difference among the groups. Robert Myles's explication of the various forms of realism in his *Chaucerian Realism* helps to clarify the way in which most thinkers may in fact be positioned along the lines of a variation of realism. Explaining that the general misunderstanding that associates realism with "Cratylic realism" limits the realist to one who believes that there is a "natural, real relationship between a word and a thing," and has "nothing to do with 'scholastic realism,'" which believes in the potential for classifying and categorizing things, Myles opens up the category of the realist to extend to all of those thinkers who are not precisely nominalists.[56] Even William of Ockham, who is often employed as an exemplar of nominalism, is a foundational, epistemological, and linguistic realist according to Myles's system.[57] Myles outlines and defines six forms of realism, which are paraphrased below and characterized by a pervasive element of possibility:[58]

1. *Foundational realism:* The belief that we live in a world of beings created by a transcendent Being.
2. *Intentionalist realism:* The belief that creation is an intentional act and that human beings tend toward their creator.
3. *Ethical realism:* The belief that the order of the universe is subject to speech or speech acts that are either "proper" or "improper."
4. *Epistemological realism:* The assumption that Being (the foundation of beings) as "reality" can be known to some degree.

5. *Semiotic* and *linguistic realism:* The assumption that signs are a "reliable means of knowing this extramental reality."

6. *Psychological realism:* The belief that "signs may reveal, to some degree, the real mental or spiritual condition of individual human beings."

For Myles, Chaucer fulfills these categories and so must be called a realist. In chapters 1 and 4, I will address the extent of Chaucer's realism more specifically. For the purposes of this introduction, I find Myles's categories useful in defining the extent to which Lacan is a realist.

Lacan is quite overt at times about the extent to which he is a realist. In "The Agency of the Letter in the Unconscious" he provokes the nominalists by attempting to take the subject at its word and when he claims that the world of words creates the world of things as well as by asserting that the unconscious is a chain of signification.[59] This would seem to place him on the side of nominalism. However, his simultaneous belief that the real is possible, acceptable, and mundane, but that truth is what disturbs, sets forth a belief in the beyond of language and leads to linguistic analysis in the search for real categories. As Alexandre Leupin has put it, "Words, for Lacan, evoke something real outside of language."[60] Despite this potential confusion and resistance displayed in Lacan's approach to the quarrel about universals, at times he comes right out and says, "I am a realist, following the tradition of the medieval scholastics."[61]

The debate about language and knowledge persistently returns to a location of theological understanding and the limits of knowability. Like an understanding of or belief in God, the study of the unconscious requires a certain degree of faith. Despite his overt claims that God does not exist, Lacan is not an atheist, and he supplements love and desire for the singular causality of a Christian God even while he engages in a discussion of God's parallel to the unconscious. Like Freud and Nietzsche before him, Lacan says that God is dead. But, diverging from Nietzsche and Freud, Lacan claims that God is dead because he was always already dead. He was dead from the beginning, and this is why creation occurs ex nihilo.[62] The notion of God as that which exists in a fragile state of Being based on our own fictional concepts asserts a theological notion of God as that which is beyond knowledge.[63] The originary point of creation does not exist, and so causality is absent leaving creation to occur as if from nothing. This would signify a disbelief in God as the creator and originator of being, and indeed forecloses the possibility of perceiving Lacan as a *foundational realist* or an *intentional realist*. Since the notion of a "unique transcendent Being intentionally creating" the world is not possible without a conception of a singular God, Lacan cannot believe in realism as foundational or intentional. Nonetheless, he does revive God in the presence of the Other, the voice of desire and the unconscious, reinscribing a form of intentionality within the subject's unconscious drive. One of the most efficient evidentiary points for this supplementation is found in *Encore*, where Lacan states that love compensates for the lack of sexual relationship and that love is bound to the image of God as the unconscious:

> The Other, the Other as the locus of truth, is the only place, albeit an irreducible place, that we can give to the term, "divine being," God, to call him by his name. God *(Dieu)* is the locus where, if you will allow me this wordplay, the *dieu*—the *dieur*—the *dire*, is produced. With a trifling change, the *dire* constitutes the *Dieu*. And as long as things are said, the God hypothesis will persist.
>
> That is why, in the end, only theologians can be truly atheistic, namely, those who speak of God.
>
> There is no other way to be an atheist, except to hide one's head in one's arms in the name of I know not what fear, as if this God had ever manifested any kind of presence whatsoever. Nevertheless, it is impossible to say anything without immediately making Him subsist in the form of the Other. (*Seminar XX*, 45)

Through speaking, by stating the word, we invoke God as the Other. By a quick slight of hand, Lacan shifts this notion of the Other as God to the Other of the unconscious address of desire. Like God, the unconscious is evident wherever there is language (the sign). The paradox of intentionality exposes the intention of the unconscious as a drive that motivates the subject to speak and act in spite of his or her conscious *intention*. If we are careful not to grant the unconscious too much power in the scene of its interaction and struggle with conscious affect, then we cannot assign *intentionality* to the unconscious drive even though there is *motivation* found in its energy. There is no precise tendency back toward a perfect being or creator, so intentional realism is not present. Nonetheless, the goal of the unconscious, its desire to fulfill itself, aims toward a particular point, an inexpressible, often unknowable point, but a point that resembles the tendency toward perfection (seen here as equilibrium).

Myles's other categories apply to Lacan's specific form of realism. To the extent that Lacan believes that speech and language partially determine the proper or improper (good or evil) order of the universe, he is an *ethical realist*. This form of realism is evident especially in chapter 1, "Singularity, Sovereignty, and the One," where I discuss Lacan's view of singularity and the One with regard to the sovereign good. Since he believes that Being (the foundation of beings) as "reality" can be known to some degree, he is an *epistemological realist*. Lacan's hyperbolic investment in *semiotic* and *linguistic realism* pervades his study of the psyche, wherein we find the unconscious to be structured like a language, and remains topical throughout this book. Similarly, the belief in language as evidence of the unconscious reveals the profundity of Lacan's *psychological realism* and is perhaps most evident in chapters 3 and 5 where the phenomenon of courtly love comes to stand in for the logical methodology of knowing the subject in the world.

Beyond these fragmentary modes of realism, a sustaining real in Lacan's theory is that of the unconscious. To say that the unconscious is a universal, however, is not the same as "universalizing" the unconscious. Recalling Boethius's distinction between the "man" as a universal and the "person" as a particular, we can perceive how the unconscious as a universal is distinct from the universalizing quality that it would have if it were applied to the "person." Since "person" is not a universal category, the unconscious cannot be universalizing; it cannot act as Jung would have had it, in an archetypal manner. Rather, the unconscious is a universal substance of each particular "man" or "woman" that is distinct and changing according to the "person." Because language is so clearly impossible in determining the differences among categories of being, Lacan sought the universal language of mathematics as a means of articulating ideas that might exceed the play of analysis. His attempt to make psychoanalysis scientific by way of the language of mathematics testifies to his belief in the potential for the real of categories.

Numerology

Lacan's investment in finding the proper mathematical formulae for his theories so that he could eliminate transference from the process of analysis and pedagogy led as well to a form of numerology. Accordingly, my chapter breakdown adheres to the limitations and possibilities of mathematical play in his system. Moving through the elements of Lacan's theory of desire, we find that his attempt to locate unity reflects his belief in the potential of the real of universals. In chapter 1, "Singularity, Sovereignty, and the One," I show, by way of an articulation of Lacan's resistance to the dialectical system, how he struggles to achieve a definition of the "One." In his search for an articulation of the sovereign good, Lacan's interpretation of Aristotle resembles the Platonism of Boethius, who first initiated the quarrel of the universals in his commentaries. As a mode of asserting the intellectual in the world within an understanding of desire and the sovereign good, Lacan refers to Geoffrey Chaucer as the father of the trope of the fool, thus providing a connection to Chaucer's own engagement with the question of realism as it opposes nominalism, seen overtly in *The Clerk's Tale*. The intersection of the search for knowledge and the process of desire is evident in the positioning of sovereignty as singularity.

Chapter 2, "Duality, Ambivalence, and the Animality of Desire," suggests that the form of ambivalence strongest in the subject is that which is caused by the subject's awareness of desire as a mode of animality. In the quarrel of the universals, the Aristotelian claim that "All men are animals" asserts a form of categorical distinction that does not sit well with the man who wants to be properly human. By engaging the hybrid human-animal and animal-human as displayed by Marie de France's *Bisclavret* and the *Mélusine* legends told by Jean d'Arras and Coudrette, the ambivalence dominant in Freud's case studies of the Wolf Man and the Rat Man come to light as medieval problematics. The impossibility of defining "man" is bound to the problem of defining "woman" and as such Lacan's pronouncement that *la femme* (the woman) must be written with a cross through it (the woman) reflects a potential for an understanding of the universals as surplus, rather than limiting, categories. As such, Lacan's choice of the scatological courtly love poem by Arnaut Daniel to articulate his theory of desire foregrounds the problem of ambivalence, even as he seeks to illustrate the work of sublimation.

Chapter 3, "Dialectics, Courtly Love, and the Trinity," reconsiders Arnaut Daniel's troubadour text in the context of other courtly love poems that alternately institute the "decency" of distance and the "obscenity" of promixity as a means of addressing the substitution of the unconscious for God in Lacan's system of desire. Whereas the scene of two limits the dialectical process and therefore glosses over sublimation, the scene of three enacts the process of sublimation and reflects the trauma inherent in the attempt to represent desire. As the troubadours reflect the tripartite system of the "alone," the "bare," the "pure," put forth by Abelard in his discussion of the universals, they also contribute to the medieval debate. By engaging their work as he does, Lacan calls attention to the poetic display of the potential for categorization with regard to the uncontainability of desire and without a consideration of God as real. This potential resides in the knot-like structure of the unconscious.

Chapter 4, "The Quadrangle, the Hard Sciences, and Nonclassical Thinking," engages the potential for teaching that which is unknowable. As Socrates reveals the limits of teaching virtue in the *Meno*, Lacan recognizes the difficulty (if not impossibility) of conveying the structure of the unconscious as it is related to desire. Seeking to use language that is precisely not subject to confusion, he attempts to formulate the appropriate *matheme* (the scientific symbolic signifier) to teach his concepts. His idealization of the hard sciences reflects his obsession with clarity even as he is aware of the limitations of symbolic expression. His search for the single cut that might untie the knot of desire and the unconscious participates in the premodern project of attempting to understand the order of the cosmos by way of mathematics and scientific instruments and devices such as the astrolabe. In Geoffrey Chaucer's *Treatise on the Astrolabe*, however, we find that even the ostensibly perfect mode of scientific inquiry is flawed, and the uncertainty that emerges demonstrates the emergence of the nonclassical within the apparently classical system of realism.

Taking up the problem of the attempt to know the unknowable order of the world, chapter 5, "The Pentangle and the Resistant Knot," perceives the emergence of paranoia in the subject who seeks to conceal the unconscious. As opposed to the hysteria of the subject who displays the unconscious without mediation, the paranoid subject attempts to control the order of the unconscious, the failure of which provides evidence for its very power and presence. Reading the protagonist Gawain from *Sir Gawain and the Green Knight* as a paranoid subject, we see how the anonymous medieval poet displays the unconscious at work. Like Daniel Paul Schreber, who attempts to control his interactions with God so that he can return the order of the world to its proper status, Gawain's manipulation of the truth reflects his need to hide his subjectivity so that he may interact with the world in an orderly fashion. The substitution of the unconscious for God further reveals the manner in which Lacan seeks to achieve an understanding of the real while maintaining an atheistic perspective.

This consideration of the perfect circle of the pentangle dovetails into a short refrain that concludes this initial investigation into Lacan's medievalism. In this "conclusion" entitled "Materiality and Spirituality/ Lacan a Thomist?" I briefly address the problem of the interaction between faith and reason by way of the letter and its literal, material, and spiritual quality. Whereas Aquinas's goal was to reconcile faith and reason so that he could better achieve an understanding of our relationship to God, Lacan's work seeks to find faith in the unconscious at the limits of reason. As a mode of connecting the material with the spiritual, the foundational structure of the real is bound to the precise materiality of the unconscious and that which is apparently abstract — the forms of the intellect. As a realist, Lacan's participation in the quarrel of the universals shows not only how he is a medievalist, but also how the medieval is still dominant in our contemporary epistemological investigations.

CHAPTER ONE

Singularity, Sovereignty, and the One

If all these goods were constituent parts of happiness, each would differ from the others; for it is the nature of parts to be different things constituting one body. But I have proved that all these goods are one and the same thing; therefore they cannot be parts. Otherwise, happiness would seem to be constituted of one part, which is a contradiction in terms.

—Boethius, *The Consolation of Philosophy*

Cruelty resists; sovereignty resists. The one and the other, the one *like* the other, pose a resistance *to* psychoanalysis; not doubt, but *just as* psychoanalysis also resists them, in the most equivocal sense of this word. Sovereignty and cruelty, very obscure things, resist differently, but they resist, one *like* the other, both without and within psychoanalysis proper.

—Derrida, *Without Alibi*

The Naked King

When, in *Seminar VII, The Ethics of Psychoanalysis,* Lacan names Geoffrey Chaucer the father of the trope of the fool, he asserts Chaucer's influence on his own participation in the quarrel of the universals and his articulation of the real of desire in the unconscious.[1] Lacan says, "A tradition that begins with Chaucer, but which reaches its full development in the theatre of the Elizabethan period is, in effect, centered on the term 'fool.'"[2]

The importance of the fool to the transition from the medieval to the early modern periods reflects the coincidental rise in the literary expression of the fool and the visibility of hegemonic sovereign powers. As Lacan puts it, "The 'fool' is an innocent, a simpleton, but truths issue from his mouth that are not simply tolerated but adopted, by virtue of the fact that this 'fool' is sometimes clothed in the insignia of the jester. And in my view it is a similar happy shadow, a similar fundamental 'foolery,' that accounts for the importance of the left-wing intellectual" (*Seminar VII*, 182). The focus of the seminar as expressed in the "Outline" to *The Ethics of Psychoanalysis* engages the statement, the king is naked. In an obvious sense, if the king is naked then he is vulnerable, open to attack or seduction, or involved in a process of exhibiting his fragility as well as his potential sovereignty.[3] As Žižek has repeatedly shown, the naked king also challenges his subjects to call attention to his nudity.[4] If the king is sovereign, his subjects will not mention to him that he is lacking clothes, and paradoxically, he retains power in his fragility. If he is not sovereign enough, his subjects will call attention to his nudity and remind him to clothe himself, thus, again paradoxically, replacing him in the proper position of the sovereign. In the face of sovereign tyranny, only the fool can tell the king that he is naked and have the king listen, laugh, decide to clothe himself or not, and move forward as if no power shift has occurred. Taken in this context, what might appear to be a relegation of Chaucer to the role of father of the fool illustrates instead an identification of the connection between ideological power, sovereignty, and the impossibility of singularity; in this case, Lacan's brief nod to Chaucer becomes an invitation to explore the manner in which Chaucer's role as a realist who often disguises himself as a nominalist assists in the development of Lacan's realism.[5]

In *The Canterbury Tales* Chaucer's Clerk represents an overt dialogue with the debate over the existence of universals. His role as a scholar, as well as the topic of his tale and the conclusion he makes regarding the difference between the category of women and the particular instance of Griselda, asserts the limits of nominalism and gestures toward an understanding of the potential for the real of universals. The Clerk is a "fool" according to Lacan's view of the necessity and significance of the role of the fool as left-wing intellectual within the context of its opposition to the "knave" who is affiliated with the "depressing" ideology of the right-wing (*Seminar VII*, 183). The representation of the Clerk contributes to an understanding of the way in which Lacan's reference to Chaucer is highly significant to the role that medieval traditions other than that left by the troubadours and the scholastics might play in an understanding of Lacan's medievalism.[6] Although he focuses primarily on the tradition of courtly love and scholasticism, he is precisely *not limited* to those articulations and representations of the Middle Ages. Indeed, without missing a beat, Lacan then compares the knave to "Mr. Everyman," buttressing the significance of medieval literature to his argument.

Considering the fact that he is often associated with the character closest to the voice of Chaucer, it seems unlikely to interpret Chaucer's Clerk as a "fool." Taking into account, however, that in the eyes of the pilgrims conceived as a conglomeration representing the "general public," one who has his head in his books while others are engaged in entertainment is quite definitely a fool, and adding to this the fact that each of the travelers is satirized in one manner or another, then the Clerk is a perfect example of the left-wing intellectual fool. The anti-intellectualism of the group is articulated by Harry Baille, whose invitation to the Clerk to tell his tale reveals the stereotypical responses of right-wing ideology to left-wing intellectuals; or, more specifically, prejudice against the scholar.[7]

"Sire Clerk of Oxenford," oure Hooste sayde,
"ye ryde as coy and stille as dooth a mayde
Were newe spoused, sittynge at the bord;
This day ne herde I of youre tonge a word.
I trowe ye studie aboute some sophyme;
But Salomon seith 'every thynge hath tyme.'
      For Goddes sake, as beth of better cheere!
It is not tyme for to studien here.
Telle us some myrie tale, by youre fey!
For what man that is entred in a pley,
He nedes moost unto the pley assente.
But precheth nat, as freres doon in Lente,
To make us for oure olde synnes wepe,
Ne that thy take mae us nat to slepe.
      Telle us som murie thynge of aventures.
Youre termes, youre colours, and youre figures,
Keepe hem in stoor til so be ye entite
Heigh style, as what that men to kynges write.
Speketh so pleyn at this tyme, we yow preye,
That we may understonde what ye seye." (*Clerk's Prologue,* 1–20)[8]

The effeminization assigned to the Clerk by the comparison to a "mayde" "newe spoused" and the pleas to be of "better cheere" combine with the request not to preach or to speak in too high a language to show the Host's classification of the Clerk as an "intellectual"; the tone, however, also suggests that Harry thinks of the intellectual as a "fool" since he cannot enjoy himself. Recall that this is core of Lacan's seminar on the ethics: to understand how the law and pleasure relate to each other and how one might achieve the sovereign good. Reading the Clerk as a "fool" provides a means of perceiving Lacan's engagement with realism as it contrasts with Chaucer's nominalism and shows the importance of the minor citation of Chaucer within Lacan's *Ethics of Psychoanalysis*. This foolishness is crucial to an understanding of the impossibility of sovereignty because, as Drucilla Cornell has noted, the "ontological elaboration of the sovereign good that classical ethics attempted is philosophically unjustifiable, even *unethical*."[9] In *The Clerk's Tale* we see how Walter's attempt at sovereign unity is unethical and how the "good" becomes the "bad" when it moves from singular identity to the masses. This question is also parallel to the question of the potential for real categories, as sovereign subjectivity is metaphorical for (and metonymical of) the question of linguistic determination of categories. Since the subject is comprised of language and the unconscious is structured like a language, the categorization of knowledge is as significant for things in the world as it is for beings.

Russell A. Peck's "Chaucer and the Nominalist Questions" suggests that Chaucer is Boethian in his approach to an understanding of universals and he develops an understanding of William of Ockham's theories that are compatible with the "moderate realism" associated with Boethius.[10] Investigating the difference between knowledge and voluntary actions, Peck shows that the difference between free will and knowledge is similar for William of Ockham's nominalist approach and that knowing is a combination of "desire, perspective, choice, and judgment" such that "willing and knowing are essentially the same act" ("Chaucer," 746). This leads then to a consideration of singularities as those objects in the world that produce knowledge by way of language. For Peck, "The knower is a viator and linguistic craftsman who, with his words, seeks a firmer base for human knowledge in the singularities and empirical realities of the created world" ("Chaucer," 746).[11]

In medieval scholasticism and in Lacanian psychoanalysis the search for the sovereign good is bound to language. The basic level of language, the signifier, both enables and prohibits an approach to the ideal of Unity in the sovereign good. In Lacan's work singularity only exists in a multitudinous form, and so, defined as a properly whole monad its instantiation is impossible. The ideal of singularity gives way to Oneness, which is a crucial element of thought that drives desire and motivates the subject to pursue knowledge. Different from singularity, we find "the One" that does exist, though only in a realist sense as the "essence of the signifier." Throughout his work Lacan speaks of and idealizes the "One." He consistently performs his realist tendencies to believe in an Ideal, while simultaneously revealing his awareness that the achievement of this knowledge as possession is impossible because the presence of the One is bound to the linguistic process. Through language the One emerges and "because every signifier, from the phoneme to the sentence, can serve as a coded message . . . it emerges as object and that one discovers that it is what determines that in the world — the world of the speaking being — One occurs *(il y a de l'Un)*, that is to say, element occurs, the Greek στοιχεῖον[12] Lacan already translates the Greek "stoicheion" for us in his statement; meaning "element," στοιχεῖον (or "stoicheion") has its origin in the opposites, the Empedoclean elements, and refers to simple bodies or entities in Plato and Aristotle.[13] By showing the Oneness of sovereignty as it opposes singularity, Lacan reflects that Unity is comprised of multiplicity.

The refrain common to *Seminar VII, The Ethics of Psychoanalysis* and *Seminar XX, Encore* that the king is naked shows that the ostensibly sovereign subject is vulnerable to the perception of others because his own desire is marked by his awareness of the desire of the Other. Even the sovereign king is subject to the demand of the Other, revealing sovereignty to be a phantasmatic projection of impossibly singular power. Sovereignty, conceived of as singularity, is also impossible as the subject exists in relation to the desires and imagined desires of others (and Others). Lacan's tenacious work toward bridging the gap between singularity and the One illustrates his adherence to realism.

In *Seminar VII, The Ethics of Psychoanalysis* and *Seminar XX, Encore,* in addition to the overt form of Lacan's medievalism in his analysis of courtly love as a model for desire, the investigation of the potential for (and limitations of) the sovereign good follows a medieval scholastic methodology. In his struggle to articulate and demonstrate the manner in which desire is bound to the classical Aristotelian concept of the sovereign good and to the drive for singularity, Lacan takes on the position of the scholastic philosophers. Sovereignty, wholeness, and desire are at their core precisely linked to the belief in Ideal forms despite the fact that we may never have pure access to these ideals in the real world. The "Outline to the Seminar" that inaugurates *Seminar VII, The Ethics of Psychoanalysis* provides the most concise definition of desire while demonstrating its elemental realism. The foundational element of desire is that "it is always desire in the second degree, desire of desire" (*Seminar VII*, 14). Desire desires itself and the perpetual drive toward fulfillment is the recognition of persistent lack. As the energy of desire, however, lack must be perceived as a fullness that serves a purpose. Similarly, the fragmentation of the subject famously delineated in Lacan's early piece "The Mirror Stage as Formative of the Function of the I as Revealed in Psychoanalytic Experience"[14] presents the subject as necessarily lacking; wholeness is neither possible nor good, despite the fact that it is ultimately and pathetically desirable. Though futile, the desire for wholeness leads the subject to attempt to find sovereignty as a mode of being in the world. The recognition of the impossibility of wholeness and singularity sublates the drive for sovereignty as an Ideal stable form, enabling the emergence of a more mutable and multiple concept of sovereignty.

Throughout *The Ethics of Psychoanalysis* (as well as the rest of Lacan's work), this foundational function of desire becomes layered with alternate instances of Lacan's medievalism such that the origin of singularity, sovereignty, and desire is often occluded; however, the clarity of these ideas in the "Outline to the Seminar" foregrounds the contribution that Lacan makes to the quarrel of the universals. Critics of psychoanalysis often pinpoint the universalizing structure of it and the attempt to move from particular instances of neurosis and psychosis to general assertions as a mode of provising potential answers and of posing new questions about epistemology and subjectivity. What these commentators miss is that psychoanalysis asserts ideas as myths that narrate structures in particular cases so that patterns may be found, but this textuality is not proscriptive. A precise difference must be marked between adherence to the possibility of the existence of universals (which is specific) and "universalization" (which is totalizing). Even when Lacan extracts and posits that the ethics he outlines have "universal validity," his definition of the universal is a Kantian one that presumes difference:

> In truth, although the response to the problem that we are proposing here is obviously illustrated in the conflict of an obsessional, it nevertheless has a universal validity; that is why there are different ethics and there is ethical thought. It is not simply the philosopher's thought alone that seeks to justify duty, that duty on which we have shed a variety of light—genetical and originary for example. The justification of that which presents itself with an immediate feeling of obligation, the justification of duty as such—not simply in one or other of its commands, but in the form imposed—is at the heart of an inquiry that is universal. (*Seminar VII,* 7–8)

Crucial to a reading of this elementary universality is the focus on *inquiry.* The question, demand, or request to alleviate suffering, to carve a space for finding happiness and living ethically, is a universal question; the particular answers, if there are any to be found, are located in the analytical ideals that manifest responses only in the realm of the Real and reflect Lacan's realism that is peppered with an awareness of the desirability and impossibility of achieving these ideals. The first three primary analytical ideals, which are specifically distinct from "idealism,"[15] are (1) the ideal of human love; (2) the ideal of authenticity; and (3) the ideal of nondependence or prophylaxis of dependence (*Seminar VII,* 9–10). These ideals might be conceived as desire, being, and singularity, and they function together as limits on the horizon of the achievement of a sovereign good. As such, Lacan's realism—his desire to find the universal sovereign good—is a mode of inquiry and an instantiation of desire itself, not a prescription or proscription for universality. The fact that he ultimately states that sovereignty is fragmentary and not unitary does not detract from the epistemological drive to believe in the possibility of the unknowable One.

The "real" or "Real" of the Imaginary, Symbolic, Real trinity is discovered in this impossible ideal space and must be distinguished from "reality" as empirical and phenomenological experienced life. The "real" is a universal defining Lacan's realism (as opposed to nominalism).[16] The real becomes a bit complicated later in the seminar when Lacan discusses the "reality principle" as opposed to the "pleasure principle" because the "reality principle" does *appear* to be bound to empirical and phenomenological existence when Lacan states that "Moral action is, in effect, grafted on to the real" (*Seminar VII*, 21). However, this reality is metaphysical and psychical (and only physical) in that it is bound to the processing of experience in the unconscious as it relates to conscious action. Since "the moral law, the moral command, the presence of the moral agency in our activity, insofar as it is structured by the symbolic, is that through which the real is actualized—the real as such, the weight of the real," sovereignty and the sovereign good are bound to the renunciation of pleasure as it is ostensibly necessary for the pursuit of moral law (*Seminar VII*, 20). Still, the universality of this endeavor remains on the level of *inquiry* and *attempt* as ideal forms of action as defined in the outline.

Lacan is thus exploring the epistemological and metaphysical fields addressed by Boethius, whose commentaries on Porphyry's *Introduction to the Categories of Aristotle* combine with his translations of Aristotle's *Organon* to initiate the quarrel of the universals. The mode of inquiry that Boethius practiced and that helped to catalyze the scholastic practices so central to learning during the Middle Ages is imitated by Lacan when he seeks to articulate the limits of metaphysical, ethical, and aesthetic knowledge. Beginning with a question surrounding the possibility of the sovereign good, Lacan also responds to Boethius's similar demand in *The Consolation of Philosophy*.[17]

Taking up the issue of confinement and persecution as a mode of addressing the problem of the law's relationship to pleasure as early as *Seminar I, Freud's Papers on Technique*,[18] embedded within an explication of the way that the unconscious appears in language by way of slips, Lacan engages the intertextual spectral trace of Boethius. He states that the Epicurean is an example of the ambiguity of discourse.

> The Epicurean introduces arguments about the function of the truth which he believes to have refuted. But these possess in themselves the virtue of truth in so far as they confirm in the listener a conviction exactly contrary to that which the Epicurean wishes to inspire in him. Furthermore, you know the extent to which a masked discourse, a discourse of persecuted speech—as a writer by the name of Leo Strauss calls it—under a politically oppressive regime, for instance, can get things across by pretending to refute arguments which in fact express its true thought. (*Seminar I*, 260)

Two main citational elements in this passage, the invocations of Epicurus and Strauss, take us back to antiquity in this search for an understanding of the law and pleasure.

First, the reference to the Epicurean understanding of the significance of pleasure to the sovereign good invokes a moment in the early recognition of the unconscious. As the enunciator of a statement that the listener hears in inverted form, the Epicurean speaker illustrates the working of the unconscious in relation to language. A properly direct and rational utterance would not come back to the listener in inverted form; rather, it would appear as clear and significant in the linear fashion designed to determine meaning and logic. The institution of pleasure, emotion, or desire with an awareness of suffering leads the subject to display a relationship to language that is neither linear nor rational but often maintains logic as significance is inverted. The emergence of "truth" (in this instance) is one that disrupts the intention of the speaker and reveals unconscious meaning, the potential for error, but also the potential for a form of truth that was not predetermined or rationally planned. In *The Therapy of Desire* Martha Nussbaum suggests that Platonists and Augustinian Christians preclude investigation of desire and the unconscious as a means of achieving the sovereign good. "For both Platonists and these Christians, digging more deeply into ourselves is not the right way to proceed in ethical inquiry. For the possibility must always be left open that everything we are and want and believe is totally in error."[19] Error, however, is necessary to the discovery of truth, as Lacan, following Socrates and the scholastic philosophers, claims throughout his work, and this reflects the significance of the deep digging that is central to ethical and epistemological investigation. Despite the desire to avoid profound internal observation and analysis, even Augustine condescends to consider his unconscious drives in *The Confessions*.[20]

Classical philosophy paves the way for investigation of the emotions and the unconscious. Even as Aristotle attempted to forward the notion that emotions and desires are forms of intentional awareness, and therefore consciously controllable,[21] the very effort to distinguish between the truth of rational emotions and the falsity of irrational emotions reveals an understanding of the layers of desire, paving the way for Epicurus to perceive the profundity of "false beliefs." Indeed, Nussbaum argues that Epicurus "discovers the unconscious" within the realm of these irrational or false desires or beliefs. This discovery is evident in Epicurus's

> understanding that the false beliefs that cause disturbance in life do not all lie on the surface of the self, ready for critical and dialectical scrutiny, as the Aristotelian seems to think. They lie deep in the soul, exercising their baneful influence, often beneath the level of consciousness. *Epicurus, in short, discovers the unconscious—a discovery after which Aristotelianism cannot ever look the same.* (*Therapy of Desire*, 133) (emphasis added)

What does it mean to say that "after the unconscious" Aristotelianism cannot look the same? Does it make a difference if the unconscious is "discovered" by Epicurus, by St. Thomas Aquinas, or by Freud? The significant point of Nussbaum's claim that the recognition of the unconscious alters Aristotelian logic is that the power of purely rational intention in the direction of thought and language is marked by pleasure and the drives. It does not matter who "discovers" the unconscious because it is bound to language. The voice of the Other in the self is always a blend of the varying ideological forces articulated in historical contexts, but the unconscious is a permanent real thing that is expressed in action.

Implicitly presaging Nussbaum's explicit insight, Lacan's work with the *Nichomachean Ethics* adds Epicurus to Aristotle to show how the two work together.[22] The *tuché* (the encounter with the real) becomes central to the unraveling and explication of this conflict between conscious and unconscious intention, action, and meaning. In *Seminar XI, The Four Fundamental Concepts of Psychoanalysis*[23] Lacan explores the *tuché* to explain the real of psychoanalysis, reinserting what Nussbaum claims is absent from Epicurus into a post-Aristotelian system. For Nussbaum,

> the practical aim to which Epicurus dedicates both ethics and philosophy of nature is characterized in a markedly un-Aristotelian way: for it involves nothing less than the complete removal of *tuché*, of vulnerability to events beyond our control, from the pursuit of *eudaimonia*. Aristotelian ethics does not give *tuché* unlimited power; in fact, it insists that the most important things in human life are not very vulnerable to reversal. (*Therapy of Desire*, 121)[24]

Lacan employs the *tuché* as a means of explicating the search for the cause of the real and reflects a Boethian approach to an understanding of intentionality and chance (or Fortune). Before demonstrating the Boethian character of Lacan's view of the real, however, it is important to show how Lacan revises the *tuché*.

Chapter 5 of *Seminar XI, The Four Fundamental Concepts of Psycho-analysis,* entitled "Tuché and Automaton," opens with a section entitled "Psycho-analysis is not an idealism," and thus reframes the three primary analytical ideals of human love, authenticity, and nondependence addressed earlier in this chapter. By calling attention to the way in which psychoanalysis is *not* an idealism, the real of the praxis of these ideals, their function within reality as universal goals is grounded in experience. Lacan translates the *tuché* precisely as "*the encounter with the real*" (*Seminar XI,* 53). Lacan begins by asking, "Where do we meet this real?" (*Seminar XI,* 53). He then posits the *tuché* as different from that employed by Aristotle, "who uses it in his search for a cause," appropriating the *tuché* and defining it as the encounter with the real that is "beyond the *automaton,* the return, the coming-back, the insistence of the signs, by which we see ourselves governed by the pleasure principle" (*Seminar XI,* 53–54). The privileging of the unconscious drive—the pleasure principle—over the apparently automatic action of the *automaton* attributes intentionality to the unconscious as it overcomes the conscious movement toward action. Limited as it is then, by the unconscious, the conscious will is confined, oppressed, even repressed in the face of the expression of the unconscious as a real. "The real is that which always lies behind the automaton, and it is quite obvious, throughout Freud's research, that it is this that is the object of his concern" (*Seminar XI,* 54). Accordingly, the automaton is never purely automatic since it is exactly motivated by the unconscious. The automaton only *appears* to be automatic and driven by an external cause; in practice the internal motivations of the unconscious drive the subject to act and speak in the world.

The problem of free will and intentionality is evidently connected to the question of chance, the chance that the unconscious real will emerge in the conscious realm, and the chance that the conscious will act on behalf of the unconscious. But again, this is only a matter of appearance, as chance is not really at stake, since the real of the unconscious is always at work in the conscious, whether it is realized or not.[25] Lacan says this when he claims, "What is repeated, in fact, is always something that occurs—the expression tells us quite a lot about its relation to the *tuché*—as if by chance" (*Seminar XI,* 54). The element of chance is only important because it shows the conscious reaction to refusing or repressing the unconscious. This is the point at which Lacan's view of the *tuché* intersects with his desire to articulate the sovereign good as a combination of the philosophical systems forwarded by Epicurus and Aristotle and reflect the arguments of Boethius.

Boethius's Neoplatonism is considered to be prevalent in his work, and this is especially evident when, in Book 2 of his second commentary on Aristotle's *On Interpretation*, he seeks to complete his work on Aristotle so that he can "return to Plato."[26] This Platonic element of Boethius's Aristotelianism is significant to his understanding of chance and refers us back to the *tuché* that is about meeting and the imperceptible difference between causality and absence of causality. As Etienne Gilson remarks, *chance* for Boethius "is still here the accidental intersection of two chains of causality that meet, without being determined to meet by any end."[27] Gilson finds that the lack of determination occurs on the level of the "human" end; once "divine" purpose enters the scene there is no longer any possibility of chance. Similarly, the unconscious, as a necessary *real* that supplements the divine force of God, leaves nothing to chance.

In *The Consolation of Philosophy*, despite the disparaging remarks made against the Epicureans and the Stoics, these elements of classical thought emerge as significant to the formation of the unity of the sovereign good. The establishment of the search for misery's solace in *The Consolation of Philosophy* initially suggests a desire to eliminate suffering and find pleasure. Of course, Boethius is warned against the notion that pleasure will lead to the sovereign good when Lady Philosophy shows the gaps in particular approaches to knowledge:

Cuius hereditatem cum deinceps Epicureum vulgus ac Stoicum ceterique pro sua quisque parte raptum ire molirentur meque reclamantem renitentempque veleut in partem praedae traherent, vestem quam meis textueram minibus, disciderunt abreptisque ab ea panniculis totam me sibi cessisse credentes abiere. In quibus quoniam queaedam nostri habitus vestigial videbantur, meos esse familiars inprudentia rate nonnullus eorum profane multitudinis errore pervertit.

[And after him [Plato] the crowd of Epicureans and Stoics and the rest strove as far as they could to seize his legacy, carrying me off protesting and struggling, as if I were part of the booty, tearing my dress, which I wove with my own hands, and then went off with their torn-off shreds,

thinking they possessed all of me. And because they seemed to be wear-
ing certain bits of my dress, some were ignorantly accepted as my servants,
and were abused by the delusions of the uneducated mob.] (*Consolation*,
I.21–30)

Lacking in the completeness of Platonic thought, the Epicureans and
Stoics nonetheless did strive to construct a philosophical system that
would account for multiplicity within singularity in the search for the
sovereign good; because they attempted to think through the limitations of purely rational control these philosophical systems are viewed
by Lady Philosophy as being potentially dangerous to the masses. However, Lady Philosophy's awareness of the unconscious and natural (Epicurean) drives comes forth when she guides Boethius toward an understanding of unity as equal to goodness.

> Neque nunc nos de voluntariis animae cognoscentis motibus, sed de
> naturali intentione tractamus, sicuti est quod accceptas escas sine cogi-
> tatione transigimus, quod in somno spiritum ducimus nescientes.

> [Nor are we now dealing with the voluntary motions of the intelligent
> soul, but with the exertion of nature, such as when we digest food we
> have taken in without any conscious thought, or when we draw breath
> in our sleep without knowing it.] (*Consolation*, III.85–89)

Boethius thus invokes the natural drives, the involuntary actions, and
the unconscious processes as a means of finding a potentially human–
divine connection that potentially represents the unconscious at work
in the discovery of the Oneness, the Unity of the sovereign good. Of
course, it is only through the combination of reason, philosophical systems, and belief in the divine power of God that the Boethian notion of
the Good may be achieved. Nonetheless, as a parallel register for God,
the natural force of the unconscious represents a means by which we
might consider free will to be located in the subject despite the tyrannical boundaries placed on it by language. L. O. Aranye Fradenburg discusses this subject in the context of allegory when she says of Chaucer's
Boece 1, prosa I that

> the group of one, the sovereign or the universal, offers a "unique" figure
> that can link the distinctiveness of objects to the *jouissance* of insentient
> generality. In Chaucer's *Boece*, the "stature" of Lady Philosophy — a
> figure of redeemed figuration, that is, of the capacity of the mind to
> know universals via images.[28]

Taking Lady Philosophy as a symbolic figure illustrates the manner in which representation depends on the potential for universals. The mind's capacity for tranference between the word and the thing binds the unconscious to free will.

The second point from the intersection of Epicurus and Strauss in Lacan's seminar calls attention to the function of free will as it is linked to and opposes persecution. By referencing Strauss, whose *On Tyranny* performed his debate with Alexandre Kojève regarding the relationship between philosophy and tyranny and the ends of history,[29] and whose *Persecution and the Art of Writing* asserts a non-Western element of philosophical investigation into the universals and freedom, Lacan gestures toward an understanding of non-Christian medieval and early modern philosophy written under oppressive systems similar to that which first motivated and then silenced Boethius. Elsewhere, in *Écrits*, Lacan refers to Strauss as a means of addressing the connection between truth and desire.

> One may read with profit a book by Leo Strauss, from the land that traditionally offers asylum to those who choose freedom, in which the author reflects on the relation between the art of writing and persecution. By pushing to its limits the sort of connaturality that links this art to that condition, he lets us glimpse a certain something which in this matter imposes its form, in the effect of truth on desire. (*Écrits*, 158)

The search for truth is clearly bound to the articulation of desire in a system of oppression. The limit case of tyrannical oppression that Strauss investigates is taken up by Lacan as a means of demonstrating the utter impossibility of freedom within language as well as the power of the unconscious. The inversion here between the effect of "truth on desire" opposes the more common understanding of the unconscious as the effect of "desire on truth," thus complicating the expression of free will.[30] If truth affects desire, then desire is subject to an external cause that supercedes the drives of desire, a confounding statement given Lacan's desire to articulate the foundational process of the unconscious with regard to an understanding of the world. Mirroring *Seminar I, Freud's Papers on Technique*, where Lacan perverts Strauss's project to disseminate knowledge about Islamic and Jewish medieval philosophy as distinct from medieval scholasticism by sandwiching Strauss between Epicurus and Augustine, here Lacan reverts to a Christianized explication of the unconscious in relation to language. The inherent connection between the spirit and the letter suggests a realist approach to language and categories:

> Of course, as it is said, the letter killeth while the spirit giveth life. We can't help but agree, having had to pay homage elsewhere to a noble victim of the error of seeking the spirit in the letter; but we should also like to know how the spirit could live without the letter. Even so, the pretensions of the spirit would remain unassailable if the letter had not shown us that it produces all the effects of truth in man without involving the spirit at all. (*Écrits*, 158)

The reference to the Word as a manifestation of Truth and the potential for the real are bound to language (logos). If language, the letter, takes precedence over the spirit, it is because the ability to articulate the spirit is dependent upon the sign. Even as he seeks to show the construction of truth as a form of linguistic presence, Lacan speaks as if one who is captivated by language and so not properly "free." In *Seminar I, Freud's Papers on Technique,* Lacan's reference to Strauss occurs in his response to Father Beirnaert's questions, leading the reader to remain within medieval Christian philosophy despite Strauss's warnings against such correlations. Lacan follows the reference to Strauss by returning to Augustine: "In short, Saint Augustine orients his entire dialectic around these three poles, error, mistake, ambiguity of speech. Well, it is as a function of this impotence of signs in teaching—simply to take up Father Beirnaert's terms—that next time we will try to get grips with the founding dialectic of the truth of speech" (*Seminar I,* 260). The medievalism here is not simply the superficial one evident in the reference to Augustine, as any reference might provide a superficial form of medievalism worthy of mention but not necessarily worthy of investigation; rather, the articulation of the slippages in language and the way in which language often misses its mark or cannot fully convey ideas is significant to the understanding and development of Lacan's realism as it is in constant tension with nominalism. His use of Strauss to explicate Freud's theory of the unconscious displaying itself in speech gestures toward the restraints that the repression imposes on the unconscious, employing broader ideological apparatuses as an example of the strength of the unconscious. Here, within the larger framework of a discussion of Augustinian sign theory that is at stake in this section of *Seminar I,* the focus on linguistic slips calls attention to the role that the real plays within the nominal, implying a connection between his own discourse and that expressed by Boethius, and in the context of engaging Catholic thought with a concern toward existentialism. It is here that we see a clear overlap between Lacan's desire to articulate the response to the question of the sovereign good and the psychoanalytical approach to language and desire.

The Fool and ~~the Woman~~

Lacan's drive to articulate and define the One and the sovereign good and the potential for the real of universal categories could have benefited from a consideration of Geoffrey Chaucer's *The Clerk's Tale*.[31] Respond-ing in part to Boethius's *The Consolation of Philosophy,* and translating the tale from Boccaccio and Petrarch,[32] Chaucer's *The Clerk's Tale* seeks to determine the relation between dialectics, the quarrel of the univer-sals, and the process of desire as it is predicated on the possibility of sin-gularity and universality. The tale illustrates the relationship between the sovereign (Walter) and his subjects (the people and Griselda). As Walter struggles to maintain sovereignty over his subjects, he is bound to their concern regarding the potentiality of his heir. Responding to their request that he marry, Walter takes Griselda, one of the many of the lower-class subjects, as his wife. He asks her to promise to obey him, which Griselda confirms with her words and her actions. Then, consciously seeking to test Griselda's honor, patience, and grace, he unconsciously puts his own sovereignty to the test as he imposes on her tyrannical limitations and orders. To the extent that his tyranny is a reflection of the fragility of his sovereignty, Walter's evil actions often appear pathetic. Perhaps even worse than his feigned marriage to another woman (his daughter) at the end of the tale is the Medea-like way in which he deprives Griselda of her children.[33] When he tells her that her children have been taken away and eaten by hounds, like Medea he performs a struggle against that which appears to threaten him. The extent to which Walter goes to test Griselda reveals his own sense of his failed singularity and sovereignty. On the contrary, Griselda's consistent patience and obedience reveal her ability to attain a position of sovereign goodness.[34] In his *Ethics: An Essay on the Understanding of Evil*, Alain Badiou perceives the potential for singularity precisely in consistency. "When all is said and done, con-sistency is the engagement of one's singularity (the animal 'some-one') in the continuation of a subject of truth."[35] Ever the good reader of Lacan, Badiou points out the connection between this consistency and the driving force of desire:

Lacan touched on this point when he proposed his ethical maxim: "do
not give up on your desire" ("*ne pas céder sur son désir*"). For desire is
constitutive of the subject of the unconscious; it is thus the not-known
par excellence, such that "do not give up on your desire" rightly means:
"do not give up on that part of yourself that you do not know." We might
add that the ordeal of the not-known is the distant effect of the eventual
supplement, the puncturing *(trouée)* of "some-one" by a fidelity to this
vanished supplement, and that "do not give up" means, in the end: do
not give up on your own seizure by a truth-process.

But since the truth-process is fidelity, then if "Do not give up" is the
maxim of consistency—and thus of the ethic of a truth—we might well
say that it is a matter, for the "some-one," of *being faithful to a fidelity.*
And he can manage this only by adhering to his own principle of continuity, the perseverance in being of what he is. By *linking* (for such,
precisely is consistency) the known by the not-known. (*Seminar VII,* 47)

Griselda, enacting pure consistency and fidelity, achieves singularity by
refusing to react to Walter's provocations. Even further, she allows
her unconscious to appear as a real in her moment of syncope upon the
return of her children.[36] As the Clerk says in his conclusion to the tale,
as an exemplar of womanly behavior, it is unlikely that Griselda can be
emulated or duplicated in other women because she stands in for the
impossible woman;[37] however, as an instance of the impossible real asserting itself by way of an understanding of the desire for Oneness,
Griselda stands in for each person's progress toward truth. Extending
this concluding statement, we find that this impossible woman is also
akin to the particularity of the woman as "person" and resembles the
representation of the category of "woman" as that which must be written
with a line through it: ~~woman~~. This suggests that the Clerk, like Lacan,
represents a consideration of the potentiality of the real as a universal
category.

As the secular scholar among the group in *The Canterbury Tales,* the
Clerk is established in the *General Prologue* as the character who is least
subject to criticism or satire among the group.[38] His is a sober voice of
scholasticism and the one that contributes to the quarrel of the universals as well as the question of sovereignty, reflecting the voice of the poet.
The Monk, the figure we would otherwise associate with the scholastic
debates, is too concerned with his gold, love-knots, and other material
effects to weigh in on the subject in any interesting manner other than
that of the excess of realism and the corruption of the church suggesting

that he would be the more obvious fool. Though he is mocked along with the rest of the group, the criticism launched against the Clerk is limited to the expenditure of his little wealth on books of philosophy.

On the surface, the Clerk appears to present a proper balance between the search for secular and divine knowledge. His long-standing knowledge of logic reflects his awareness of dialectics, and his "Twenty bookes, clad in blak or reed, / Of Aristotle and his philosophie" (*General Prologue*, 294–95) are material evidence of the abstract knowledge of classical philosophy such that it is not impossible to believe that his speech is indeed "Sownynge in moral vertu, . . . / And gladly wolde he lerne and gladly teche" (*General Prologue*, 307–8). However, the mere visible presence of his knowledge, the fact that he has learned logic (long ago), and his stereotypical "scholarly" appearance do not attest to the knowledge that is imperceptible. He may, in fact, carry his books and segregate himself in the process of study as a means of signifying the process of metaphysical and dialectical study so that he need not engage in its utterance. The incompleteness of his degree, read by Jill Mann as evidence of his status as an "eternal student" who "performs the role of the ideal scholar" and is an "ideal representative of the life of study," also provides evidence for the apparent gaps in his knowledge.[39] His persistent engagement with scholastic study does not lead to the movement from the university to the church. The forms of knowledge that determine his repertoire, however, reveal an awareness of the limitations of nominalism and a longing for the solace of realism and universals. Despite his dedication and perpetual study of classical secular philosophy, the Clerk's epistemophilia does not seem to find its satisfaction in philosophy. That is, philosophy does not console him. Either the Clerk is a bad scholar, a "fool" who is also a "knave" and therefore a "scoundrel," or the fissures in his philosophical system signify his participation in the quarrel of the universals and render him a more proper "fool."

The Clerk's tale combines with his own response to reflect the disjunction between his awareness of the limitations of dialectics and his awareness of the impossibility of achieving the categories of the real. This ironic reversal of potential, or achieved, sovereign subjectivity plays with the master/slave dialectic in such a manner that the dialectic itself becomes subject to the sovereignty of a universal singularity beyond dialectics. Walter's attempt to master Griselda, in true Hegelian fashion, is met with his dependence on the servant; however, Griselda's mastery over Walter is not bound to a dialectical engagement with him. Rather, Griselda escapes the dialectics of master and servant because she is bound instead to her oath, a nominalist utterance that achieves the universal because it is indicative of the imperceptible real of her faith.

The Clerk, however, does not seem to understand this epistemological web. Philosophy's failure to console the Clerk motivates him to seek a justification for singular sovereignty as that which may achieve universal signification. Rescuing Walter from the potential accusations that he is simply sadistic and evil, the Clerk shows how, through the process of tormenting Griselda, he learns how to lead his people. At the beginning of the tale Walter is precisely neither sovereign nor free; rather, his actions and decisions are dictated by the will of his people. His own fears of losing singular sovereignty over himself give way to his fear of losing sovereignty over the "many" that he rules, such that his decision reveals the illusion of both forms of sovereignty.

> "Ye wol," quod he, "myn owene peple dere,
> To that I nevere est thoughte streyne me.
> I me rejoysed of my liberte,
> That seelde tyme is founded in marriage;
> Ther I was free, I moot been in servage." (*Clerk's Tale*, 143–47)

Walter's consent is marked by ambiguity. The people are constraining him by way of their demand, but they also are dominating him by requesting that he choose to give up his sovereignty. When he says, " 'But nathelees I se youre trewe entente, / And truste upon youre wit' " (*Clerk's Tale*, 148–49), Walter's faith in the many of the group is bound to his need to serve them. This is a precarious position because, as the Clerk later comments, the people are "stormy."

> Unsad and evere untrewe!
> Ay undiscreet and chaunhynge as a fane!
> Delitynge evere in rumbul that is newe,
> For lyk the moone ay wexe ye and wane! (*Clerk's Tale*, 995–98)

An overarching theme of the One in relation to the Many pervades Eugene Victor Wolfstein's *Psychoanalytic Marxism*[40] and sheds light on the manner in which the intellectual as "fool" plays a significant role in pointing out and altering the tyrannical forces of the naked king.

> The One and the Many is a problem of many levels. At least for now, our concern is with these two: the political and the psychological. The political

problem has various forms. The Many are hoi polloi (the masses) and
are viewed as morally inferior by the One, the aristocrat, intellectual, or
philosopher. Or reverse the perspective: The Many are the masses, the
people, the wretched of the earth who view the One — the ruling class,
the State — as their oppressor. Alternatively the masses are absorbed into
the State, leaving the individual who would speak for them isolated,
without constituency, outside the effective unity of the One and the
Many. Yet again, the masses come to constitute a political movement, of
which radical intellectuals are an organic part. If successful, it shatters the
existing social order and reforms the one as the common interest and
life of the Many. (*Psychoanalytic Marxism,* 93)

In *The Clerk's Tale* Walter's interactions with the people show their
power and his impotence, revealing the lack of singularity and sovereignty in the "One." His attempts to please the people are thwarted by
his own sense of his precarious power such that he seeks the sovereign
power over Griselda as a supplement for that which he cannot have in
his more general rule. Having become aware of his dependence on his
people and his precise lack of sovereignty, he consents to marry despite
his fear that where he was free, he will now be in servitude. His solution
to the relinquishment (or the always already lack) of sovereignty with
regard to the many of the masses is to seek pure sovereignty over the
"one" of Griselda.

Griselda's singularity is evident in her ability to uphold the promise
she makes to Walter to obey him. When asked to give him full sovereignty, Griselda says, " 'I swere that nevere willingly, / In werk ne thought,
I nyl yow disobeye, / For to be deed, though me were looth to deye' "
(*Clerk's Tale,* 363–65). Departing from the many performative speech
acts, oaths, contracts, and pacts that are broken throughout literary history, Griselda keeps her promise. She adheres to the Kantian categorical
and universal imperative to obey, suggesting to Walter that his is a perfect meeting of human law and divine law. Griselda's transferal from her
father's house to Walter's domain, back to her father's house and back
again, reflects the shift from the domain of human law to that of divine
law (though both forms reflect the Law of the Father). Contrary to the
determination that obedience is submission, however, Griselda's obedience is upheld by her singular subjective sovereignty that is marked by
her kept promise. In a move that prefigures the dangerous paradox of
Hobbes's approach to the state and subjectivity, Griselda attains sover-

eignty through apparent submission to the Law. Griselda's kept promise reflects her belief in the power of language to signify a real beyond, and her actions demonstrate the power of this universal.

As such, her power is precisely distinct from the form of sovereignty that the Wife of Bath claims women desire. The Wife of Bath prefigures the famous Freudian question of female desire by presenting the knight's quest to find the answer to the question "what do women want?" It might be tempting to parallel this question with the precise question asked by Freud, Lacan, Felman, and many others, "what does a woman want?" As similar as the two questions may appear, they are quite distinct; there is a world of difference between the signifiers of a generalization of "women," the universal category "the woman," and the particularity of "a woman." If women in general want sovereignty as *The Wife of Bath's Tale* tells us, "Wommen desiren to have sovereyntee /As wel over hir housbond as hir love, /And for to been in maistrie hym above" (*Wife of Bath's Tale*, 1038–40), this desire does not necessarily transfer to the particular desires of a singular woman, nor does it characterize the crossed-out universal category of "the woman."

In *The Wife of Bath's Tale,* for instance, sovereignty is given to the fairy/hag not because the rapacious knight gives her the choice between being young, beautiful, and potentially unfaithful or old, ugly, and faithful, but rather because she is able to maintain a consistent identity once the choice is made. Giving her the chance for sovereignty, the knight says

> "I put me in youre wise governance;
> Cheseth youreself which may be moost pleance
> And moos honour to yow and me also.
> I do no fors the wheither of the two,
> For as yow liketh, it suffiseth me." (*Wife of Bath's Tale*, 1231–35)

Because she is willing to alter her form, to change her being, the fairy/hag in *The Wife of Bath's Tale* does not exhibit the type of singular, consistent sovereignty that is performed by Griselda. Despite her status as a supernatural figure, the fairy/hag cannot meet the impossible standards that Griselda apparently establishes. When the Clerk comments on his tale, stating that

> This storie is side nat for that wyves sholde
> Folwen Griselde as in humylitee,

For it were inportable, though they wolde,
But for that every wight, in his degree,
Sholde be constant in adversitee
As was Griselde. (*Clerk's Tale*, 1142–47)

The Clerk's commentary on his tale and the impossibility of finding a woman who might equal Griselda is so ridiculously misogynist that it simply can't be true! Griselda's pain is perhaps overlooked because the ultimate tragedy of the tale is precisely located in the impossibility of achieving the singular, real, sovereign status that Griselda achieves, not because woman is evil or even inherently flawed, but rather because we are caught in the world of nominalism. As an impossible version of woman, Griselda stands in for the universal category of "the woman" that must be written with a line through it and appears to represent the limitations on universal categories.

In *Chaucer and the Universe of Learning*, Ann Astell provides a thorough argument for the centrality of the Clerk as a character who represents secular knowledge and whose figure affects *The Canterbury Tales* both through his absence, which leads other characters to call attention to him, and through his image as ideal, which challenges others to maintain a high standard of textual integrity. According to Astell and J. Burke Severs, such respect is shown for the Clerk through the consistency of representations in the other clerks among the tales (including, for instance, Nicholas in *The Miller's Tale*, Aleyn and John in *The Reeve's Tale*, Jankyn in *The Wife of Bath's Prologue*, the clerk at Orleans, and Aurelius's brother in *The Franklin's Tale*).[41] This representation of a group of secular scholars reveals a growing community of study, suggesting that "Chaucer's four ideal pilgrims are not simply a conservative bow to the three estates of feudal social order, but rather an original vision of the new social order being shaped by the book-learning fostered preeminently at the universities. In a uniquely open-ended way, the Clerk of Oxenford represents an independent fourth estate, not a simple subdivision of the *cleri*."[42] This group formation of secular scholars is highly significant to the development of literacy, to the dissemination of knowledge and texts, as well as to the political and cultural movements of the fourteenth and fifteenth centuries (and beyond). In order to identify itself precisely as a group, lay study needed to distinguish itself from ecclesiastical study. The process of this distinction is fraught with an understanding of philosophy as distinct from and bound to theology.

As a secular but Christian poet, and as a clerk himself, Chaucer displays this struggle throughout his work, but most obviously in his representation of the Clerk of *The Canterbury Tales*. This idealization of the pursuit of knowledge should not be seen as counter to the "mainstream" group perception of the Clerk as a fool. Rather, it coalesces with the resistance present in the pursuit of intellectual goals as contrary to the banality or perversity of other forms of endeavors.

The Clerk has been read as both Chaucer's self-inscription into his poetics and as the projection of that which he is careful to avoid. Rather than pin down the way in which the Clerk does or does not properly signify Chaucer's view of his own role as a poet, secular scholar, and clerk, however, the crucial significance of the Clerk's description, his tale, and his own interpretation of it is found in the struggle between realism and nominalism, and the concomitant desire to find the solace of a theological faith in universals as it is confronted with the awareness of nominalist limitations and the dialectical process. *The Clerk's Tale* exhibits the quarrel between realism and nominalism such that the universal category is shown to be an obscure object of desire.

The Clerk, a student of philosophy whose knowledge is incomplete, departs from his secular learning to find meaning in his tale by way of its imitation of the Job story. According to Jerome the Bible is a "literary corpus" in which Numbers contains "the mysteries of all arithmetic" and the Book of Job contains "all the laws of dialectics."[43] Indeed, the Book of Job is a central text for medieval writers. Its theme of the conflict between human will, chance and fortune, and divine forces is imitated and translated throughout the Middle Ages by authors including but not limited to Isidore of Seville, St. Gregory, Bede, Boethius, Aquinas, the Gawain poet, Chaucer, and Langland.[44] Since Chaucer brings many of these elements together intextually, his poetics provide a dense and economical locus for a discussion of the quarrel about universals.

In *Job, Boethius and Epic Truth*, Astell delineates a powerful argument expanding the notion of epic and showing the conflict in the Clerk's translation of the Griselda story directly from Petrarch's Latin version, but also from Boccaccio's *Decameron*.[45] In her reading, Walter is simultaneously the benevolent God from Boethius and Satan who torments Job; Griselda is also fragmented in her representation in which she is a combination of the figures of Lady Philosophy and Job. The Christian conception of the Job story pits Satan against God, showing how Job overcomes his lack of faith to find unity and solace in proper faith such that God and good triumph over Satan and evil. The Judaic interpretation of the tale perceives God as a singularity that is both malevolent and munificent, good and evil in one. The initial bet that God makes with Satan illustrates his arrogance as well as his desire for competition and the need to beat Satan at his own game. The acts that cause Job to suffer are attributed to God, as the figure of Fortune, the hand of good and evil that Lady Philosophy explicates to Boethius. Indeed, Boethius's account of God is in accord with the Judaic understanding of God's potential for good and evil.

The way in which the God of Job is interpreted is significant to the understanding of the roles of Griselda and Walter in *The Clerk's Tale*. Walter seeks to attain the status of God, and the Clerk represents him as the sovereign force capable of giving and taking away, in whom Griselda must have utter faith and patience in order to prove her worthiness as a wife. The Clerk's reading of the story, though, is misleading, as Walter's need to test Griselda, as well as his dependence on the people he rules, renders impossible any singular sovereign status. Instead, Griselda's actions, her pure duty, obedience, reflect her belief in the real of universals, making her ontologically singular and sovereign. Unlike "real" women, however, Griselda manifests this singularity and sovereignty by inhabiting the totalizing position of the slave and so overcoming her position as slave in a properly dialectical fashion. Lacan's pronouncement that "the woman" must be written with a line through it resembles the Clerk's warning that "no woman like Griselda can exist" so closely that we must see in it an understanding of the universal categories that is more nuanced than Hegelian dialectics or a belief in singularity allow.

However, like the illiterate Wife of Bath, the hyperbolically literate Clerk also seems to misinterpret his tale. Aside from frustrating the reader who wants the Clerk to be accurate, insightful, and pedagogically sound, the secular moral of *The Clerk's Tale* reflects the limits of his education and a need for theology in his philosophical system. Although his narration shows that Walter is convinced by empirical evidence, the Clerk says, "don't believe it," it can't happen, demonstrating his own refusal of the potential for knowledge gained through the senses—singular forms of knowledge—to transfer to understanding and become universal. As such, *The Clerk's Tale* asserts a nominalist view of ontology (especially female ontology), even while revealing a *hope* for the universal potential (which may begin with male sovereignty). Another name for limiting female subjects to the particular and nominal and rendering male subjects universal is, of course, misogyny.

The Clerk's concluding observation that no real woman could live up to the ideal of patience embodied and exemplified in and by Griselda uncannily resembles Lacan's claim that "the woman" does not exist. In fact, the utterly imaginary and impossible standards set for Griselda by Walter and the ostensibly perfect performance by Griselda assert an ideal category of woman as nonexistent and reintroduce the category of "the woman" as a real precisely because her singular sovereignty provides evidence of the unconscious at work. It would be simple to determine Griselda's humanity if we could find evidence of her repression in the tale. Her stoicism, however, does not leave room for a reading of precise repression. Griselda's stoicism throughout most of the tale renders her silent and disengaged from action, discourse, or agency. Rather, her unconscious and the expression of her emotions are reserved for the moment of reunion with her children. Until her cathartic moment, when her children are returned to her, she is defined precisely by her refusal to participate in an emotional display or response to Walter's sadistic ploys to test her virtue.

While performing singularity and sovereignty, Griselda's stoicism participates in the conspiracy of the masses' refusal to tell the king that he is naked. On the one hand, her stoicism participates in a performance of her enslavement to Walter. Shadia Drury points out in her reading of Kojève and Strauss that stoicism "allows the slave to convince himself that he is free simply by thinking that he is free, or by having the abstract idea of freedom."[46] Reflecting the implicit process of repression at stake in Stoicism, Drury continues:

> In this way, the slave becomes convinced that the fact of slavery is unimportant. Stoicism tries to deny the conflict between the ideal of freedom and the reality of slavery by relegating the actual world to the status of nonbeing. In this way, Stoicism becomes an exercise for inaction. It convinces people that there is no need to change the world or the state in order to realize the abstract idea of freedom. It insists that man is free even though he is everywhere in chains. (*Alexandre Kojève,* 31)

In light of this awareness of the oppression inherent in Stoicism and in light of the torture that Griselda withstands, it is nearly impossible to deny that Griselda is enslaved to Walter. Her performance of patience, love, and loyalty must be the result of some element of repressed desire for free action (*Clerk's Tale*, 1050–65). On the other hand, however, Griselda's actions are precisely *not* representative of stoic behavior. If there were any sense of repressed desire in her actions, Walter would have perceived this as a lack in her love for him. Either she is such a good slave that she has no alternative desire other than to love Walter, as he finally comes to believe, or her unconscious reveals itself despite her best efforts.

The latter case is clearly illustrated in the text when Walter reveals to her that he has been testing her all along and returns her children to her; Griselda experiences a cathartic syncope, revealing the eruption of her unconscious.[47] Walter says,

> "I have doon this deed
> For no malice, ne for no crueltee,
> But for t'assays in thee thy wommanheede,
> And nat to sleen my children — God forbeede! —
> But for to kepe hem pryvely and stille,
> Til I thy purpose knewe and al thy wille." (*Clerk's Tale*, 1073–78)

And Griselda responds by swooning: "Whan she this herde, aswowne doun she falleth" (*Clerk's Tale*, 1079). Her swooning reasserts her singularity even as she is in the process of being drawn in by Walter, who finally perceives her to be dedicated to him. As such, she finds her place within herself as one of solitude and protection. According to Derrida, "When I say that *I* tremble, I mean that *one* trembles, the 'one' or the 'on' trembles, whoever it is trembles: because the injustices of this justice can concentrate its violence in the very constitution of the *One* and of the *Unique*. Right where it can affect everyone, everyone and anyone, whoever."[48] The representation of the "I" as the "One" is not found in every instance of ontological presence, however. Derrida's point about the uniqueness of trauma is significant; however, the Oneness or singularity of Being must exist already for the moment of trauma, trembling, or syncope to be precisely distinct and distinguishing of the *I* as the *One*.[49] Griselda was One before, and so her syncope is read here as a reassertion of that one *in spite of* Walter. Although the Clerk inserts his narrative voice to comment on her swooning, he presents it as if she is merely performing "woman" to the best possible extent: "O which a pitous thing it was to see / Hir swownyng, and hire humble voys to here!" (*Clerk's Tale*, 1086–87).

At this point in the symptomatic eruption of Griselda's unconscious syncope, it is important to consider the potential reasons for her catharsis. Is she swooning in response to the extent to which Walter went to test her patience and loyalty, or to the cruelty of his actions? Or is she (as the Clerk sees her) swooning because she is so happy and in utter surprise that her children are returned to her safely? Her first actions upon awakening from her swoon are to clutch her children close and kiss them, suggesting the immediate presence of them in her mind even while she is where she isn't—in her moment of syncope. Having given up the solidity of her singularity as that which was for and against Walter, Griselda appears to discover a new Oneness with respect to Walter because her children have been returned to her.

> "Grayntmercy, lord, God thanke it yow," quod she,
> "That ye han saved me my chiuldre deere!
> Now rekke I nevere to been deed right here;
> Sith I stoned in youre love and in youre grace,
> No fors of deeth, ne what my spirit pace!" (*Clerk's Tale*, 1088–92)

However, the immediate *repetition* of her swooning suggests that she has not quite regained her status as singular or sovereign and she is, instead, transferred from the realm of the ideal woman to the realm of the real woman who experiences unconscious drives and who finds those drives to control her will. She says,

> "O tender, o deere, o yonge children myne!
> Youre woful mooder wended stedfastly
> That crueel houndes or som foul vermyne [Petrarch's hounds]
> Hadde eten yow; but God of his mercy
> And youre benyngne fader tenderly
> Hath doon yow kept"—and in that same stounde
> Al sodeynly she swapte adoun to grounde. (*Clerk's Tale*, 1093–99)

What is described as her "sudden" fall is also the fall of one who is engaged in the process of assimilating the unconscious with the conscious. Having proven herself to be the perfect, stoic being, Griselda now lets go and allows her repressed unconscious to affect her actions. She must become human in order, then, to be placed next to the naked king whose sovereignty is neither pure nor singular. As two fragmented entities that sit next to each other on their thrones, "married" Walter and Griselda finally enter a relationship wherein their mutually incomplete being complements each other as they sit side by side. The repetition of the marriage between Walter and Griselda is significant as it reveals the automatic repetition of the unconscious as *tuché* appears within it, and it points to the investment that the law has in the unconscious.

Performing a perfect mode of repetition, the introduction to *Seminar XX, Encore* echoes the outline to *Seminar VII* on the *Ethics*.[50] As the outline to the *Ethics* tells us that the king is naked, we learn in *Encore* that "Law does not ignore the bed"; this reconfiguration and extension of the Law in relation to sexuality makes the statement that the king is naked a bit more obvious: the king is naked, and we should always think of sovereignty in terms of sexuality; the bed is bound to the social strata of the Law, and both are fragile domains, and the sovereign good should be approached with an awareness of this fragility.

Lacan therefore returns to the movement from Aristotelian ethics to Bentham's utilitarianism and the theory of fictions to focus on the materiality or "use-value" of language. "It is from that standpoint that I return to question the status of being, from the sovereign good as an object of contemplation, on the basis of which people formerly believed they could edify an ethics."[51] This is telling of the similar focus on sovereignty and the One that are central to the introductory lecture, which happens to be called "On *Jouissance*." Combining desire, sexual difference, and the discourse on sovereignty and ethics, Lacan asks, "Is Eros a tension toward the One?" thus properly placing in relief the imbrication of knowledge and desire.

> People have been talking about nothing but the One for a long time. "There's such a thing as One" *(Y a d' l'Un)*. I based my discourse last year on that statement, certainly not in order to contribute to this earliest of confusions, for desire merely leads us to aim at the gap *(faille)* where it can be demonstrated that the One is based only on *(tenir de)* the essence of the signifier. *(Seminar XX, 5)*

This "One" is also the One of the sexual rapport *(Seminar XX, 7)*. Moving quickly to an awareness of dualism, Lacan points out that the "requirement of the One, as the *Parmenides* strangely already allowed us to predict, stems from the Other. Where there is being, infinity is required" *(Seminar XX, 10)*.

The duality that remains, the two "ones" of Walter and Griselda, shows that the first part of their marriage is an extended courtship. The marriage really begins at the end when Griselda, through her stoicism, is allowed to overcome it and take her place beside the sovereign. The *earning* of this place exhibits the conflict of tenderness and resignation. Therefore, when he crowns her as he has not previously done throughout their marriage, "In a clooth of gold that brighte shoon, / With a coroune of many a righe stoon / Upon hire heed, they into halle hire broughte, / And there she was honoured as hir oghte" (*Clerk's Tale,* 1117–20), he actually enforces the removal of Griselda from her sovereign place of singularity and places her in (impossible) relation to him, enacting his final and most tyrannical moment in the story. This removal of Griselda from her singularity upholds a traditional notion of sovereignty and shows how the Clerk is appealing to hierarchical structures. As L. O. Aranye Fradenburg has written,

> "Basic separation" (Kristeva's term), distance, absence, the disembodied quality of our objects of belief—in short, lack—is not necessarily given, nor is it a liability for a sovereign: the sovereign is created as distant, and the distance allows him or her to be desired in a particular way, as Ideal, as Extraordinary. And yet the distance of the ideal nonetheless requires "corporealization," "sensualization," if the Extraordinary is to have fully at his or her disposal a power of conviction, a reality so beyond question that it becomes superreality. This experience I will call "sovereign love." Sovereign love is a means of creating, and shaping the creativity of, desire or aspiration; but sovereign love can thereby shape desire so that its creativity, its economically and socially productive power, may be laid open to interference, even forestalled. The sovereign's mixing of lack and fullness—whereby the sovereign may be desired as inaccessible ideal, *and* loved as flesh—enables the subject to feel simultaneously at one with, and free of, power.[52]

A parallel register for the articulation of the relationship between Griselda and Walter, the status of Griselda as singular, sovereign, and universal and Walter as the dependent, dialectically engaged, figure, is found in Lacan's theory of desire. A simple understanding of the Walter-Griselda master-slave dialectic shows how their relationship is precisely *not* one of courtly love, since, in the conclusion of the tale, the two are positioned next to each other in a synthetic fashion. As such, there is a lack of the proper element of desire in the tale. Desire instead emerges as the need to find singularity and sovereignty in subjectivity.

We are not yet in the realm of courtly love poetics; rather, we are in the realm of the definition of the real. Recalling the limitations of the dialectical process that opened this chapter, we can see how Lacan contributes to an understanding of the overlap between the quarrel of the universals and courtly love, and *The Clerk's Tale* (among other tales) posits the limitations of the dialectics of desire in the history of philosophy and theology.

Mirroring and representing Lady Philosophy, Griselda's precise singularity allows her to attain a form of universal subjectivity that Walter's precarious and dependent sovereignty prevents him from reaching. Griselda's wisdom reveals the location of the universal within the dialectics of theory and practice, good and evil, or sovereignty and submission. Her actions demonstrate Lady Philosophy's explanation of higher knowledge and understanding:

> The intelligence knows the objects of the lower kinds of knowledge: the universals of the reason, the figures of the imagination, the matter of the senses, but not by using reason, or imagination, or senses. With a single glance of the mind it formally, as it were, sees all things. Similarly, when reason knows a universal nature, it comprehends all the objects of imagination and the senses without using either. For reason defines the general nature of her conception as follows: man is a biped, rational animal. This is a universal idea, but no one ignores the fact that man is also an imaginable and sensible object which reason knows by rational conception rather than by the imagination and senses. Similarly, although the imagination begins by seeing and forming figures with the senses, nevertheless it can, without the aid of the senses, behold sensible objects by an imaginative rather than a sensory mode of knowing.
>
> Do you see, then how all these use their own power in knowing rather than the powers of the objects which are known? And this is proper, for since all judgment is in the act of the one judging, it is necessary that everyone should accomplish his own action by his own power, not by the power of something other than himself. (*Consolation,* 111)

The engagement with the categorical distinctions of Aristotle's *Organon* reflects the play among the ability to determine a universal category and the awareness of its disruption by multiplicity of forms.[53] The precise extent to which this description of universals is formalist is complicated by the dialectics of the thing and its representation in the imagination. Boethius finds realism and universals to be possible by way of dialectics. Since the mind is capable of conceiving a form without access to the phenomenal realm, potential for the real exists. This Boethian approach prefigures the revised version of phenomenology as potentially Ideal in Lacan's work. Unlike the later scholastics, the element of empiricism is marginal to a view of phenomenological experience as real although it might not be positively proven in the physical realm. This is due, of course, to the strength of the unconscious, which certainly takes in and responds to external stimuli from the symbolic realm, but also, in return, assigns significance to the symbolic from the realms of the imaginary and the real. This partially explains the impossibility of singularity and pure sovereignty in Lacan's system; it also explains the way in which Griselda's stoicism, if not a symptom of active repression (i.e., foolery), places her in the position of the purely fictional and impossible woman.

CHAPTER TWO

Duality, Ambivalence, and the Animality of Desire

Freudian dualism finds its strongest expression in this impossible
harmonizing of amorous space, in the fractured space of lovehate.
— Julia Kristeva, *Tales of Love*

Whereas Chaucer's Clerk's representation of the naked King Walter is a
figurative understanding of the fragility of sovereignty, Marie de France
presents a more literal example of nudity in the king's chambers in *Bisclavret*. In this *lai*, it is not the king who is naked, but his supplement,
the werewolf Bisclavret who displays rationality as an animal and animality when he is human. Although the subject and the king are altered
in the movement from Chaucer's *The Clerk's Tale*, addressed in chapter 1,
to Marie de France's *Bisclavret*, we should not take the difference to be
one of the literal versus the figurative, because all language is necessarily
metaphorical; rather, the difference in the fragility and nudity of the king
and his subjects should be read on the level of the difference between
the search for sovereignty and the struggle with ambivalence. In both
cases, we remain in the realm of the discussion of universals, and in the
debate begun by Boethius about the potential for genus and species.
It is important then, to recognize that the beginning of this chapter
repeats the assertion that the king is naked and the insistence that "Law
does not ignore the bed" put forth in Lacan's search for the articulation
of the sovereign good. Further tangling this already complex web of ideas
is the manner in which the articulation and prohibition of categories
leads to Lacan's formulation that "the woman" must be written with a

cross through it "~~the woman~~." Taking "~~the woman~~" as a particular representation of Being in the world allows an understanding of the ambivalent struggle to determine the status of real and nominal categories. As Drucilla Cornell confirms in "Rethinking the Beyond of the Real," the real is equal to the crossing out of Being (~~Being~~).[1] An understanding of the animality within humanity and the humanity within animality will help to illustrate how this crossing out of Being alters what has been taken as Lacan's misogynist statement that "the woman" must be written with a cross through it. Instead of being viewed as Lacan's failure, his assertion may be perceived as a contribution to the debates over universal reals.

Put forth as a conflict that is precisely *not* dialectical, ambivalence presumes the possibility of two discrete "ones."[2] Love and Hate, Eros and Thanatos, attraction and repulsion, conscious and unconscious, body and mind, as well as obscenity and decency, and even "man" and "animal" are dual expressions and entities that we have, of late, taken to be dissolved of their antagonistic binary status. In a post-structuralist, post-deconstruction, even postdialectical world of thinking, it is difficult to conceive of these dualities in their separate binary forms.[3] For the moment, however, it is necessary to suspend an awareness of the deconstruction of dichotomous systems and return to this conception of two distinct entities that engage each other antagonistically in order to understand the weight of ambivalence as it contributes to the perception of the unconscious and desire as a *real* universal category as well as to the manner in which we might read Lacan's configuration of ~~the woman~~ as a maintenance of the universal category rather than its elimination.

As a mode of expressing the conflict of desire to find singularity within humanity, ambivalence emerges in the problematic element of the animality within man. As Abelard, following Aristotle and Boethius, says, "Si est homo, est animal" (if it is a human, it is an animal).[4] Further, in order to determine the propriety or the real of being as that which is bound to desire as an involuntary force, the structure of ambivalence foregrounds subjective fragmentation. The contradictory and mutually present sensations of horror and pleasure at the mental or phenomenological engagement with the animal are not only expressions of ambivalence toward an external "animal" distinct from the "man," they also point to the ambivalence that the subject feels toward herself. An understanding of these processes will assist in the epistemological and ontological definition of the human who is a desiring subject and the manner in which categories emerge as real within the Lacanian system.

Ambivalence is most clearly seen in the history of psychoanalysis in Freud's case studies of "The Rat Man" and "The Wolf Man."[5] In both cases, the unconscious struggles with its own desire to balance animality within the rationality of the human. In order to achieve a properly rational approach to being and the world, the subject's attempt to eliminate the "natural object" that is the unconscious. Chris Powici characterizes this succinctly in his essay "A Wolf Sublime." "For Freud," says Powici, "the 'natural object' is of course the unconscious, and the unconscious is 'natural' only insofar as it is 'animal.'"[6] Recognition of the unconscious, if not subject to proper repression or sublimation, emerges as a feeling of traumatic ambivalence. In Freud's case history of the Rat Man we find the subject expressing "horror at pleasure of his own of which he himself was unaware" (*Three Case Histories*, 27). This ambivalence manifests itself as neurotic activity, obsession with attempting both to harm and to protect the object of his affection.

> A battle between love and hate was raging in the lover's breast, and the object of both these feelings was one and the same person. The battle was represented in a plastic form by his compulsive and symbolic act of removing the stone from the road along which she was to drive, and then of undoing this deed of love by replacing the stone where it had lain, so that her carriage might come to grief against it and she herself be hurt. (*Three Case Histories*, 50)

Further, the obsessional quality of the neurosis manifested in statements involving positive and negative wishes; "if he said, 'May God protect him,' an evil spirit would hurriedly insinuate a 'not'" (*Three Case Histories*, 51). Freud diagnoses the Rat Man as an obsessional neurotic, who cannot stop imagining the various and contradictory impulses and scenarios that he feels because his own relation to his desire is ambivalent. Following a similar structure of desire as a combination of attraction and repulsion, the Wolf Man experienced ambivalence with regard to animals due to his own relation to his desire, which is formed in response to "affectionate abuse" (*Three Case Histories*, 217). The Wolf Man's neurosis takes on the form of anxiety-hysteria, wherein he is terrified of the animals that he loves so profoundly. Both subjects are bound in the duality of ambivalent systems of desire.

In the discussion of his case, Freud recalls another patient whose grandfather, while playing affectionately, would say that he "would cut open their tummies" (*Three Case Histories*, 217). The Wolf Man's obsession with two fairy tales — *Little Red Riding Hood* and *The Wolf and the Seven Little Goats* — is read by Freud as pointing toward a profound fear of having the stomach cut open. "In both [tales] there is the eating up, the cutting open of the belly, the taking out of the people who have been eaten and their replacement by heavy stones, and finally in both of them the wicked wolf perishes" (*Three Case Histories*, 216). Later, we will return to the manner in which these two case studies of animal-phobia and attraction-repulsion, by illustrating the structure of ambivalence, also reveal how the real emerges when repression and sublimation are not working properly. For the moment, the establishment of ambivalence as an inhibitor of singular subjectivity, and so reflective of the subject's duality, is apparent in the fear of having the belly cut open as it recalls the history of the bees that is so crucial to the development of humanity as it is bound to and opposes animality.[7]

To begin this discussion, then, we enter the finely tuned world of the geometrically advanced bees. The tale of the bees is a long one with a rich philosophical history. In Plato's *Laws* the bees are subject to discussion as a farmer's property and they are protected from poisoning by a neighbor.[8] In the *Republic* the bees are a metaphor for the masses while the dominating class is perceived as the apiarist.[9]

The modern discussion is focused on the bees as a mode of explicating the difference between the animal and the human as well as the elements of animality within the human. Leading the swarm that circulates around the honey pot of this problem is Martin Heidegger, who locates the bees as instinctively bound to their food. After Heidegger, Lacan focuses on the honey pot as a mode of goodness and fullness in the search for knowledge and the cause of desire. Jacques Derrida takes up the question of animality and its relation to the subject as being in the world with relation to ambivalence in *Of Spirit*.[10] Giorgio Agamben follows with a discussion of the captivation of the bees as evidence of the animality within the subject bound to the Other in *The Open*,[11] returning the line of thought to the question of democracy and free will addressed in Plato's *Republic*. Before moving on to the manner in which this line of inquiry predicates and is predicated by the ambivalence and duality of sexual difference in courtly love as an instance of desire, it is important to pay homage to this discussion as it illustrates the process of desire as purely animal instinct that nonetheless threatens the subject because of its abject, tragic, and ambivalent character.

Contrary to human subjects, the bees are not ambivalent; they have no mind/body or soul/body split. Their desire is simply, and terrifyingly, horrifically, abjectly, inexorably, similar to the process of desire in humans, but without the self-awareness or metacritical distance that causes trauma in the desiring subject. The expression of the desire of the bees is precisely like desire in that it seeks its satisfaction, which is impossible. The difference between the bees and the human desiring subject is that the bees appear to be happy in their pursuit of enjoyment. The human subject suffers at the sight to excess precisely because it is never enough to fill the gaping belly. Lacan mocks us and challenges us when he claims in *Seminar VII, The Ethics of Psychoanalysis* that he is bringing us honey. "Honey is what I am trying to bring you, the honey of my reflections on something that, my goodness, I have been doing for a number of years."[12] The "goodness" of the "my" that Lacan uses as a mode of self-reflection is also the "goodness" of the sovereignty of being that is as stake in his seminar. His attempt to bring honey, as he tells us, is fraught with difficulty and lures us into the slippery realm of desire.

> If the communication effect here sometimes presents difficulties, reflect on the experience of honey. Honey is either very hard or very fluid. If it's hard, it is difficult to cut, since there are no natural breaks. If it's very liquid, it is suddenly all over the place—I assume that you are all familiar with the experience of eating honey in bed.
>
> Hence the problem of pots. The honey pot is reminiscent of the mustard pot that I have already dealt with. The two have exactly the same meaning now that we no longer imagine that the hexagons in which we tend to store our harvest have a natural relationship to the structure of the world. Consequently, the question we are raising is in the end always the same, i.e., what is the significance of the word? (*Seminar VII*, 19)

Despite his awareness of Heidegger's work on the bees and animality, he is stuck in the sticky world of language. Remaining at the level of the distinction between human and animal as a linguistic one, Lacan obscures a clear understanding of the way that desire itself is reflected in the experiment with the bees and Heidegger's investigation into the animality/humanity duality. Instead, Lacan moves from this point to discuss the moral quality of the real and the fragility that lies therein. To slow the argument down a bit, Derrida and Agamben assist in an understanding of the way that the actions of the bees reflect the process of desire.

In *The Open* Agamben says, "The mode of being proper to the animal, which defines its relations with the disinhibitor, is captivation *(Benommenheit)*" (52). He continues, then, to refer to the experiment with the bees that Heidegger takes from Uexküll, "in which, a bee is placed in front of a cup full of honey in a laboratory. If, once it has begun to suck, the bee's abdomen is cut away, it will continue happily to suck while the honey visibly streams out of its open abdomen" (*The Open*, 52). As a mode of explaining the ambivalence of the pleasure/pain of desire, this image of the bee, obliviously eating the honey while his abdomen has been cut open, foregrounds the horror of the fullness and lack in desire itself. Is the bee so transfixed, so captivated by the honey that it does not notice its sliced tummy? Or is it so aware of the impossibility of becoming full (due precisely to the incision) that it desperately attempts to eat enough to fill the emptiness? Since, unless we are trained apiarists, we do not know the language of the bees, and the bee cannot answer this question for us, we are left to speculate about the connection between the animal drive and the human drive. For Heidegger the animal drive precludes recognition. What Agamben describes as the captivation of the bees is, for Heidegger, a lack of recognition:

> This shows convincingly that the bee by no means recognizes the presence of too much honey. It recognizes neither this nor even — though this would be expected to touch it more closely — the absence of its abdomen. There is no question of it recognizing any of this; it continues its instinctual activity *(Trieben)* regardless, precisely because it does not recognize that plenty of honey is still present. Rather the bee is simply taken *(hingenommen)* by the food.[13]

Agamben goes on to discuss the mode of captivation that holds the bee before the honey as Heidegger perceives this to be an openness and yet a prohibition from engaging with the world. For both Heidegger and Agamben, the perseverance in the bees is one that signals a symbiotic connection between the animal and the world. The "openness" reveals a lack of threshold by which the subject — the bee — might recognize its fullness, thereby enabling more of the world to enter and affect its being. This openness does not account for the ambivalence of the scene as it is represented and mirrors the human attribute to desire; rather, it is action as tenacity, the drive for fullness, and the pure pleasure in that fullness. What Lacan might perceive in this moment is too horrifying to admit, and so he focuses on language. For Lacan, the ethical question of the relationship between animal and human is precisely bound to language. Prefiguring Derrida's *Without Alibi*,[14] immediately after the attempt to bring us honey, Lacan writes:

> This year we are more specifically concerned with realizing how the ethical question of our practice is intimately related to one that we have been in a position to glimpse for some time, namely, that the deep dissatisfaction we find in every psychology—derives from the fact that it is nothing more than a mask, and sometimes even an alibi, of the effort to focus on the problem of our own action—something that is the essence and the very foundation of all ethical reflection. In other words, we need to know if we have managed to do anything more than take a small step outside ethics and if, like the other psychologies, our own is simply another development of ethical reflection, of the search for a guide or a way, that in the last analysis may be formulated as follows: "Given our condition as men, what must we do in order to act in the right way?" (*Seminar VII*, 19)

I juxtapose this passage immediately with the reflections of Heidegger and Agamben on the bees, not only because it follows Lacan's shift from honey to the word, but also because it poses the question of the difference between the human and the animal. What might we do "as men" (read here as "humans") to act properly? Well, to begin, we should stop cutting open the abdomens of bees to see what happens. Lacan perceived this with specific regard to language and the problem of cutting. In *Television*, Lacan reveals that the experiment with the bees influences his thinking about metaphysics in relation to ontology and epistemology.[15] Locating and "grounding" the "unconscious in the exsistence of one more subject for the soul," Lacan then explicates, "For the soul as the assumed sum of the body's function. A most problematic sum, despite the fact that from Aristotle to Uexküll, it has been postulated as though with one voice, and it is still what biologists presuppose, whether they know it or not" (*Television*, 10). The continuity from Aristotle to Uexküll calls forth the materiality of the unconscious seen as it is in somatic symptoms. Lacan then develops a mode of thinking through the body[16] that exhibits proof of the unconscious at work in the subject.

> In fact the subject of the unconscious is only in touch with the soul via the body, by introducing thought into it: here contradicting Aristotle. Man does not think with his soul, as the Philosopher imagined.
>
> He thinks as a consequence of the fact that a structure, that of language—the word implies it—a structure carves up his body, a structure that has nothing to do with anatomy. Witness the hysteric. This shearing happens to the soul through the obsessional symptom: a thought that burdens the soul, that it doesn't know what to do with. (*Television*, 10)

The developing relationship among the body, the soul, language, and the unconscious persistently returns to a scene wherein conscious and rational intentionality gives way to unconscious drives. What then happens between the instantiation of desire as an impulse and the expression of desire as a linguistic or performative utterance? How do we express desire and act ethically at the same time? This latter question appears to be at the core of the problem. If our desires are animal and without consideration of moral or ethical laws, dictates, or maxims, then how can they exist simultaneously with our ethical being in the world? Lacan implies these questions and Derrida asks them overtly.

According to Derrida, the experiment on the bees marks the bees' desire in relation to an "other." Here, the question of Being as spirituality and animality is not bound or predetermined by ideological imposition as it is for Agamben, and it is not led by the primary process of desire that we see in Lacan's reading; rather, for Derrida, the bee is eating because it is *searching*. "[T]he animal does not have enough world, to be sure. But this lack is not to be evaluated as a quantitative relation to the entities of the world. It is not that the animal has a lesser relationship, a more limited access to entities, it has an *other* relationship" (*Of Spirit*, 49). This split consciousness, presenting the bees in relation to themselves as others, renders the bees subjects who, like human split subjects, experience ambivalence. In this sense Agamben is faithful to the psychoanalytical materiality presented in Heidegger's phenomenology. Agamben perceives and forwards the relationship of the bees to need and desire in the world, whereas Derrida extends this ambivalence to a metaphysical relation of the bee to spirit.

> The animal *has* and *does not have* a world. The proposition seems contradictory and logically impossible, as Heidegger recognizes. . . . The logical

contradiction between the two propositions (the animal does and does not have a world) would mean simply that we have not yet sufficiently elucidated the concept of world—the quilting thread of which we are following here since it is none other than that *of spirit.* Spirituality, Heidegger insists on this, is the name of that without which there is no world. It is therefore necessary to manage to think this knot which laces together the two propositions: the animal has no world, the animal has a world. And therefore the animal has and does not have spirit. (*Of Spirit*, 50–51)

The ambivalence of the animal in relation to the world is bound, for Derrida, to the improperly formulated notion of spirit in the world. For every other aspect of this statement that is loaded with potential for analysis, it is important in the context of the discussion of the real of universals and the unconscious as an aspect of the animality within humanity because of the significance of ambivalence between having and not having world and spirit. In his next, and slightly longer, formulation of the centrality that this ambivalence takes in the scene of the being in relation to the world and spirit, Derrida calls forth the unconscious as a real element of animality.

In *Zur Seinsfrage* . . . Heidegger proposes to write the word Being under a line of erasure in the form of a cross *(Kreuzweise Durchstreichung).* This cross did not represent either a negative sign or even a sign at all, but it was supposed to recall the *Geviert,* the fourfold, precisely, as the "play of the world," brought together in its place *(Ort),* at the crossing of the cross. The place, for Heidegger, is always a place of collecting together *(Versammlung).* The lecture on "The Thing" (1950) deciphers in this play of the world—recalled in this way by an erasing of "Being"—the becoming-world of the world, *das welten von Welt,* the world which is in that it worlds (itself) or makes itself worldy *(Die Welt ist, indem sie weltet).* (*Of Spirit*, 52)

By Being in the world, even the Thing portrays an instantiation of the unconscious as worldly. This understanding of Heidegger is crucial to a reading of Lacan's statement that "the woman" must be written with a line through it: ~~the woman~~.

Why Lacan never openly admits his indebtedness to Heidegger on this point is not clear, especially since he is overt about the Heideggerian influences behind the development of the Thing *(das Ding)* as a real. If Lacan had called attention to this Heideggerian understanding of Being as multidimensional and the fact that this Being is represented by crossing out the signifier of the universal, then the debates over his antifeminism would have been easily solved.

If we read Lacan's positing of "the woman" as ~~the woman~~ in a Heideggerian fashion, then the very question of the universal category of Being opens to the "play of the world" and to the manifold becoming of the Being in the world. This would assist in an understanding of the Oneness of the Woman that we struggled to articulate in chapter 1, and it would also, more importantly perhaps, lead to a profound definition of the category of the universal as real. In a moment I will embark on this analysis and demonstrate the process of ~~the woman~~ as Being with regard to the animality in the "man." First, though, the enigma of the apparent simplicity in an enunciation of the category of ~~the woman~~ as a multidimensional real universal must be prohibited by something, or logic would state that Lacan would simply have referred to Heidegger to explain his point. The fact that he *does* refer to Heidegger, but not in this manner, shows the extent to which, despite the many times that Derrida seems to be behind Lacan, on this particular issue it takes Derrida's view of Heidegger to show us what Lacan means when he writes ~~the woman~~.

As Derrida cites Heidegger, we find the initial passage that leads to the Derridean understanding of the crossing-out as manifold being. Heidegger says:

> When we say that the lizard is stretched out on the rock, we should cross through *(durchstreichen)* the word "rock," to indicate that while what the lizard is stretched out on is doubtless given him in *some way (irgendwie),* but is not known [or recognized] *as (als)* rock. The crossing-through does not only mean: something else is apprehended, as something else, but: it is above all not accessible *as entity (überhaupt nicht als Seiendes zugänglich).*[17]

Suddenly, Lacan's reluctance to cite Heidegger on this point becomes clear. As he perceives elements of the world, rocks, matches, pots, vases, to be Things in the world, they nonetheless do not have the character of life in the world as that which consists of a being with an unconscious. Lacan wants strictly to distinguish between the animal-human as one who has and can articulate an unconscious and the animal—lizard/wolf/rat/bee—as one who does not have an unconscious; further, these animal forms are separate from nonanimate beings such as "rock."[18]

In his discussion of *Das Ding* in *The Ethics of Psychoanalysis* Lacan insists on the difference between the animal as real and the human as struggling to achieve the real but whose engagement is problematized by the necessity of the symbolic. "When we seek to explore the frontier between the animal and the human world, it is apparent to what extent the symbolic process as such doesn't function in the animal world" (*Seminar VII*, 45). And this points toward the limitations of psycho-analysis: "That man is caught up in symbolic processes of a kind to which no animal has access cannot be resolved in psychological terms, since it implies that we first have a complete and precise knowledge of what this symbolic process means" (*Seminar VII*, 45). At this limit of the psychoanalytical understanding of animality and subjectivity, we are thrown into a different realm of discourse that engages the potential for universals such that we might access the real. And, in this place the Thing, *Das Ding*, the "beyond-of-the-signified," the real, obeys the order of necessity and emerges (*Seminar VII*, 54). This may be what Heidegger means when he says that the "rock" is not accessible as an "entity" because it is not representative of a complex system that has significance to us as a conscious/unconscious blend of being. What Lacan takes him to mean, however, is that these Things, which exist in the world in fact, have enormous significance to *our* unconscious behavior as we seek to possess and interact with things in the world.

Lacan's understanding of Heidegger is therefore quite different from Derrida's reading, which perceives a prohibitive split between the entity as nonaccessible and the speaking subject. In Derrida's view:

> Erasure of the name, then, here of the name of the rock which would designate the possibility of naming the rock itself, *as such* and accessible in its being-rock. The erasing would mark in *our* language, by avoiding a word, this inability of the animal to name. But this is first of all the inability to open itself to the *as such* of the thing. It is not of the rock *as such* that the lizard has experience. That is why the name of the rock must be erased when we want to designate what the lizard is stretched out upon.... Here the erasure of the name would signify the non-access to the entity as such.[19] ... The crossing-through recalls a benumbedness *(Benommenheit)* of the animal.... It does not have access to the difference between the open and the closed. (*Of Spirit*, 53–54)

What we can see from the difference between Derrida's characterization of Heidegger, which leads us to a better understanding of Lacan, and

Lacan's characterization (or noncharacterization) of Heidegger on this point specifically is the difference between Derrida as a nominalist and Lacan as a realist. With regard to the animality of the drives and the status of the human subject, Lacan unwittingly reveals the dirty little secret that he is a humanist. Derrida and Agamben agree that the animal, for Heidegger, is captivated, numbed, or experiencing "benumbedness." For Derrida, this means that the animal experiences no ambivalence between the open and the closed. For Agamben, the animal is open precisely to the possibility of being closed. In Lacan's system, the differentiation between the subject with an unconscious and the subject without an unconscious takes precedence over the determination of ambivalence. "There is no unconscious except for the speaking being. The others, who possess being only through being named — even though they impose themselves from within the real — have instinct, namely the knowledge needed for their survival. Yet this is so only for our thought, which might be inadequate here" (*Television*, 9).[20] Only the subject with an unconscious that speaks can express and even perhaps experience ambivalence precisely because ambivalence has the character of the subject as human attempting to account for and contain its animality. The recognition of the inadequacy of this formula prevents Lacan from being anthropocentric, but he does, nonetheless, work from that presumption in the progress of the articulation of analysis.

Agamben's formulation of this problem is helpful in understanding the categorical distinctions at work here:

> [I]f the caesura between the human and the animal passes first of all within man, then it is the very question of man — and of "humanism" — that must be posed in a new way. In our culture, man has always been thought of as the articulation and conjunction of a body and a soul, of a living thing and a *logos*, of a natural (or animal) element and a supernatural or social or divine element. We must learn instead to think of man as what results from the incongruity of these two elements, and investigate not the metaphysical mystery of conjunction, but rather the practical and political mystery of separation. What is man, if he is always the place — and, at the same time, the result of ceaseless divisions and caesurae? (*The Open*, 16)

As in Lacan's system, the distinguishing factor between human and animals for Agamben is language.[21] When he imagines the nonspeaking man, however, Agamben takes the line of inquiry into a realm wherein we can reconceive of the category of the human as a universal, and he heads us toward a reading of the famous "nonspeaking man," the Werewolf.

Becoming Human

Marie de France's *Bisclavret* participates in the debate over universals by representing the ambivalence of the animality with the human. When the "animal" becomes "human" by getting dressed in the king's chambers, the position of ambivalence within sovereignty and the potential for categories becomes evident.[22] Of course, these categories are always linguistically bound.

R. Howard Bloch traces the etymology of the name "Bisclavret" to demonstrate Marie's investment in exploring the limits of linguistic significance and play.[23] In *The Anonymous Marie de France* Bloch provides the philological history that traces the different elements of the name.

> Joseph Loth claims that it derives from the Breton *bisc,* meaning "short," and *lavret,* "wearing breeches or short trousers." Heinrich Zimmer relates it to the Breton term *bleiz lavret,* "speaking wolf." Th. Chotzen derives it from *bleidd Ilafar,* "the dear little speaking wolf" or *le bon loup fatidique.* H. W. Bailed explains the form *bisclavret* as *bleiz laveret,* "rational wolf." Finally, William Sayers proposes *bleiz claffet,* "wolf-sick, afflicted with lycanthropy," as the term "claff" is associated with leprosy. (82)

Working from this etymological survey Bloch's solution is to divide the name into *bis,* meaning "again," and *clavret,* meaning a "nail" or a "key," therefore suggesting that the significance of the name is reflective of the multiplicity of language and the surplus of meaning (*Anonymous Marie,* 82). Bloch's gesture toward the play and mutability of language and Marie's awareness of it is seductive and implies that all of the meanings are available and possible at alternating moments in, and from varying perspectives of, the text. Taken together, in their plurality and their singularity, they point to the uncanny quality of the idea of the "speaking wolf," which, surprisingly, does not appear uncanny at all in Marie's *lais.* The diminutive form proposed by Chotzen of the "dear little speaking wolf" relates that the sublime elements of the uncanny moment that are reflected by the speaking animal (or automaton) are, in fact, not sublime at all; rather, they are contained within the system of linguistic play that defies singularity and exhibits mutability—they are made cute and small, like a little pet wolf whose string one pulls to hear a message.

Language itself need not be seen here as the crucial difference between animals and humans or as the difference that leads to sovereign power of one species over another.[24] On the contrary, the term "rational wolf" is a terrifying and sublime image since it ascribes to the animal the ability to use logic and therefore potential cunning over another.[25] It also points toward a more fluid connection between the wolf and the "man." Since many speaking subjects are not necessarily precisely "rational" subjects, and since rationality itself is dependent upon language, the "rational wolf" threatens the sovereignty of human life, perhaps even suggesting that its inversion is simple — that the rational is not rational at all, but irrational and motivated by libidinal drives.[26]

In the prologue to *Bisclavret,* Marie defines the werewolf as being "a savage beast," who, "While his fury is upon him / he eats men / does much harm, / goes deep in the forest to live."[27] The cannibalistic impulses and actions of the werewolf, the animalized-human, are hidden in the dark of the woods as an element of the fragmented self that cannot be shared with the community. In the tale, Bisclavret's secret is disclosed to his wife, who is unhappy with his absence for three days of the week. She loved him very much, but was quite disturbed that "during the week he would be missing / for three whole days, and she didn't know / what happened to him or where he went" (*Bisclavret,* 25–27). Fearing that he is being unfaithful to her, Bisclavret's wife finally asks him where he goes when he disappears. Seeking to disclose her fears and questions regarding his fidelity, Bisclavret's wife is afraid of his anger even before she discovers that she might have a reason to fear him. She states,

"I'd like very much to ask you one thing —
if I dared;
but I'm so afraid of your anger
that nothing frightens me more." (*Bisclavret,* 33–36)

Bisclavret's response is kind and generous given the accusation launched against him by his wife, when he holds her and states that the reason for his silence is that the curse will be placed upon him if he reveals his mutable and animal existence. His fear for his own subjective status is clear: "'Harm will come to me if I tell you about this, / because I'd lose your love / and even my very self'" (*Bisclavret,* 54–56). Despite his trepidation, Bisclavret does reveal his secret to his wife, telling her "everything" about his metamorphosis and alternate existence (*Bisclavret,* 63–67).

In the sense that inconsistency is a form of infidelity, Bisclavret's hybrid, animalized humanity does in fact reflect his infidelity even though he does not "have a lover" (*Bisclavret*, 51). As we saw in chapter 1, in Alain Badiou's view, "consistency is the engagement of one's singularity (the animal 'some-one') in the continuation of a subject of truth."[28] However, Bisclavret's consistency here is precisely a hybrid reflecting the animality within the human and the human within the animal. In this sense, *singularity* does not represent consistency; rather, the fragmentation of the subject as consisting of multiple parts, in this case "two" parts, the animal and the human, is more properly aligned with Badiou's notion of the truth-process as that which is faithful to a fidelity; even further, the pursuit of desire, the refusal to give up on one's desire, is evident as Bisclavret has no choice but to persevere in "being what he is" (*Bisclavret*, 47). As such, the desire for singularity is again revealed to be a futile search since desire itself prevents such simplicity.

Although he is traumatized by his metamorphosis, and reveals ambivalence toward his own animal subjectivity, Bisclavret negotiates his duality because his clothes return him to his human status. The drives of the beast within the human are dangerous to the precarious and thinly veiled rational sovereignty of the subject, and Bisclavret wants to protect the hiding place of his mutability. His wife then asks a strange question regarding the limits of his animality when he is in the werewolf form and wondering whether he is clothed or naked when he is transformed into a werewolf. When he tells her that he "goes naked" she becomes invested in learning about where he hides his *vestements.*[29] The sovereignty that he holds while clothed appears to give way when he is in the denuded state that Agamben calls "bare life." Disclosing his secret, Bisclavret renders himself vulnerable and endangers his "self" as a sovereign subject.

In *Homo Sacer,* Agamben's reading of *Bisclavret* illuminates the political implications of the fragmented subject and his/her connection to the exhibition of free will and power.[30] Agamben's well-conceived and subtle argument linking the appearance of a loss of control as "bare life" with the sovereignty of sovereign power itself makes sense of Bisclavret's ability to mutate and return to his "human" status, while maintaining power as an animal. Appropriating Carl Schmitt's point about the state of exception,[31] Agamben writes:

[T]his lupization of man and humanization of the wolf is at every moment possible in the *dissolutio civitatis* inaugurated by the state of exception. This threshold alone, which is neither simple natural life nor social life but rather bare life or sacred life, is the always present and always operative presupposition of sovereignty.

Contrary to our modern habit of representing the political realm in terms of cititzens' rights, free will, and social contracts, from the point of view of sovereignty, only bare life is *authentically political.* (*Homo Sacer,* 106)

Agamben's assertion renders Bisclavret's alternate life as a werewolf crucial to the development of the subject as sovereign and as a necessarily political subject within the context of a community, which may be seen as, he says, "the city" or as a "community" that is developed in the process of a relation between one subject and another. Despite this necessity, Agamben wisely perceives the incompatibility of the savage or animal with the "community" of "rational" human culture. "What unites the surviving devotee, *homo sacer,* and the sovereign in one single paradigm is that in each case we find ourselves confronted with a bare life that has been separated from its context and that, so to speak surviving its death, is for this very reason incompatible with the human world" (*Homo Sacer,* 100). Rather than stupidity, terror ("she was terrified of the whole adventure" [*Homo Sacer,* 99]), sheer evil deception, or even her own desire to love her admirer and consort in the plan to denude and destroy Bisclavret, perhaps this incompatibility of bare life and its political context reveals Bisclavret's wife's reasons for being afraid of his metamorphosis. His animality cannot coexist with his sovereign life as a human and her life with him because it challenges her concept of the wholeness of their contractual and cultural (political) marriage bond.

The animal, the cannibal, the drives, and the precise "humanness" that these "flaws" reflect *must* be excluded in order for Bisclavret's wife to maintain a conception of herself as sovereign. What she does not realize, however, is that through this exception, through the very exclusion and elimination of her husband and her unfaithful, bigamous marriage to the knight who steals her husband's clothes, she exhibits her own desire in a more precise sovereign form that carries with it a different approach to bare life. When his former wife's nose is cut off, she is rendered denuded and her beauty is "unmasked." Her "nosiness," either a symptom of her lack of faith in Bisclavret, or a symptom of her own inability to be faithful, is also reflective of the necessary connection between bare life and sovereign power, fragmentation and the appearance of wholeness, as well as animality and humanity.

The dissonance between the animal and the human is not as wide a gap as it might appear in Marie's tale. The king perceives humanity within the animal because of the performance of obedience.

> he saw the king
> and ran to him, pleading for mercy.
> He took hold of the king's stirrup,
> kissed his leg and his foot.
> The king saw this and was terrified;
> he called his companions.
> "My lords," he said, "come quickly!
> Look at this marvel —
> this beast is humbling itself to me.
> It has the mind of a man, and it's begging me for mercy!"
> (*Bisclavret,* 145–54)

If an awareness of gratitude and hierarchical order determine the rationality of the animal in Bisclavret, then his appearance as an animal is subordinate to his sense of order. The initial terror experienced by the king illustrates the uncanny and ambivalent character of the animal who is human. The king, however, is able to process this information quickly and takes Bisclavret's actions for their symbolic meaning, thus placing the human in the animal as that which can convey meaning without speech. Bisclavret's symbolic actions lead the king to conclude that " 'This beast is rational — he has a mind' " (*Bisclavret,* 157). Rationality in this case is not limited to speech, but it does depend on symbolic expression. As Bisclavret's actions are consistent, the king is led to recognize love between the two:

> he was so noble and well behaved
> that he never wished to do anything wrong.
> Regardless of where the king might go,
> Bisclavret never wanted to be separated from him;
> he always accompanied the king.
> The king became very much aware that the creature loved him.
> (*Bisclavret,* 179–84)

If the king knows that Bisclavret loves him, then these actions also indicate that the king loves Bisclavret in return. The properly domesticated animal is a perfect subject to the king. His rationality, as evidence of his humanity, also enables his actions to be taken as those of desire, reconciling the apparent animal and human duality and giving proper *will* to the animal. As such, when Bisclavret attacks the knight who has married his wife, he is granted voluntary intention as a rational subject who is taking revenge on one who has wronged him, placing the animal in the position of the ethical subject with desire. After he has attacked the knight,

> All over the palace people said
> that he wouldn't act that way without a reason:
> that somehow or other, the knight had mistreated Bisclavret,
> and now he wanted his revenge. (*Bisclavret*, 207–10)

Properly domesticated, the animal behaves like a human and so is not threatening even in his violence, which is attributed causality. In this way, he avoids the position of ambivalence that Bisclavret's wife exhibits in her actions and in her subjection to the king's explicit wishes on behalf of the mute Bisclavret.

Though she has betrayed Bisclavret, as a human reacting to a human, the process of torture to which she is exposed foregrounds the animal within the human power that the king wields, and the human within the animal who betrays, as the wife is forced to speak to "tell what she knows."

> he took the wife
> and subjected her to torture;
> out of fear and pain
> she told all about her husband. (*Bisclavret*, 263–66)

In this position as the tortured victim who has oppressed an other, the wife supplements Bisclavret's voice; she is the animal who does speak, and Bisclavret is the human who does not.[32]

The king in *Bisclavret* is apparently a good king, who is comfortable enough in his sovereign role to bring a "rational animal" to his court, and to allow him to use his chamber for potential transformation after he has shown shame by way of his reluctance to transform his identity in the presence of the king. The image of Bisclavret's metamorphosis gives new meaning to the refrain, the king is naked. Bisclavret enters the king's chambers as an animal denuded of his humanity and emerges clothed and with the ability to speak restored, thus restoring his humanity. This generosity is reflective of the king's own awareness (conscious or unconscious) of the imbrication between bare life and sovereign power, animality and human rationality. To the extent that the king enables Bisclavret's return to the court as well as his transformation, the text supports Agamben's positions that "Sovereign violence is in truth founded not on a pact but on the exclusive inclusion of bare life in the state. And just as sovereign power's first and immediate referent is, in this sense, the life that may be killed but not sacrificed, and that has its paradigm in *homo sacer*, so in the person of the sovereign, the werewolf, the wolf-man of man, dwells permanently in the city" (*Homo Sacer*, 107). The difference between Bisclavret's wife's terror and that felt by the king upon his encounter with Bisclavret in the woods is the precise difference between the fear of the animal within the human and the human within the animal. Both elements are shown to be precious in the text, and the wife's condemnation for her own terror is more dramatic because her love should be the love of bare life, when she is in search, instead, of sovereign power. Similarly, the king's munificence is evident in his acceptance of bare life (even if it remains subject to him in the form of a master/servant relationship), when he might typically be invested in sovereign power; the king's wisdom and the wife's failure then, mirror each other in their acceptance and refusal, suggesting that sovereignty is bound to an awareness of its fragility and fragmentation.

One of the significant textual elements that has not yet been explored here is the synaesthetic shift from the wife's need to gaze at Bisclavret's secret, her jealously driven epistemophilia that becomes transformed into her nosiness (epistemophobia), and the removal of her nose (her castration) that is then carried on to her children in a Lamarckian manner. As a signifier of Bisclavret's wife's curiosity, physical beauty, and nobility, the nose's removal represents a mark of her infidelity. More interestingly, it is a form of rape and castration that condemns the betrayer to betray herself, on a daily basis through her own life and in the future lives of her children. As Bisclavret's wife rendered him impotent in the form of the werewolf, he now in turn eliminates her ability to avoid the presence of bare life in her otherwise fictionally solid sovereignty. She must live with the fragmentation and fragility that she so feared in her husband's mutability and animality.

The need to *see* manifested as an involuntary scoptophilic drive also exhibits an ambivalent desire to control that which one sees. In this way, one fights to put up a barrier against seeing so that one is either blind to what one sees, or one eliminates the scene (rendering it obscene, or out of sight). In the case history of the Wolf Man, Freud describes scoptophilia as a sexual drive wherein the subject desires to see the other in a denuded form. According to Freud, "The child, as we have seen, was under the domination of a component of the sexual instinct, scoptophilia (the instinct of looking), as a result of which there was a constant recurrence in him of a very intense wish connected with persons of the female sex who pleased him — the wish, that is, to see them naked" (*Three Case Histories*, 23). As much as it is compelled by desire, this drive is also replete with a sense of repulsion and a fear of what might occur if the wish is fulfilled.[33] The appearance of the erotic instinct is simultaneously met with the "revolt against it" (*Three Case Histories*, 24). The strength of both forces gives life to the ambivalence at work here. The conscious understanding of the drive is met with a counterpoint that renders the wish one that is abject and improper to the human subject who is attempting to control his will, and that emerges as the animal that one fears and loathes. At stake in this dynamic is the problem, as we have seen, of faith and trust in the self and in the other.

Stealing Woman

The punishment for refusing to trust one's partner is imposed on the betrayer, the one who cannot trust and who holds too dearly to the need to see. As we will "see" momentarily, in the Old French romance *Mélusine*, however, the punishment falls on the victim. In both cases, a theft is at stake. Bisclavret's wife commissions her new lover, the knight, to steal his clothes. In *Mélusine*, Raymond "steals" a glance at his wife through a hole in the wall to discover her secret hybrid human form. Both the wife of Bisclavret and the husband of Mélusine discover what they hoped never to find, a presence where they hoped there was absence. Their discovery, whether linguistic, textual, textile, or visual, presents them with the horror of the presence of the animality and drives within the human that they hope will be rational, faithful to subjective wholeness, and so properly "human."

In his essay on obsessive actions and religious practices, Freud discusses the clandestine nature of the rituals that neurotics perform as a means of disavowing their lack. He compares the secret actions of the obsessive to Mélusine who hides her physical metamorphosis into a serpent, showing only her intact feminine body to the public. Freud's interpretation of the legend places Mélusine within the popular view of her during the early 1900s. He states that she is "A beautiful woman in a mediaeval legend, who led a secret existence as a water-nymph."[34] Freud's romanticized account of Mélusine conceals the vast history behind her legendary status as the maternal origin of France.[35] Although Lacan does not directly address the legend, he extends Freud's interest in the legend by exploring the secret nature of sexuality. A reading of Lacan's view of the phallus as signifier within an impossible sexual relation as a crucial aspect of his historiographical project that interprets medieval texts and concepts as a means of uncovering desire in the history of philosophical thought may be enhanced by an analysis of the history and context of the medieval legend of Mélusine.

The fourteenth-century Old French prose text of Mélusine, *Le Roman de Mélusine* (1393), by Jean d'Arras and its somewhat more overtly philosophic poetic translation by Coudrette present the mythical history of Mélusine.[36] Represented as the phallic-mother who instantiates the impossibility of writing "the woman," Mélusine demonstrates that despite her long lineage and multiple existence, she cannot (neither as a particular, the woman, nor as general, the nation) become a categorical "real."[37] And yet, the very textuality of the long history both within and surrounding *Le Roman de Mélusine* supports a presentation of it as a *real*. The texts are based on a legend about a woman who at birth is given by her mother a serpent tail that shows itself on Saturdays. Along with this tail her mother gives her supernatural powers that enable her to construct a broad lineage and gain control over vast geographical regions. The stipulation of maintaining her powers states that they will be removed and her lineage will fall if she allows anyone to witness her metamorphosis. Throughout the text the curse or blessing given to Mélusine by her mother is alternately called a gift and a punishment.[38] When Mélusine marries Raymond, she says that she will grant him happiness and prosperity as long as he agrees never to spy on her on Saturdays. He agrees to the contract and the couple lives well and prospers, producing many children who succeed in populating various realms of France. Urged by his brother, who is suspicious of the virtue of all women, Raymond begins to get jealous of the time that Mélusine takes to herself and wonders if she is being unfaithful to him. Ultimately, Raymond breaks his vow to leave her alone on Saturdays and, piercing a hole in an iron wall surrounding her bath, he sees her serpent tail. He thus gains the knowledge of her bodily change, beginning a curse by which she will eternally remain in the form of a serpent and their lineage will fail to prosper. She dies a human death but supernaturally remains to perpetually watch over the outcome of her lineage and sing a song of lament over her loss. Raymond laments his own loss and his betrayal of Mélusine.

Versions of the Mélusine legend abound in French, Germanic, and English literary and historical traditions. Moving from the fourteenth century to the twentieth, Mélusine's tale is constantly rewritten as a literary tale as well as an incorporation of that tale within historical narratives of the history of France. Specifically, the production of Mélusine as a mythical history of the lineage of the Lusignan family affects a larger sense of nationalism in histories of France written in the late nineteenth and early twentieth centuries.[39] Mélusine figures in various genealogical surveys of the political effects of the Lusignan family.[40] Invoking the image of the mirror, both Beauvais and Bourgogne recall a concept of the mimetic process in history. Additionally, Baudot notes that Froissart echoes the Mélusine tale when he writes about the marriage of Charles III to Isabeau de Bauviere, suggesting that historical narrative mirrors the mythical narrative. Froissart, following the example of Mélusine, marks the aristocracy with the discursive identity of fictional characters.[41] Baudot constructs a genealogy of the Mélusine text, placing it in the context of other literary products for the duke of Berry including texts by Marie de France and Christine de Pizan. Significantly, all three productive lines (the Marian *lais*, Christine's texts, and the Mélusine story) interweave "history" with "myth."[42] Editing the Coudrette prose version, *Le Roman de Mélusine ou Historie de Lusignan par Coudrette* (1982), Eleanor Roach writes that the text wants to present itself alternately as a fiction (or romance) and as a history.

During the sixteenth century the historian Mezeray says, "not knowing [Mélusine's] real history, we have invented marvelous tales concerning her."[43] The tale itself demonstrates a fascination with the curiosity and desire for self-knowledge that leads to a concern with documenting history. The epistemophilia indicated by Coudrette's prologue unfolds in the narrative as that which drives Raymond to break his vow never to mistrust Mélusine despite her secretive habits on Saturdays. As the prologue states, human intellect endeavors to learn and know things, be these things of love or reproach, and especially if it concerns the seeker of knowledge closely. According to Coudrette, the philosophers and their noble metaphysics seek to know the truth.[44] In Raymond's voyeuristic moment this desire to know the self leads to a love of the myth of the other that drives history to produce records of its lineage.[45]

Illuminations of the tale from the Middle Ages through the Victorian era increasingly represent the demonic and monstrous side of Mélusine as one that is precisely decent and expected for a woman. The image from Baudot in the 1900s presents Mélusine as a romantic figure recalling the Lady of Shalott more than the "evil" Luxuria or Bathsheba from the earlier texts. This transformation in textual images corresponds to the transforming perception of Mélusine as historical matriarch who is also demonic, and as a woman who is inherently demonic. It also reflects the developing romanticizing of the Middle Ages that accompanies the formation of the discipline of medieval studies in the early nineteenth century.[46]

This complex citational and revisionist history is central to an understanding of the way in which Mélusine's apparent absent causality leads Raymond to perceive her in a state of animality and the manner in which this reflects the ambivalence at stake in the definition of "the woman" (~~the woman~~) as a potential universal real. Since he is not familiar with the "gift" bestowed on Mélusine by her mother, and he simultaneously assumes that Mélusine's serpentine appearance is due to an evil or poisonous force (such as infidelity or a curse), rather than associating her body with the positive and productive attributes that it carries, Raymond perceives a lack of origin or causality in her being and takes her for a demon. When Raymond sees his wife in her hybrid woman-animal state, he reacts violently; unlike the king who sees Bisclavret as an animal who is also human, Raymond sees his wife as the abject, revolting, and threatening human who is also animal.[47]

The play with the voyeur and exhibitionist in the various mirror scenes used to illuminate *Mélusine* demonstrates the constant return to the mirror as a place of self-construction. The moment of seeing remains traumatic, only assuming its shock value retroactively.[48] Indeed, Raymond is shocked when he sees the horrible truth *(l'horrible vraiment)* of Mélusine's reptilian tail.[49] Bedazzled by the blue and silver colors of her serpent's tail, Raymond cries out to God, becomes silent, and actively closes the hole he has made with his sword. Playing the role of the voyeur, Raymond must expect his gaze to find the absent phallus. The voyeur looks partly in the hopes of *not seeing* what he anticipates. In fact, Raymond's experience directly counters what Lacan (following Freud) describes as the trauma of the primal moment—the finding of the object that one hopes to see as absence. Raymond seeks the absence that will enable his fantasies to continue growing in his mind. He finds in place of this absence the fullness of Mélusine's phallic power. Her bodily presence leaves no room for imagination. Rather, it embodies that which the voyeur's imagination could expect to find. Where Raymond expects a shadow, he finds the powerful subject who constructed his city and provided him with a lineage, and a body that blends the demonic with the angelic in such a way that confounds him, threatening his very sense of the reality of his life. His gaze foregrounds the violence of the love relationship by enacting the disjuncture between his expectation and the fulfillment of his desire.[50]

In her reading of postmodern love, Catherine Belsey asks, "Is desire a matter of fact or fiction?"[51] As a text that combines myth with historical fiction, *Mélusine* aids in the revealing response "Both and neither." When Raymond discovers Mélusine in her bath and sees her serpent tail, his perception of her is altered. Her "essence" as a categorical real, however, has not changed; she remains the same being that he loves. Nonetheless, his empirical witnessing of her bodily form as the phallic mother causes him to reevaluate his relationship with her. The love that bound him to his wife was based on a fiction of her identity. The reality of her physical being and her habit of altering it is a knowledge that Raymond cannot process. His very real desire was based on a fictional view of his wife.[52]

The scopic moment of witnessing Mélusine, for Raymond, and in the illuminations that consistently accompany the various manuscripts, play on the etymology of *obscene* as that which exists outside the realm of the gaze. Mélusine is consistently placed both outside of the gaze and at its center. Like Bisclavret, Mélusine is undone by the breach of contract, preventing her from controlling the manner in which she is perceived. In this way, she is an appropriate symbol on which to cathect a view of medievalism as that which searches for what is hidden and, as in Poe's "The Purloined Letter," continually in plain sight.[53] Mélusine's phallic tail leading to her association with abject monstrosity symbolizes the form of the knot that historiography assumes under Lacan's theory of desire.

Crucial to an understanding of Lacan's medievalism is the way in which his view of history leads to a particular canon of literature that constructs the history of subjectivity. Any attempt to sublimate animality will result in its emergence in a different, potentially more threatening form that will carry with it the force and power of the symptom that returns from the place of repression. But this is precisely what does not work in the scene of ambivalence. As we will see shortly, when sublimation fails, ambivalence prevails.

In *Seminar XI, The Four Fundamental Concepts of Psychoanalysis,* Lacan addresses the problem of the voyeur as ambivalent that Freud initiates in his case study on the Wolf Man.[54] Speaking of the moment that Jean-Paul Sartre discusses as that of the thief trying to peer into a keyhole, Lacan reconfigures the moment to interpolate the thief as the voyeur.

> What he is trying to see, make no mistake, is the object as absence. What the voyeur is looking for and finds is merely a shadow, a shadow behind the curtain. There he will phantasize any magic of presence, the most graceful of girls, for example, even if on the other side there is only a hairy athlete. What he is looking for is not, as one says, the phallus — but precisely its absence. (*Seminar XI,* 182)

This desire to see the absence of the phallus, the ambivalence of the desire to see and to see that there is nothing to see, is precisely the problem that Bisclavret's wife and Mélusine's husband Raymond share in their horror at the view of their respective partners in their various states of animality. On a physical level, one may speak of the way in which Bisclavret and Mélusine become the phallus when they shift into the forms of werewolf and half-woman, half-serpent. They represent the horror of the presence of the phallus as animal drive and the signifier of the uncontrollable element of desire. Taking this somewhat crude reading further, we might consider the way in which the phallic inhabitation and exhibition in the animality (lupization and reptilization) of both characters is more threatening and confrontational when we imagine the role that they play in challenging the sovereignty of the subject, the other, and illustrate the pure fragmentation and fragility of subjectivity itself. Although neither Bisclavret nor Mélusine are actively infidelitous to their partners, it might be asserted that the accusation of infidelity is appropriate if fragmented subjectivity is threatening to the love between the subjects. It is irrelevant to Bisclavret's wife and to Raymond that Bisclavret and Mélusine are not engaging in sexual relations with an "other," because they are instantiating (and so loving) the other within themselves. Despite his rational wishes, Bisclavret must give over to his drives to hunt and consume his prey (his *human* prey). The fact that Mélusine is found "in her bath" illustrates both her need to make her animal-self hygienic, as well as her potentially narcissistic or potentially pleasurable engagement with her body. Both Bisclavret and Mélusine maintain distance and difference through their participation in their own drives reflecting the threat of animality.

Lacan's reading of courtly love takes up Freud's classical view of the feminine abject as monstrous other and renders visible that which was hidden—the impossibility of a sexual relationship and the mourning and sublimation that are involved in an awareness of that lack.

Scatology and Ambivalence

In Freud's case study of the Wolf Man, we see an ambivalent relation to the scene of courtly love in the Wolf Man's simultaneous display of pleasure and repulsion, holiness and scatology. The Wolf Man's sadistic fantasies emerge in the form of masochistic ones that allow him to identify with the suffering of Christ on the cross. His subjective fragmentation is a result of his persistent ambivalence, which does not allow for the incorporation of various forms of desire into a singular one. As Freud remarks,

> No doubt was left in the analysis that these passive trends had made their appearance at the same time as the active-sadistic ones, or very soon after them. This is in accordance with the unusually clear, intense, and constant *ambivalence* of the patient, which was shown here for the first time in the even development of both members of the pairs of contrary component instincts. Such behaviour was also characteristic of his later life, and so was this further trait: no position of the libido which had once been established was ever completely replaced by a later one. It was rather left in existence side by side with all the others, and this allowed him to maintain an incessant vacillation which proved to be incompatible with the acquisition of a fixed character. (*Three Case Histories*, 209)

The alternate forms of courtly love expressed by the Rat Man and the Wolf Man in their neurotic behavior, and embodied poetically in the verses that Lacan cites by Jaufré Rudel and Arnaut Daniel (which we will see in chapter 3), reflect the ambivalence at the core of desire. As a two-fold ambivalence, that within the subject and that which is in relation to another subject, this ambivalence is transformed into a symptomatic display of attraction-repulsion, wherein love and hate become "lovehate," "one" becomes "two," and "two" appear never as "one" but rather as the square root of negative one. Because the Wolf Man displaces his horror onto the animal-object, we are enlightened about the relationship between animality and subjectivity within the process of ambivalence.

The articulation of desire that Lacan first uses to express courtly love in *Seminar VII, The Ethics of Psychoanalysis* similarly suggests that animality is present in humanity through the excess and surplus of the female body. The overt ambivalence displayed by Arnaut Daniel in the scatological poem that Lacan analyzes as a model of courtly love performing the process of desire in *Seminar VII* marks woman as a site of ambivalence.

Ambivalence is predicated on the ability to locate two discrete entities, two "ones." Without the possibility of singularity, or "the one," the conflict between two cannot exist. If, as Lacan insists, the "One" is the "essence of the signifier," then how might two of these essences enter into a relation with each other? Fundamentally, if we take the maxim "*il n'ya pas de la rapport sexuel*" at its word, then there is no moment or place where two essences taken as signifiers succeed at entering such a relation, thus eliminating the possibility of two; we must acknowledge that there can, in fact, be only *one* essence of the signifier, and this essence, this transcendental universal *is desire.*

In the first prominent citational instance of troubadour poetics that marks Lacan's assertion of courtly love as anamorphosis, he does not focus on a common display of the distance and idealization of the love object so popular to an understanding of courtly love poetics. Instead, he takes up a scatological text by Arnaut Daniel that resembles a fabliau more than it does a properly generic troubadour poem. Lacan's choice to find a courtly love poem that resembles a fabliau calls attention to the obscene within the divine and ideal. His assertion that courtly love is "not at all platonic," perplexing when one considers troubadour poetics as pastoral, makes sense when the agonism of the concurrent sacred and profane aspects of courtly love are addressed. To focus on the fabliau as a genre would place Lacan's discussion within the "low" or bawdy genre and reverse the implications of his argument, which finds precisely the necessity of the obscene in the articulation of love for an Other.

The conservative historical authority of the "high" mode of poetic expression invests Lacan's argument with the element of seriousness that is necessary to intervene in scholastic debates. Further, Lacan's attempt to usurp the position "knowledge" has played in the history of philosophy and replace that repressed state with the fullness of desire requires that his discourse participate within that history. Notably, this move is not simply "subversive" as many contemporary arguments that adhere to notions of inside and outside would have it. Rather, Lacan's comment that the state of courtly love itself involves obscenity deploys his notion of the *extimate*—that which is simultaneously intimate to the subject and external to it.

Lacan's statements about the function of language in relationship to "the death of God" provide insight regarding his choice of the scatological troubadour poem to display his theory of desire. The extension of sexual terminology into metaphors that apparently have nothing at all to do with sexuality leads him to the conclusion that "sexual symbolism in the ordinary sense of the word may polarize at its point of origin the metaphorical play of the signifier" (*Seminar VII*, 169). In the discussion immediately preceding this conclusion, Lacan investigates the gap that exists between the signifier and the signified in the instance of metaphor. "Why," he asks, "do we use some slang expression that originally had a sexual significance in order to evoke metaphorically situations that have nothing to do with sex?" (*Seminar VII*, 168). The response to this question exists in the lack associated with female sexuality and the gap that resides in the utterance of the metaphor. On the surface, it would seem that Lacan is indeed marking a misogynist claim that equates the gap in signification with the hole in women. However, the argument, leading both to the notion of the death of God as always already given and to the impossibility of the sexual relation, instead employs the example of female genitals as precisely that which replaces gaps in signification and sexuality with fullness.

In the example of courtly love poetics that Lacan chooses to illustrate his theory of desire, Bernart refuses to participate in a sexual relationship with Lady Ena on the basis of her excess. That surplus of desire takes on the form of an overwhelmingly negative response to sensory stimulation. The response to this phenomenological saturation displayed by Arnaut's lover to Lady Ena's physicality explicitly reveals the unconscious processes that prevent the completion of an erotic relationship between a male and a female (i.e., there is no sexual relationship).[55] Bernart is confronted with visual, olfactory, tactile, auditory, and gustatory horror.[56] The fear of coming back from the venture into the Lady's cavern blind from the smoke combines two of these sensations. The combination of the desire to maintain one's role as a poet and the refusal to "put his mouth to that trumpet" reveals the link between textual and sexual production in Arnaut's poem. The ethical dimension of the poem plays on this level of sexuality and textuality when Arnaut writes that "he who puts his mouth to that pipe" should not "be a favorite." The fear associated with the moment during which the poet loses his ability due to his sexual encounter with the wrong woman is further reflected by the relationship between synesthesia and the fear of death in poems by Arnaut and other troubadours.[57]

The abjection associated with the repulsive surplus of the woman's body does not transfer to the seducer who guards against the scene of sexuality, and so animality, by failing to engage in it. The notion that it is better to be in exile than to submit oneself to the horrors of the surplus of woman further supports the attempt to preserve the self in the face of the excess of the other. In that sense, Arnaut's poem differs from traditional courtly poetics in the additional way that it refuses to participate in the master/slave dialectic. Arnaut's advice to Bernart is precisely that he should not participate in fulfilling the desires of the other if the result is the subjection of the self. Rather, the lover should maintain himself and refuse to participate in a scene of love that would threaten his distinct subjectivity.

The excess released by Lady Ena that terrifies the poet and warns Bernart away from the orifice suggests that emptiness is, indeed, full. The fear of being the object upon which the Lady excretes her "rust colored substances" and her "piss" reveals the apprehension of locating himself beneath her.[58] If a necessary part of courtly love etiquette is to subject the self to the Lady and to demean the self in order to achieve or earn the Lady's love, then the obscenity in Arnaut's poem clearly rejects the manners expected of the courtier. This poem exposes the anticourtliness of the courtier, rendering the troubadour (he who "blows") one who also refuses entirely to subject himself to that role.[59] In that sense, Arnaut's poem is perhaps the epitome of courtly love.

Arnaut's text reveals that the function of courtly love depends on the impossibility of the complete sexual encounter. In the poem, that impossibility occurs due to the abject figure of the female. The contrast between the idealized Lady of most courtly love poems and the monstrous and excessive Lady Ena in Arnaut's poem shows how both sides of distancing (extreme attraction and idealization, or extreme repulsion and denigration) fulfill the same function.

> Though Lord Raimond, in agreement with Lord Truc Malec, defends Lady Ena and her orders, I would grow old and white before I would consent to a request that involves so great an impropriety. For so as "to put his mouth to her trumpet," he would need the kind of beak that could pick grain out of a pipe. And even then he might come out blind, as the smoke from those folds is so strong.
>
> He would need a beak and a long, sharp one, for the trumpet is rough, ugly and hairy, and it is never dry, and the swamp within is deep. That's why the pitch ferments upwards as it continually escapes continually overflows. And it is not fitting that he who puts his mouth to that pipe be a favorite.
>
> There will be plenty of other tests, finer ones that are worth far more, and if Lord Bernart withdrew from that one, he did not, by Christ, behave like a coward if he was taken with fear and fright. For if the stream of water had landed on him from above, it would have scalded his whole neck and cheek, and it is not fitting also that a lady embrace a man who has blown a stinking trumpet.
>
> Bernart, I do not agree in this with the remarks of Raimon de Durfort, in saying that you were wrong; for even if you had blown away gladly, you would have encountered a crude obstacle, and the stench would soon have smitten you, that stinks worse than dung in a garden. You should praise God, against whomsoever seeks to dissuade you, that he helped you escape from that.
>
> Yes, he escaped from a great peril with which his son also would have been reproached and all those from Cornil. He would have done better to go into exile than to have blown in that funnel between spine and mount pubic, there where rust colored substances proceed. He could never have been certain that she would not piss all over his snout and eyebrows.
>
> Lady, may Bernart never venture to blow that trumpet without a large bung to stop up the penile hole; then only could he blow without peril. (translated in *Seminar VII*, 162)

The overt sexuality and excess of sensuality within Arnaut's poem metaphorically reflects the meeting place of obscenity and divinity.[60] The synaesthesia that conflates "pitch" and "ferment" juxtaposes sound with smell in a manner that calls attention to the pervasive nature of the phonetics emitting from the Lady's "holes." The cunt and anus are inter-changeable in this scene of seduction-prohibition. This interchange is typical of fabliaux wherein the male often cannot distinguish between the vaginal and rectal orifices.[61] Such a poetic description of the female body in courtly love poems, however, is rare. If the rhetoric of Arnaut's poem falls into the genre of fabliau, then what about the poem places it within the genre of courtly love? Is this distinction important? Or is it merely a by-product of Lacan's choice of the courtly love text as the subject of his articulation of desire? What role does obscenity play in Lacan's theory of desire?

The impossibility of the sexual relationship in the general scheme of courtly love poetics is crucial to his theory of the lack in sexual relation-ships. To the extent that he attempts to employ courtly love on many levels as the basis for his theory, he renders the sexuality and textuality of the troubadour poets equal to the system of desire. The example he cites ex-ceeds its role as metaphor when he makes love and poetry coterminous.

> As opposed to what Freud maintains, it is man—I mean he who happened to be male without knowing what to do with it, all the while being a speaking being—who approaches woman, or who can believe that he approaches her, because on that score there is no dearth of convic-tions.... But what he approaches is the cause of his desire that I have designated as objet a. That is the act of love. To make love (faire l'amour), as the very expression indicates, is poetry. But there is a world between poetry and the act. The act of love is the male's polymorphous perversion, in the case of speaking beings.[62]

Reading Arnaut's poem as a text about the process of creating courtly poetics illustrates its adherence to traditional notions of the trouba-dour poems that characterize them as self-referential, metapoetic con-structs that have little, if anything, to do with the practices of love and sex in "real" life. Yet, Lacan's poetic choice of Arnaut's scatological, physical, and obscene text to discuss the process of desire reveals that even in a scene where copulation between two subjects does occur, there remains an impasse—the impossibility of a sexual relationship.

If Lacan's example foregrounds the way in which knowledge has cov-ered over desire in philosophical history, then it also serves to reveal the way in which studies of courtly love have occluded the physical and obscene, favoring a Platonic ideal that is not evident when the whole of the oeuvre is considered. Lacan's now (in)famous pronouncement that "there is no sexual relationship" reveals as much about desire as it does about the history of philosophy and its discursive practices that he claims have repressed desire. In a scene where a direct consideration of desire reveals the very impossibility of its completion and wholeness, perhaps the discourses that sublimate desire are as direct as their detours.

Lacan's struggle to uncover the truth of desire reflects his similar determination to situate his theory of desire within a feminist ideology. Having been the focus of attacks by feminists during the late 1960s and throughout the 1970s, Lacan sought a way to ensure that his theory would reinforce, rather than contradict, the feminist agenda. His own efforts in this realm led him to the conclusion that there is no possible sexual relationship.[63] One consequence of this theory is that the performance of sexuality and desire is tethered to the violence of a language that cuts up what it addresses and represents. The scatological courtly love poem that Lacan makes his example for the articulation of desire, opposed as it is to traditionally ascetic lyrics of love, is necessary to a reading of polymorphous sexuality. The fabliaux, poems in which obscenity is expected, are not appropriate examples for Lacan's theory precisely because they do not shock the auditor into listening to the scene of seduction.[64] The use of obscene language and situations in the courtly love text juxtaposes the high genre of courtly love with the low language of the fabliau, rendering a genre that is situated in between traditionally expected medieval literary forms. Binding the scatology of Arnaut Daniel's poem to his larger theory, Lacan shows the relationship between courtly love as excessive and the animality of the drives.

> The historians of poets who have attacked the problem cannot manage to conceive how the fever, indeed the frenzy, that is so manifestly coextensive with a lived desire, which is not at all Platonic and is indubitably manifested in the productions of courtly poetry, can be reconciled with the obvious fact that the being to whom it is addressed is nothing other than being as signifier. The inhuman character of the object of courtly love is plainly visible. This love that led some people to acts close to madness was addressed at living beings, people with names, but who were not present in their fleshly and historical reality—there's perhaps a distinction to be made there. They were there in any case in their being as reason, as signifier. (*Seminar VII*, 214–15)

The very "inhuman" character refers back to the problem of the animality within desire; if it hasn't been obvious so far, the abjection of the woman in Arnaut's text is akin to the horror of the animality within the self. The terrifying proximity of the very real flesh and mucous of the woman in Arnaut's text serves as a close-up that is too close, leaving the lover unable to focus on the other and rendering him overcome by sensation that is too much to process. This "too much" of the closeness of reality must be resisted and so ambivalence, the hatred of the desire within the self, enters the scene as a form of negativity. Attraction-repulsion at the animality within the human leads the subject to disappear as a human and respond from the position of the animal. As Lacan says,

> We find ourselves here faced with a sudden reversal, a strange reaction. Heaven knows that Arnaut Daniel went a long way in the direction of lending the greatest subtlety to the pact between lovers. Doesn't he push desire to the extreme point of offering himself in a sacrifice that involves his own annihilation? Well. He is the very same one who turns out to have written a poem, however reluctantly, on a subject that must have concerned him in some way for him to have taken so much trouble with it. (*Seminar VII*, 163)

The form of desire and the literary history of courtly love form a multi-dimensional frame that exceeds the limits of signification. The excess of scatology, then, is the only refuge for a moment too replete with lack to contain itself.

At stake for Lacan in Arnaut's poem is the notion that the subject must subject himself to the other in the scene of desire. As Lacan asks "Doesn't he push desire to the extreme point of offering himself in a sacrifice that involves his own annihilation?" he misses the fact that Arnaut is advising the refusal of self-annihilation. Arnaut is clearly arguing that Bernart should not sacrifice himself in the scene of courtly love; he should refuse this animality and retain his human status. Where Lacan perceives sublimation and annihilation of the self, Arnaut asserts that such subjection and sublimation of desire should be eliminated from the scene of desire. Unless we account for repulsion as a form of sublimated attraction (which may very well be the case) sublimation seems to be precisely refused in Arnaut's scene of the limit-case of courtly love where the lover is repulsed and fails to participate in the sexual encounter. If Arnaut sublimates his desire at all, it is in the creation of a poem about his own resistance. In this sense, then, courtly love does instantiate sublimation. Instead of approaching the woman directly with desire or repulsion, he translates that desire/repulsion into a literary object. If linguistic articulation is the symptom of the working out of ambivalence, then the poem is an expression of ambivalence. However, if the poetic expression takes the form of a dialectical sublimation reflecting the simultaneous presence of contradicting forces working against the appropriate processing of desire's conflicts, then we have an instance of the courtly love poem as equal to the expression of desire in the scene of analysis.

The subject in analysis (the analysand) speaks and simultaneous sublimates her desire. Sublimation exists in a tenuous relationship to language because language is always already an obstacle to the thing itself, an intermediary between the real of the idea and the real expressed in the world. When the obscene word enters the scene of signification, sublimation becomes difficult to recognize. One is tempted to state that in the scene of obscene language there is no sublimation. As Lacan states in regard to Arnaut's poem, "just blow in that for a while and see if your sublimation holds up."

The surplus of bodily horrors is met in Arnaut's poem by a correspondingly excessive refusal to participate in a sexual relationship with Lady Ena. Arnaut's speaker describes the bodily horrors of Lady Ena in a way that only one who has been proximal to her could. To know that "he would need the kind of beak that could pick grain out of a pipe. And even then he might come out blind, as the smoke from those folds is so strong" reveals an awareness of the grandiosity and overwhelming stench of Lady Ena's genitalia. Further, to state that "the trumpet is rough, ugly and hairy, and it is never dry, and the swamp within is deep" implies that the speaker has seen and felt her. Such sensory response to the materiality of Lady Ena's genitals focuses on her body in a way that courtly love poetics do not. Even granting the possibility that the sensory awareness does not come firsthand, but is speculated by the speaker in Arnaut's poem, such a detailed description of the body incorporated matter into courtly love poetics. Lacan's use of Arnaut's obscene courtly love poem defies the imposition of traditional Freudian readings of female genitalia as consisting of, or reminding of, lack. When the lover in Arnaut's poem confronts or seeks to avoid the "Lady," he calls attention to anything but lack. The surplus of sensory affects imposed on the male speaker reflects the excessive features of the female genitalia to which he is exposed. This surplus is in direct contradiction to the readings of medieval fabliau and farce that perceive feminine sexuality as lack.

Throughout *Seminar VII, The Ethics of Psychoanalysis* Lacan's analysis of desire and knowledge vacillates between Aristotelian ethics and the poetics of courtly love. He alternately claims that desire is most overtly expressed and revealed by courtly love poetics, and that its ethical function is better explicated by Aristotle than by the troubadours.

> [Courtly love] is a highly refined way of making up for *(suppléer a)* the absence of the sexual relationship, by feigning that we are the ones who erect an obstacle there too. It is truly the most amazing thing that has even been attempted. But how can one denounce the fake?
>
> Rather than dwelling on the paradox of why courtly love appeared during the feudal era, materialists should see therein a magnificent occasion to show, on the contrary, how it is rooted in the discourse of loyalty *(féalité)*, of fidelity to the person. In the final analysis, the "person" always has to do with the master's discourse. Courtly love is, for man—in relation to whom the lady is entirely, and in the most servile sense of the word, a subject—the only way to elegantly pull off the absence of the sexual relationship.
>
> It is along this pathway that I shall deal—later though, for today I must break new ground—with the notion of the obstacle, with what in Aristotle's work—whatever else may be said, I prefer Aristotle to Jaufré Rudel—is precisely called the obstacle. (*Seminar XX, 69*)

The focus on courtly love gives way to the rhetoric of philosophy. Although he employs courtly love as his prime example of sublimation and the obstacle of desire, he reverts to the Aristotelian notion of the obstacle. What is the difference between the two descriptions of the obstacle, such that Lacan would depart from his subject of analysis to buttress his argument with Aristotle's writings? Is this difference vast enough to warrant such a digression? Or is the digression merely a rhetorical ploy to remind his students of the rich philosophical history behind the literary example he studies?

Aristotle's commentary on the obstacle in the *Nichomachean Ethics* reveals the manner in which it reflects the desire for knowledge.[65] In his definition of pleasure Aristotle maintains an awareness of the spatial and temporal movement at stake in an analysis of the obstacle. He distinguishes, however, between pleasure and movement, stating that pleasure is precisely not a movement. Movements take time and are partial and fragmented, whereas pleasure must be whole and complete at each moment it is experienced. Having explored the relationship between the sensation of pleasure and the perfection of the sensory apparatuses, Aristotle then wonders why pleasure is intermittent and difficult to achieve.[66] His response is that pleasure is dependent upon activity and activity is not always good.

> One might think that all men desire pleasure because they all aim at life; life is an activity, and each man is active about those things and with those faculties that he loves most. . . . But whether we choose life for the sake of pleasure or pleasure for the sake of life is a question we may dismiss for the present. For they seem to be bound up together and not to admit of separation, since without activity pleasure does not arise, and the attendant of pleasure completes every activity.[67]

The obstacle here takes on the form of inaction or the performance of activities that are not inherently good. On the surface, it seems that Lacan is disavowing his central subject to shift his focus from courtly love poetics toward Aristotelian ethics. What appears to be a shift, however, is ultimately a performance of the union between his articulation of desire, its cause and its impossible limit, and the way in which it will come to supplement the history of knowledge. By reminding the audience that Aristotle also discusses the ethics of pleasure (and implicitly desire), he brings the history of desire and the history of knowledge into the same discursive system. He also recalls the problem of categories and shows how ~~the woman~~ is a reference to the manifold of being as a human who is an animal, rather than its lack.

From One to Three: Dialectics and Desire

When Lacan announced in *Seminar VII, The Ethics of Psychoanalysis* that the woman, "*la femme*," could only be written with a line through it (~~la femme~~), he became the target of numerous criticisms of his entire work based on what was interpreted as an antifeminist statement. Lacan's criticism (and not without other assistance provided by the analyst himself) became phallocentric, even phallogocentric, patriarchal, and hegemonic. Since the oral performance of the seminar on the *Ethics* coincided with the publication of his *Écrits*, wherein he outlines the theory of the signification of the phallus as the singular signifier and the universal category of power and knowledge, his critics had plenty of fodder (word of mouth and word of text) for their arguments. Lacan's claim, however, that "the woman" can only be written with a line through it was a statement about the category of woman, as an impossible category, equal to the impossibility of God and the Sign, which also could only be uttered while simultaneously being eliminated.

As I suggested in the beginning of this chapter, Heidegger's crossing-out of the Thing (das Ding) assists in an understanding of the elimination of "the woman." The woman, the Sign, and God are all impossible categories because their reality is bound to their surplus; the categorical term cannot contain the differences within the thing itself. The manifold element of the crossing-out that is evident in Heidegger's understanding of the Thing as Being in the world is reflected in the excess of being that is the surplus of desire.

Since he was heard in the *Ethics* to have eliminated women as a category, rather than to have eliminated the generalizations that lead to antifeminism as he arguably intended, Lacan attempted to rectify the misinterpretations of his theory of desire, woman, and the limits of knowledge in *Encore*. In a typically peripatetic manner, Lacan presents his own struggle with realism and nominalism in this text. As the *Ethics* were meant to outline the way in which medieval poetics revise Aristotelian dialectics and to show how both contribute to an understanding of psychoanalysis, *Encore* repeats the pattern but approaches the question of universals more directly. In several quite direct statements, he claims that there is, in fact, reality and there are indeed universals. "Reality is approached with apparatuses of *jouissance*" (*Seminar XX*, 55), and on the contrary, "There's no such thing as a prediscursive reality. Every reality is founded and defined by a discourse" (*Seminar XX*, 32). The occurrence of "One" is significant to an understanding of the elimination of the category of "the woman" and the manner in which, despite what appears to be a superficial refusal of the real of universals, this crossing-out of "the woman" in fact reflects Lacan's belief in the universal of humanity, while the particularity of the "person," "the woman" must be approached as discrete and singular entities. This perception of Lacan as a humanist emerges from his play with categories and the manner in which desire itself, although presumed and reported to be dialectical, does not achieve synthesis or unity because of its dependence on the signifier.

Considering the element of ambivalence in the desire to see the precise absence of the phallus, the horror that Raymond experiences when he perceives that Mélusine *has* and *is* the phallus, and the presence of phallic animality as embodied by Bisclavret in Marie de France's *lai*, we can see how the unreality of the phallus reflects the reality of the unconscious and the desire for ontological categorical (universal) status in the subject who seeks to account for animality within humanity. By perceiving the Fort/Da of the present-absence of the phallus in the voyeuristic scene that reveals the animality within the human, the phallic function as a prosthetic signifier for the real of desire also reflects the way that the real of the unconscious is hidden and appears. What the subject ultimately searches for in looking for the phallus as absence is the ability to control a perception of the unconscious drives. The pain and trauma of ambivalence toward the object of desire and within desire itself prevents sublimation from working properly and leads to neurosis. As the Wolf Man says in his autobiography, the neurotic function displaces or bypasses the real of reality and focuses instead on crossing-out the real of the unconscious.

> A sufferer from neurosis is trying to find his way back into normal life, as he has come into conflict with his environment and then lost contact with it. His emotional life has become "inadequate," inappropriate to outer reality. His goal is not a real known object, but rather some other object, hidden in his unconscious, unknown to himself. His affect bypasses the real object, accessible to his consciousness.[68]

As a limit case for the phobia of the animal within, the Wolf Man substitutes his experience of the real with hallucinatory fantasies of his persecution by animals. The focus on the animal becomes too strong for the proper function of sublimation to allow him to integrate his dual consciousness of his animality and humanity into a coherent (yet fragmented) subjective existence. In fact, by displacing or bypassing the processing of the duality at work in the animal within the human, the Wolf Man represents a desire for a more concrete and discrete categorization of the difference between "man" and "animal," one that might read, "all animals are animals" and "all men are men" wherein men have sovereignty over animals. The impossibility of this formula and the universal category "all men are animals" is too traumatic for the Wolf Man's desire. As such, instead of distancing himself from the animal, he assumes an overdetermined relation to the ambivalent structure of his desire to be human and continues to feel horror at his own pleasure. Therefore, he renders himself "two" rather than "one" and instantiates the problem of the self in relation to the other within the self, the very mode of desire as articulated by Lacan.[69]

The question of the "two" as dependent upon two "ones" is at the core of an understanding of desire and the ontological status of the subject as a human who is an animal. Lacan's comments on the Being of the subject coalesce around the problem of the nothingness of subjectivity and the impossibility of properly naming that nothingness. In the following passage, the conflation of being and sexuality by way of the term "copula," which inevitably recalls "copulation," centers on the impossibility of articulating the lack in subjectivity.

> Ontology is what highlighted in language the use of the copula, isolating it as a signifier. To dwell on the verb "to be" — a verb that is not even, in the complete field of the diversity of languages, employed in a way we could qualify as universal — to produce it as such is a highly risky enterprise.
>
> In order to exorcise it, it might perhaps suffice to suggest that when we say about anything whatsoever that it is what it is, nothing in any way obliges us to isolate the verb "to be." That is pronounced "it is what it is" (*c'est ce que c'est*), and it could just as well be written, "idizwadidiz" *(seskecé)*. In this use of the copula, we would see nothing at all. We would see nothing whatsoever if a discourse, the discourse of the master, *m'être*, didn't emphasize the verb "to be" *(être)*. (*Seminar XX*, 31)

How different is Lacan's term "idizwadidiz" *(seskecé)* from "Whatdo-youcallit"? The homonym in French for "idizwadidiz" *(seskecé)*, "c'est ce que c'est?" reverses Lacan's commentary on being to reinvest it with the question fundamental to his graph of desire, *Che vuoi?* From "it is what it is," Lacan gleans "what is it?" and we are reminded of the question that haunts desire: "what is it that it wants?" The language of this passage moves quickly from being to dwelling to the interrogation of the subject, to a question of the master who has not properly guided the subject. From nothingness we return to the desire of the other and its influence on the desire of the speaking subject. The ontological problem of dwelling calls into question the limits and possibilities of desire as its universal articulation is prohibited in the animal-human resistance to proper symbolization. As such, Lacan seeks to express the formula for the sexual relation (or lack thereof and therein) mathematically as $\sqrt{-1}$ (this will be addressed in chapters 3 and 4). Of immediate importance is the precise manner in which the "one" becomes the "two" and the way in which this reflects the potential for Being as the copula.

> When you try to read the theories of mathematicians regarding numbers you find the formula "n plus one" ($n + 1$) as the basis of all the theories. It is this question of the "one more" that is the key to the genesis of numbers and instead of this unifying unity that constitutes two in the first case I propose that you consider the real numerical genesis of two.[70]

To get to "two" we must first have "one."

> It is necessary that this two constitute the first integer which is not yet born as a number before the two appears. You have made this possible because the *two* is here to grant existence to the first *one*: put *two* in the place of *one* and consequently in the place of the *two* you see *three* appear. What we have here is something which I can call the *mark*. You already have something which is marked or something which is not marked. It is with the first mark that we have the status of the thing. It is exactly in this fashion that Frege explains the genesis of the number; the class which is characterized by no elements is the first class; you have one at the place of zero and afterward it is easy to understand how the place of one becomes the second place which makes place for two, three, and so on. The question of the two is for us the question of the subject, and here we reach a fact of psychoanalytical experience in as much as the two does not complete the one to make two, but must repeat the one to permit the one to exist. The first repetition is the only one necessary to explain the genesis of the number, and only one repetition is necessary to constitute it. The unconscious subject is something that tends to repeat itself, but only one such repetition is necessary to constitute it.[71]

The evidence of the unconscious as a real is dependent upon this "two" as an instance of repetition. If duality is predicated on the possibility of singularity, there must be two "ones" to arrive at "two," and as such, both singularities must exist in precise distinction from each other. The discernibility of duality within two singularities is often represented by binary opposites. The histories of scholasticism and psychoanalysis are dependent upon the categorization of singular elements to determine definitions by which those elemental structures or ideas are denoted and recognized.

What is perhaps most striking in the scene of two as an expression of ambivalence with regard to the animality within the human is the appearance of what seems to be an inherent connection between the struggle for "humanity" and the existence or expression of desire as a courtly phenomenon. *Bisclavret* and *Mélusine* are both courtly romances that configure desire as that which cannot properly reach its goal because of the abject horror bound to the search for pleasure. Similarly, the Wolf Man and the Rat Man both present elements of courtly seduction-prevention in their cases. The Rat Man's ambivalent feelings toward the "lady" who is the object of his desire and repulsion manifest themselves as obsessive thoughts about serving her in the manner of a vassal. Proper to the scene of courtly love, the lady resists the Rat Man's advances, and when she becomes ill, he believes that his desires caused her sickness. His projected fantasies take the form of revenge at having been rejected, and he imagines himself saving the lady by helping her husband. The mediator of the husband, standing in for the king, places the Rat Man in a triangular relation to his desire, which, as we will see, is dominant in the system of courtly love. Additionally, he puts himself in a position of the possessor of *caritas* when he imagines that he "did the lady some great service without her knowing that it was he who was doing it" (*Three Case Histories*, 53). What Freud perceives here is that the proper fantasy of courtly desire is bound to repression. The fantasy then emerges as an expression of sublimated desire. In this case, the desire for revenge becomes shifted to a desire to be of assistance to the lady, and therefore to be seen (by himself or others) as powerful because he is needed.[72] Rather than perceive his ambivalence, the Rat Man's fantasies show that "he only recognized his affection, without sufficiently appreciating the origin and aim of his magnaminity, which was designed to repress his thirst for revenge" (*Three Case Histories*, 53). As such, the Rat Man fantasizes about a properly courtly scene, but he cannot achieve it because of the ambivalent character of his drives. To move from ambivalence to dialectics, we need to assert the third element of desire and its sublimated force by way of the language of courtly love. The scene of courtly romance is not enough to get beyond ambivalence; rather, what is at stake is the poetic representation that occurs in the linguistic utterance of desire and the awareness of the other within the self. To get to Three, then, to get beyond the two "ones" of the Aristotelian element of the quarrel over universals, we need to move toward the articulation of desire that Lacan sets forth in his discussion of Hegelian dialectics.

CHAPTER THREE

Dialectics, Courtly Love, and the Trinity

> A gaze, that of Beatrice—that is to say, a threefold nothing, a flutter-
> ing of the eyelids and the exquisite trash that results from it—and
> there emerges the Other whom we can identify only through her
> *jouissance:* he whom he, Dante, cannot satisfy, because from her, he
> can have only this look, only this object, but of whom he tells us that
> God fulfills her utterly; it is precisely by receiving the assurance of
> that from her own mouth that he arouses us.
>   To which something in us replies: annoyance *(ennui).*
>   —Jacques Lacan, *Television*

The triangulation of desire is exhibited in three different ways in psychoanalysis and medieval studies. First, the triangular configuration of desire is represented in the scene of courtly love. Second, the triangulation
of the Trinity is expressed in the formula of the Father, the Son, and the
Holy Spirit. Third, the triangular mathematical structure of the dialectical process (thesis-antithesis-synthesis) reflects the ideal of the triangle
as wholeness. This chapter will investigate the role of courtly love in the
intersections of medieval studies and psychoanalysis; and to this complex of triangulation, those of us in the humanities who are not comfortable in the field of mathematical inquiry can begin with annoyance.

The role that annoyance plays in the search for the proper articulation of desire emerges from the frustration caused by the feeling of ambivalence. Even worse than the duality of ambivalence, which depends
on the possibility of two discrete "ones," is the scene outside of dualism
in which one is not ambivalent at all, but nonetheless cannot properly

achieve a union with relation to an other. The threefold "nothing" of the dialectic produces excess and "exquisite trash" in the subject who desires. In this triangular dialectical structure, the excess is often represented, as it is in the epigraph above, as God—the impossible object of desire. Struggling to overcome distance that, like Zeno's paradox, cannot be overcome often leads to frustration and annoyance. In all three of the structures defined above, one seeks a synthesis of apparently opposite binary systems. The fact that, in any moment of synthesis, some sort of sublation or sublimation occurs reflects the frustration of the threefold system. Something is always given up, repressed, or eliminated in the dialectical system. As we will see through the analysis of Lacan's attempt to follow the dialectics of desire, this is precisely why desire does not ultimately adhere to the dialectical system.

The Middle Ages as Object of Desire

Annoyance is evident in the public debate about courtly love and its role in our understanding of the Middle Ages that William D. Paden and Don A. Monson perform in the outstanding medieval journals *Speculum* and *Exemplaria*. Between 1999 and 2002 Paden and Monson engaged in a critical debate about the representation of the Lady in troubadour poetics that illustrates their own symptomatic frustration with the object and subject in courtly love poetics. Rather than address the particulars of the debate (which readers can find for themselves) I want to focus here on the repetition and insistence, as well as annoyance, that emerge from the performance of their argument about the function of the poetic representation of the Lady in courtly love poems. Already reproducing a debate with a "thick history," Paden and Monson approach a determination of the Lady in courtly love poetics either as a literary figure that is historically contextualized and specific (Monson) or as a literary figure that might transcend specific temporal and spatial (as well as fictional) context (Paden). Most crucial for an understanding of the dialectics of courtly love poetics and the relationship between psychoanalysis and medieval studies is the very fact that this debate is performed between 1999 and 2002, a time when the stakes of theory are said to have already been assimilated within medieval studies. More than the subject of the Lady within troubadour poetics, what is evident from this argument between two medievalists is the need to assert a method by which we might approach texts from the Middle Ages.

Because repetition is important here, the titles of the essays put forth by Paden and Monson are worth citing. The debate begins with Paden's "The Troubadour's Lady as Seen through Thick History."[1] Monson responds with "The Troubadour's Lady Reconsidered Again."[2] Monson then publishes "The Troubadour's Lady, Yet Again,"[3] showing his own frustration (annoyance) with the formulation "yet again"; he implies, "I am tired of this, I am frustrated with this, let's move on." And Paden simultaneously (and in the same issue of the same journal) publishes two essays entitled "The Troubadour's Lady, One More Time," and "The Troubadour's Lady, a Summing Up."[4] The immediate repetition and the preemptive closure of Paden's publications reflect his own annoyance with the debate, therefore bringing rhetorical force to it. At stake in the argument is the difference between perceiving history through a cultural studies lens of "thick history" and approaching the text on the level of the particularity of the signifier. In fact, both Paden and Monson reveal an understanding of medieval texts and ideas as culturally thick because language is always at the core of representation. Their performance demonstrates that they are both right about the mode of approaching troubadour poetics. The rhetorical display is singular to the performative moment in the history of the circulation of the journal *Exemplaria,* and simultaneously, an understanding and illustration of the thickness of history is made evident. The Middle Ages and the Lady represented in troubadour poetics both function as the impossible object of desire that produces the symptom of writing (critical or poetic). Paden and Monson emerge as troubadours; loving the Lady of the Middle Ages by way of their literary criticism and their engagement in the dialectical structure of the debate performs their approach to their object of desire and the concomitant obstacle to it.

The contemporary nature of the symptomatic expression of the dialogue about the woman within courtly love poetics itself reflects the dialectical process at stake in the troubadour poetics. This too, illustrates and results in annoyance. Why have we not overcome the debates that were central to the troubadours? Why should literary criticism replicate, repeat, and imitate the debate poems (the *tensons*) popular among the troubadours? These questions are of course loaded, and the answer is that the symptomatic expression of the need to explicate the "reality" of the troubadour poetic experience testifies itself to the function of the unconscious as a transhistorical thing. More than the representation of the Lady, what is at stake in the debate between Paden and Monson is the way that we approach an understanding of the Middle Ages. Paden makes it clear that the debate is really about how one conceives of "reality" in the Middle Ages, as the text or as something outside of the text.[5] "Thick history" of course is Clifford Geertz's term, and in Paden's words, it refers to "the play of successive intervening perspectives on our own perceptions and the consequent need to consider revising our views."[6] There is always an obstacle to our analysis of medieval poetics, not merely because of the problems asserted by historical distance, but also because language itself is always a supplement.[7] In this sense the artificial end imposed on the argument with Paden's "The Troubadour's Lady, a Summing Up" serves to open rather than close discussion about the Middle Ages as an object of inquiry and affection, as well as irritation. Annoyance should not be underestimated as a weak form of aggression.[8] It, in fact, is the power of repressed or sublimated aggression that emerges from the scene of desire as it seeks to adhere to a dialectical process.

Annoyed with Lacan?

The "threefold nothing" that catalyzes the gaze of annoyance and its play with "oneyance" reflects Lacan's assertion that the scene of desire in courtly love supplements the absent sexual relationship as well as the absence of God. As the "threefold nothing" the Trinity emerges in Lacan's view of the Father, the Son, and the Holy Spirit as the play of the subject engaged in the attempt to understand his or her desire; that is, to understand the manner in which desire functions in the unconscious and emerges in the conscious by way of language, which, in turn, reflects the play of presence and absence. The obsessive quality of the repetition in troubadour poetics illustrates the sublimation of annoyance and the supplementation of that aggressive emotion with passive longing and the tenacious expression of desire. Annoyance also emerges as envy of the subject who appears satisfied. As the woman who is attributed the power to experience *jouissance*, Dante's Beatrice is the object of a projected longing for a union with God that, through an unfair twist of events, only the woman can have. Through this projection of the potential for wholeness by way of *jouissance* onto the woman, sexual difference becomes loaded with the impossibility of a union, with God or with an other. Two beings who are separate can only come together momentarily, and even (or especially) when the "first troubadour," Guillaume IX, claims that he has fucked one hundred and eighty-eight times in just over a week, he remains a subject engaged in the impossibility of a sexual relationship and paves the way for the popularity of the troubadour obsession with *amor de longh* (distant love) that Jaufré Rudel helped to popularize and perfect.[9]

Despite the secular quality of troubadour poetics that is so important to an understanding of the process of desire and to Lacan's system, the articulation of *jouissance* reasserts Christianity into the discussion of courtly love and desire. In fact, the general focus on the importance of the precisely secular nature of the erotics expressed by the troubadours conceals the manner in which their articulation of desire forwards a conception of desire itself as a universal category. Overcoming the duality of ambivalence, the troubadours engage the process of sublimation to express the utter impossibility of locating the cause and object of desire and move toward the tripartite scheme of dialectics. Desire circulates within the knot of the unconscious, toying with the dialectical process and anamorphosis to reveal the limitations on the sexual relationship and language that render desire its own absent cause. Where ambivalence maintained a distinction between opposite emotions in the scene of desire, dialectics, sublimation, anamorphosis, and ultimately the baroque character of the knot of desire depend on the idea of synthesis.

In the history of medieval literary criticism courtly love is read as precisely dialectical.[10] Typically the master/slave dynamic is seen to be at the core of readings of desire and courtly love within a psychoanalytic framework.[11] According to this traditional reading, courtly love expresses desire by imagining the necessary other and addressing that other through poetics. The culmination of such an experience of expressed desire is, indeed, dialectical as the subject's recognition of the self is found in the mutual recognition between the self and other. "They recognize themselves as mutually recognizing one another."[12] The process of identification and mutual recognition involves a dualistic process of awareness that involves the desire to present the self in a manner that will please or repulse the Other. The monologic quality of the troubadour poem, however, puts up a barrier prohibiting such mutual recognition, despite the fact that so many of the troubadour poems exist in *tenson* (dialogic) form, wherein a poet creates two speakers who debate over the possibility of a sexual encounter.[13] Identification is at play in the *tenson:* the speaking subject imagines an other being responding to his/ her words. Nonetheless, the poet of the *tenson* is always responsible for putting words into the other's mouth. This in fact is precisely a model of a monologue of desire wherein the self asks *Che vuoi?* "what do you want of me?" Desire aims at singularity. Desire's aim, however, is bound to encounter the obstacle to its own achievement and therefore to recognize the gap between itself and its object.

The process of desire that Lacan wants to call dialectical ultimately exceeds the structure of dialectics and takes on the form of the One as that which is comprised of Many, and so a universal. Lacan displays and insists upon adherence to a dialectical method in his essay collected in *Écrits* "Subversion of the Subject and the Dialectic of Desire in the Freudian Unconscious"[14] (September 1960) where he provides a topography of desire and its limits. In this essay he presents his initial references to courtly love, its dialectical impossibility, and its source for his theory of desire. At work behind this mathematized scheme of desire is Lacan's investment in mapping the structure of the unconscious and showing it to be a real universal category. Binding the unconscious to a combination of faith and reason, and inserting theology into the field of psychoanalysis, Lacan suggests that the unconscious begins with Aquinas.

> In the Freudian field, in spite of the words themselves, consciousness is a feature as inadequate to ground the unconscious in its negation (that unconscious dates from St. Thomas Aquinas) as the affect is unsuited to play the role of the protopathic subject, since it is a service that has no holder. (*Écrits*, 297)

The discursive limits of desire and its lack become the focal point of psychoanalysis whose dependence on the Hegelian dialectic transforms the history of knowledge into the process of uncovering the desire that has been sublimated. Extending the theoretical beginnings of desire into a system of thought and practice, Lacan maintains the elements of Hegel's philosophical enterprise. The presence of the Other remains the sovereign Master; the Law transforms from the Hegelian State Law to the Freudian Law of the Father; the State is seen as the macro version of the nuclear family; religion, spirit, desire are addressed in a way that eliminates their absolute quality and supplements the problem of the impossible and phantasmatic for the certainty of Spirit. Lacan reveals the way in which elements of thought may be dialectical without claiming a broader absolute system of dialectics.

As Lacan develops a visual and quasi-scientific chart of desire, he moves toward a potential understanding of the abstract concept of desire as material and practical. In this foundational essay, "Subversion of the Subject and the Dialectic of Desire in the Freudian Unconscious" the graphs that he develops map out intangible elements including the subject, temporality, change, distance, and proximity, as well as the signifier and the potentially *real* of the signified. The first graph (see Figure 1) displays the situational proximity between desire and the subject as the signifier mediates it.[15] The signifying chain is exhibited as an arc full of movement and change and marking the limits of that slippage. The circularity and slippage that Lacan finds in the play between O (the "locus of the signifier's treasure") and s(O) (the "punctuation in which the signification is constituted as a finished product"), added into the visible field in the second graph, resembles the dialectical process (*Écrits*, 304). As a synthetic moment wherein the two established fields engage in the movement and recognition, the O and s(O) create dimension in the articulation and instantiation of desire. Language as the sum of signification and its inherent sliding reflects the inability to represent

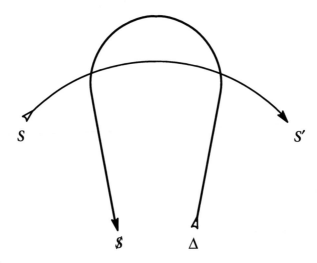

Figure 1

things as they are. The awareness of impossible direct representation asserted by Saussure in his *Course in General Linguistics*[16] is fundamental to Lacan's reading of the lack within language that provides the basic outline for his theory of desire.

In the second graph (see Figure 2) Lacan complicates his notion of the play between O and s(O), adding to the formula the "I(O)" and the "$\mathcal{S}$" (the barred S of the retrograde vector), as well as the "e" and the "i(o)." The problems of linguistic signification and representation transfer here to the impossibility of self-recognition. The complexity in this graph derives from the temporal play between the retrograde effect of the moving vector and the future perfect tense. In Lacan's words, "This is a retroversion effect by which the subject becomes at each stage what he was before and announces himself — he will have been — only in the future perfect tense" (*Écrits*, 306).[17] This is important to medievalists because it explicates the way that we approach our object of inquiry, and it is important to desire because it is the way that desire functions in the conscious awareness of that which has gone unnoticed or has been repressed. The temporalities of the retrograde and the future perfect tenses within language and within historical time intersect to create a "rear view." In the temporal dislocation of self-perception appears the impossibility of knowing oneself: "in this 'rear view' *(retrovisée)*, all that the subject can be certain of is the anticipated image coming to meet him that he catches of himself in his mirror" (*Écrits*, 306).[18] The anticipation of seeing one's own image promises a mode of knowing that always necessarily involves *méconnaissance*.[19] This breach of self-knowledge will ultimately play a crucial role in the function of desire.

Until this point, Lacan follows a Hegelian path along which self-consciousness or "consciousness-of-self" can only be achieved through the sublation, identification, interdependence, and recognition of the master/slave dialectic. (If he departs from this path at all, it is only to comment cynically on the hopelessness and bondage that remain within such a dialectical system of desire and the process of self-knowledge.) Need is a "subjective opacity" that unleashes or produces desire (*Écrits*, 311). Lacan determines that the desire of the subject is determined by an identification with the desire of the Other that leads to the staggering question: *Che vuoi?* "what do you want?" or "what do you want *of me?*" This question becomes interpreted by the subject as: "What does *he*

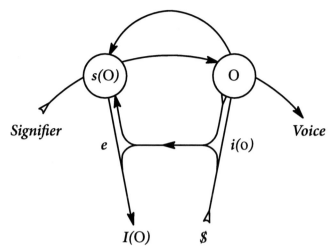

Figure 2

want of me?" showing the incorporation of the other into the self, and leads to Figure 3 (*Écrits*, 312). The question of subjectivity complicates the structural graph of desire by interrogating it and the alienation found therein. Lacan persists in his adherence to a Hegelian notion of consciousness of self even while his own theory begins to show the limits of that system to his own articulation of knowledge and being. Visually, the graph is presented beneath the *Che vuoi?* whose arc is suspended over the signifier and the Other, therefore performing a sublation of signification to the question of the other's desire.

The impasse of regression affects and constitutes the conscious and unconscious realms of desire. The inner workings of the paradoxical situation in which fantasy remains potentially singular while signification assumes multiplicity applies to the spheres of language and subjectivity. The notation *($◊o)* demonstrates that the treasure of signifiers "proceeds from demand when the subject disappears in it" (*Écrits*, 314). Next, demand (or, as Alexandre Leupin has recently retranslated it, "request") also disappears.[20] A cut, or suture, remains where demand and the subject have been removed, reminding the subject of what once was present. Within this cut the drives appear in their erogenous forms, emerging from the awareness of the lack of wholeness in physical and psychic subjectivity and signification. For medieval studies, this moment often appears as the insertion of knowledge into unknowable gaps.

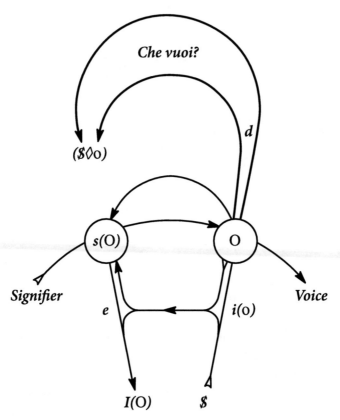

Figure 3

Attempting to define a particular poetic moment by way of the author's biography or by way of legal documents or historical notations often symptomatically supplements the lack left in historical traces.

The difference between Figure 3 and the completed graph (see Figure 4) is equal to the difference between the demand (request) and its disappearance that results in the mark of the cut. The objects that present themselves as evidence of the cut share their lack of a specular image and/or alterity (*Écrits*, 315).[21] Desire for that which is missing erupts. In this completed graph (the sum of the theory of desire) Lacan's discourse begins to resemble that employed when he speaks of the Middle Ages: "It is to this object that cannot be grasped in the mirror that the specular image lends its clothes. A substance caught in the net of the shadow, and which, robbed of its shadow-swelling volume, holds out once again the tired lure of the shadow as if it were substance" (*Écrits*, 316). "[T]his object" is not only the cut or suture that reminds the subject of its lack; it also represents the play with signification wherein signification reminds its reader or auditor of its multiplicity and the play with epochs, whereby that which becomes sublated remains present not only as a trace, identificatory object, or alterity, but whose suture recalls the past that is embedded within the present. The play with the retrograde and future perfect tenses also recalls the Freudian return of the repressed and the complimentary anticipatory view of the future returning to affect the past.

The chains of signification and desire are complete according to Lacan's final graph. What remains to be addressed, however, is the complex relationship between signification and desire that exceeds the form of metaphor or analogy. This remainder—seen at its core as the problem of mediation—is precisely the crucial difference between Lacan's

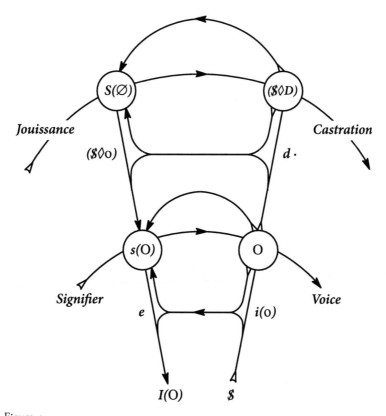

Figure 4

theory and the system of Hegelian dialectics. Notably, it is also the point at which Lacan's investment in adhering to Hegel's system is most overt.

Lacan attempts to address the remainder of his formula algebraically, yet his numbers never quite compute. What he calls dialectical actually involves more features and axes than Hegelian dialectics. Whereas the dialectic has two axes and may incur minor features, the main point involves the process of reconciling apparent dichotomies — master/servant, self/other, etc. Identification, for instance, is certainly a dialectical process;[22] the aspects of desire described by the graphs, however, narrate a different history of desire; the vectors do not fulfill the form of the dialectic. The role of Hegel's master/servant dialectic is crucial to Lacan's articulation of desire.

> The master brings himself into relation to both these moments, to a thing as such, the object of desire, and to the consciousness whose essential character is thinghood. And since the master, is (a) qua notion of self-consciousness, an immediate relation of self-existence, but (b) is now moreover at the same time mediation, or a being-for-self which is for itself only through an other — he [the master] stands in relation (a) immediately to both (b) mediately to each through the other.[23]

Desire here resembles courtly love and the identification and projection at play in its discourse. The poet (the master) subjects himself to the Lady (the slave) as a means of attempting to seduce her. In so doing, the master renders himself the slave of the Lady and raises her to the position of ideal master. Both roles are interdependent and both are mediated, not only through the representation of the ideal image of master and servant, but also through the mediating force of language. Euphemism confounds this relationship, enabling the poet to imitate the position of subjected slave when he ultimately maintains control and the position of master by speaking indirectly and conveying duplicitous messages that render his desire mysterious even as it is in the process of being articulated.[24]

The lack that is caused by the excess in Lacan's version of Hegelian dialectics is expressed by the mathematization of the sexual relationship as $\sqrt{-1}$. Perhaps this absence of the sexual relation, coupled with the failure of desire to properly conform to dialectics, explains his recourse to the example of courtly love, which is characterized by a lack of synthesis. As he says,

The invention of courtly love is not at all the fruit of what people are historically used to symbolizing with the "thesis-antithesis-synthesis." There wasn't the slightest synthesis afterward, of course—in fact, there never is. Courtly love shone as brightly as a meteor in history and afterward we witnessed the return of all the *bric-à-brac* of a supposed renaissance of stale antiquities. Courtly love has remained enigmatic.[25]

Despite the apparent applicability of the dialectic to courtly love and Lacan's theory of desire, both the poetic and the philosophical explication of Lacan's theory of desire resist the dialectical system. Is Lacan claiming that in Hegelian dialectics there is never a synthesis? In courtly love and sexual relationships there is never a synthesis? That the historical association of the dialectical process is inaccurate in its claim to a synthesis? That courtly love has been "invented" or constructed to exhibit a dialectical process that it does not accurately exemplify? That courtly love is dialectical or that it is not dialectical? If courtly love is the basis for his articulation of desire, and desire is dialectical, then the logical conclusion to the syllogism would be that courtly love is dialectical; yet, it is not.

Clearly something has gone awry in the analysis of desire as it relates to and is dependent upon the example of courtly love. Lacan's reliance on the example of courtly love poetics suggests that the theory of desire whose ultimate claim will be "there is no sexual relation" must return to the linguistic and poetic utterances forming the basis of that theory. As the graph began with the problem of linguistic signification and ends with a view that, like signification, subjectivity also necessarily misses its mark, the example Lacan needs to support his theory is found in the aesthetic and political union of poetry itself.

Lacan's use of Hegelian dialectics explicitly relates desire to language such that mediation becomes the primary and crucial distancing split between the signifier and the signified and between one lover (being) and another. In Adorno's words, "Dialectics—literally: language as the organon of thought—would mean to attempt a critical rescue of the rhetorical element, a mutual approximation of thing and expression, to the point where the difference fades."[26] The necessity of the dialectical system for the articulation of a theory of desire that relies on linguistic problems seems clear. Yet Lacan's simultaneous adherence to and difference from dialectics in the explication of his theory remains problematic.

Hegel's philosophy of the dialectic involves a view of knowledge that is based on a particular notion of consciousness of self and desire. The implicit view that consciousness is distinct from the self resembles the subject formation in Lacan's terms. "This dialectical process which consciousness executes on itself—on its knowledge as well as on its object—in the sense that out of it the new and true object arises, is precisely what is termed Experience" (*Hegel*, 52). More obviously, the process of psychoanalysis takes as its focus "experience"—seen here as the residues and totality of daily life in the conscious and unconscious realms. The master plan of psychoanalysis would then resemble a philosophical project that demands the dialectic. There is, however, a difference. Language causes a crease in the smooth fold of the dialectic and imposes its refusal to cooperate with concepts onto the theory of subjectivity and desire. Hegel is aware of the role of desire within the dialectical process of knowing and being. His view of the self as becoming conscious of itself—the experience of Consciousness—relies on desire (*Hegel*, 53).

Mediation, however necessary, is not described precisely as language. In Hegel's words, "I have the certainty through the other, *viz.,* through the actual fact; and this, again, exists in that certainty through another, *viz.,* through the I" (*Hegel*, 55). If being "in-itself" and being "for an other" might possibly coincide and become coterminous, mediation must play a unifying role. Epistemologically, this form of self-consciousness is required to approach a concept of truth. As Hegel says, "This opposition of its [self-consciousness's] appearance and its truth finds its real essence, however, only in the truth—in the unity of self-consciousness with itself. This unity must become essential to self-consciousness, i.e., self-consciousness is the state of *Desire* in general" (*Hegel*, 65). Note here that Hegel does not say self-consciousness *is* desire, a claim that would render it Lacanian and solve the problem of the relationship among desire, knowledge, and subjectivity for once and for all; rather, he says that self-consciousness is *the state of desire—in general,* and the only state that can lead the subject to any other form of absolutism or generality that Hegel perceives to be ideal.[27] This state of being of desire is the precise locus for Lacan's intervention into dialectics.

Finally, Hegel appears to equate self-consciousness with desire without the aid of a mediating qualifier.

And self-consciousness is thus only assured of itself through sublating this other, which is presented to self-consciousness as an independent life; self-consciousness is *Desire*. Convinced of the nothingness of this other it definitely affirms this nothingness to be for itself the truth of this other, negates the independent object, and thereby acquires the certainty of its own self, as true certainty, a certainty which it has become aware of in objective form.

In this state of satisfaction, however, it has experience of the independence of its object. Desire and the certainty of its self obtained in the gratification of desire, are conditioned by the object; for the certainty exists through canceling this other; in order that this canceling may be effected, there must be this other. Self-consciousness is thus unable by its negative relation to the object to abolish it; because of that relation it rather produces it again, as well as the desire. The object of desire is, in fact, something other than self-consciousness, the essence of desire; and through this experience this truth has become realized. (*Hegel,* 69)

At once eliminating mediation from self-consciousness, Hegel supplements it with another barrier to direct affect. The process of sublation inserted into this scheme enacts its own form of mediation, removing the rhetoric of mediation and replacing it with the conceptual dynamic that states such an equation cannot exist.

The difference between the beginning and the end of the paragraph on the self-consciousness and desire of the master is the difference between the elision of desire and its projection (or expulsion) from the dialectic. At the conclusion of this paragraph, Hegel writes: "What mere desire did not attain, he now succeeds in attaining, *viz.,* to have done with the thing, and find satisfaction in enjoyment. Desire alone did not get the length of this because of the independence of this thing" (*Hegel,* 75). Hegel's insistence on the independent nature of the process of becoming self-conscious accounts for that primacy of the imagination within the system wherein mutual recognition may occur. However, the state of his argument becomes highly precarious, as his either/or logic reads a bit like a choose-your-own-adventure novel.

"Since the object is in its very self-negation, and in being so is at the same time independent, it is Consciousness. In the case of life, which is the object of desire, the negation *either* lies in an other, namely, in desire, *or* takes the form of determinateness standing in opposition to another external *individuum* indifferent to it, *or* appears as its inorganic general nature" (*Hegel,* 69). The first difference between Hegel's system and the Lacanian version of desire obvious within the passage is the notion that "life" is the object of desire. Negation, the inexorable next step, is rendered so general and potential as to ensure its occurrence. The multiplicity of either/or(s) vows that negation will ensue. That multiplicity causing absolute universalizing negation alone distinguishes Hegel's formulation from Lacan's. Combined with the perversion of desire in the form of an "other," the difference between desire in Hegel's account and Lacan's reading of desire's dialectical foundations becomes evident. The blending of "in an other" and "in desire" locates desire's agency in a particular subject. This view of desire's agency is in direct contradiction to Lacan's theory of desire wherein one thing that is certain is that desire cannot be located in a subject.

Lacan's commentary on Hegel and his desire to adhere to the dialectical system is a symptomatic display of his project that seeks to uncover the way in which philosophical discourse has sublimated desire. Rather than pursue a systematic and synchronic line of philosophical engagement, Lacan deploys those systems most fundamental to the history of philosophy, appropriates their methodologies, and exhibits the central role desire plays beneath more explicit claims to knowledge. In so doing, he does not distinguish precisely between knowledge and desire; rather, he reveals the way in which a discussion of knowledge is always necessarily a discussion of desire. The role the dialectic plays within this intervention within philosophical history is obscured by the focus on sublimation, erotics, and the literary language of courtly love poetics. Ultimately, the difference between desire as a linguistic form of expression and love as it is enacted within daily life denotes the difference between the dialectical quality of the concept of desire and the limits of the dialectical system to the articulation of desire.

The dialectics of Lacan's theory of desire alter Hegelian dialectics by layering various systems of knowledge on top of each other. When he writes, "In this respect: that desire becomes bound up with the desire of the Other, but in this loop lies the desire to know," Lacan complicates the apparent simplicity of the loop (*Écrits,* 301). By layering the desire to know on top of the dialectical loop of desire between two subjects, a kink is inserted into the loop, leaving a knot in the chain of signification. Adding epistemophilia (the desire to know) onto the process of desire reveals the way in which desire and epistemology are bound or knotted together. Yet, Lacan creates a knot within the loop and fails to account for that knot (*Écrits*, 301). Due to this knot in the otherwise smooth dialectical process, Lacan's approach to the dialectic is manifold where Hegel's is absolutist. Although he claims to follow a Hegelian dialectical process in his theory of desire, Lacan instead relies on the dialectic to alter it. This revision is crucial to the distinction between Lacan's belief in the potential for the real of universals and the form of singular, absolutist universality that Hegel expounds.

The distance between Lacan and Hegel is significant to the openness of Lacan's theory. Whereas for Hegel, the appearance of being is never "creation *ex nihilo,* but is, rather a moment in the development of a Concept *(Begriff),*"[28] Lacan's view of creation as precisely ex nihilo liberates the subject, object, and being from a predetermined and preorganized teleological process. When synthesis is impossible, precise singularity and absolutism are also impossible. We are left, instead, with a dialectical process that reframes its components so that the elements that are sublated emerge uncontrollably in the knot-like structure of the Many within the One. The real of the unconscious and desire remain, but they are disguised as fragile nominalist presences. To the extent that desire is manifold, it cannot be singular; it is, however, an instantiation of the One, as an ideal.

The lack of a materially present other in the scene of courtly love enables the lover to participate in a play where identification and projection construct the other. A prime example of the narcissism involved in the *tenson* form of the courtly love poem appears in Lombarda's text that reveals a feminine voice that challenges the subordinating categorization of woman as mirror to man. A debate poem, the *tenson* gives voice to two subjective positions. Lombarda plays with this form as she employs the image of the mirror to undermine its objectifying metaphorical implications. Interrogating the blind acceptance of the mirror's significance, Lombarda requires her interlocutor and seducer to pay attention to language. Contrary to the customary alternating stanza pattern of the troubadours, Lombarda's *tenson* is split into two sections, revealing a consciousness of dialogic form that reflects her awareness of the structural (as well as the symbolic) function of the mirror. In the first section of the poem, Lombarda gives voice to Bernart Arnaut d'Armagnac, allowing him to present his desire. By creating a voice to which she can respond, Lombarda plays on the notion that woman's language is simply the mirror response of man's sign, and she reinvents the scene of seduction only to show that gender roles do not matter in the courtly love dynamic: *the relationship is always already impossible* regardless of the speaker's subject position.

Interrogating the assumption of the Lady as mirror, Lombarda demands of Bernart, "What's the mirror where you stare?" The implications of this question not only tell Bernart that his offer of love is narcissistic, but also displace the notion that the "woman" is the mirror reflecting his gaze. Rejecting the narcissism found within identification, Lombarda seeks to be perceived as she is. This refusal to play into the scene of identification and Lacan's little fable of the mirror stage supports the notion that Lacan's theory of desire extends beyond the confines of the dialectical system. By removing the mise en abyme in which reflection and self-knowledge are impossible, Lombarda challenges desire to develop a shift toward signification and subjectivity that is not quite so slippery as the infinity of lack that results from two mirrors being placed opposite one another. As such, Lombarda's reference to the "mirror with no image" refers both to the screen of limits preventing one from seeing another and the refusal to see subjectivity as that screen.

Lacan's differentiation between the obscene courtly love poem and the fabliau defies the imposition of traditional Freudian readings of female genitalia as consisting of calling attention to lack. When the lover in Arnaut's poem confronts or seeks to avoid the "Lady," he calls attention to anything but lack. In Arnaut's poem that Lacan reads as a central figure for the articulation of desire, the surplus of sensory stimulation felt by the male speaker in the presence of Lady Ena illustrates feminine excess. Lack is merely a defense reaction to the hyperbolic phenomenological stimuli against which Arnaut's speaker cannot protect himself (except by way of language). How does this representation of woman as lack affect a reading of troubadour poetics whose euphemistic term "nothing" conceals and reveals the female body? Repeatedly in troubadour poetry we find a poet discussing the "nothing" that comprises his text. The "nothing" of courtly love poetics represents Lacan's (in)famous statement that the woman does not exist.

The notion of "blowing" into the "funnel" implies the emptiness that constructs the female anatomy. The idealization of the Lady in typical courtly love poems intersects with the overdetermined materiality of Arnaut's poem when her body is perceived and described as abject.

Lacan's description of the courtly love process still remains within the dialectical system when he accounts for this reversal of excess and lack.

> The idealized woman, the Lady, who is in the position of the Other and of the object, finds herself suddenly and brutally positing, in a place knowingly constructed out of the most refined of signifiers, the emptiness of a thing in all its crudity, a thing that reveals itself in its nudity to the thing, her thing, the one that is to be found at her very heart in its cruel emptiness. That Thing, whose function certain of you perceived in the relation to sublimation, is in a way unveiled with a cruel and insistent power.[29]

The "emptiness" of the Lady shifts her in an anamorphotic manner from idealized to abject. In both cases, the obstacle to a sexual relationship takes the form of language. The emptiness of the signifier reflects the process of desire as that which seeks impossible synthesis.

Lacan's insistence that courtly love is more than a metaphor for desire and that it actually enacts the process of desire in language replaces the empty center of being with the signifier. In so doing, he implicitly calls attention to the poetic and literary function of desire in courtly love. The history of discourse about nothing in courtly love poetics supports a reading of the genre as metapoetic. Guillaume IX states that he will compose a poem about nothing. "I will compose a song about nothing / nothing about me or anyone else, / there will be nothing about love or youth (3.2–4) [Farai un vers de dryt nîen; / Non er de mi ni d'autra gen, / Non er d'amor ni de joven].[30] The focus on "nothing" as absence, however, calls forth the ironic presence that in fact is found here. As we saw in chapter 2, the apparent lack of woman is ultimately an instance of excess; similarly, calling attention to the lack of center or subject in the poem about "nothing" Guillaume IX foregrounds the way in which he speaks precisely about *something*. What the speaker calls attention to is his own subjective absence in the face of the *something* (some *thing*) of desire.

As Thomas Pepper argues in "The Story of I/I," "I" is accompanied by *nothing*, which comes to the poet as he is sleeping on his horse. According to Pepper, "From exactly nothing, the poet brings forth an agent — still hiding here, sleeping in the verb, the first word of the poem . . . as well as *vers*, nothing, anyone else, love, youth, anything else, before, sleep horse" ("Story of I/I," 143). From this focus on the absence of subjectivity in the production of a discursive agent, we find the potential for a discussion of the creation of the subject as if from nothing. In order to achieve this understanding of the subjective creation ex nihilo, Pepper compares Guillaume's poem to the Book of Genesis and the act of coming into being:

> To push the comparison with the first chapter of Genesis further (and why not, as a point of comparison? Is it here, the heresy of the Troubadours, the reason why the Church wiped them out?), the lack of the nominative of the first person pronoun in the first half of this poem re-enacts—but in human song—the way in which god, in the beginning, is either described as doing something in the third person ("and he created . . ."), or as being present in an exhortation ("lux fiat"). ("Story of I/i," 145)

The goal of achieving a secular understanding of the subject in relation to the world displaces the focus on the divine to assert a coming into presence of existence poetically.[31] As such, the relation of the subject to desire is driven by the understanding of desire as a real category that the apparent nothing of the unconscious attempts to displace as nominal. The precise refusal to name that which is evident as being, and being that motivates and controls the subject, reflects the representation of the unconscious as an element that makes the subject and that is always already exposed in language. Similarly, the refusal to name the poem calls attention to its status as a creation produced from love. Following Guillaume IX, Raimbaut takes this refusal to name literally when he gives his poem a non-name:

> I conclude my Whatdoyoucallit
> for that is how I've had it baptized;
> since I've never heard of a similar thing,
> I use the name that I devised. (32.36–39)[32]

The "devised" name, *Whatdoyoucallit,* presents a metapoetic perspective in which the poet signifies the unique quality of the words he has joined to compose a poem. The life of the poem is created by the poet's decision to write. Its matter or name is meaningless in comparison to the presence it assumes as textual production.

The focus on *nothing* in Guillaume's seventh poem reflects this negative awareness of the unconscious as a real.

> It has always happened to me thus
> that I never enjoyed what I loved,
> nor shall I do it, nor ever did I;

For knowingly
I do many things when my heart says to me:
"All this is nothing."

[A totz jorns m'es pres enaisi
c'anc d'aquo c'amei no•m jauzi,
Ni o farai, ni anc non hi fi;
C'az essïens
Fauc maintas rens que•l cor me di:
"tot es nïens."] (13–18)

In this passage the speaking heart should be interpreted as the unconscious voice erupting into conscious awareness. When the speaker hears
the other speaking within himself and saying "all this is nothing,"
he laments the inability to find pleasure where he thinks it is properly
located. His awareness of his fragmented desire leads him to conclude
that absence resides within desire. The presence of love is always inadequate to the fulfillment of desire, such that a dehiscence between desire
and love is evident in the perpetual longing for the object of desire. In
love the poet thinks he should be fulfilled; however, because his desire is
always for that which is beyond his reach, the presence of love is necessarily an imposition on the fantasy of the scene of the love relationship.
The poem is the symptom of and the solution to this loss. The literary
supplement stands in for the impossibility of the sexual relation. As the
real of the signifier, desire also then raises itself, by way of poetics, to the
level of the real.

The distinction between love and desire comes to light when we consider the impossibility of the sexual relationship. In the scene of two
subjects engaging with each other, the desire for unity is forever thwarted
by the recognition of fragmentation. Love itself becomes a product of
this recognition of lack, and so we find the lovehate ambivalence as a
mechanism that exhibits the frustrated attempt to know, have, or be
with an other.[33] Lacan's theory of desire is dependent on representational signs and their concurrent impossibilities. For Lacan, "Love itself . . . is addressed to semblance. And if it is true that the other is only
reached if it attaches itself *(qu'a)* . . . to *a*, the cause of desire, then love is
also addressed to the semblance of being. That there-being is not nothing. It is attributed to *(supposé à)* that object that is à" (*Seminar XX*, 92).
The desire for the location of the being as real encounters the prohibition of the object of its drives in the form of the *objet a*, the cause of

desire. The articulation of desire foundational to troubadour poetics reflects the manner in which this division between desire and love instantiates the impossibility of the sexual relationship. Indeed, as Lacan asks "What is courtly love?" he explains that it is precisely a mode of substituting for the sexual relationship: "It is a highly refined way of making up for *(supplier à)* the absence of the sexual relationship, by feigning that we are the ones who erect an obstacle thereto" *(Seminar XX, 69).* The refinement and, later, the "elegance" of courtly love are present even in the scatological examples because of the complex formation of the system of sublimation that allows the subject to discuss the lack of desire and the absence of the sexual relationship with reference to the propriety of "love."

In "The Scene of Two" Alain Badiou[34] shows how the attempt to find a union in love in order to fulfill desire is met with the imposition of the sexual relationship as what Lacan calls the square root of negative one. Love imposes a contract as well as a construct on the uncontrollable presence of desire.

> [L]ove comes to assert . . . that it is from the being of the subject that the object, as cause of desire, has the singularity of its presentation, and finally, the charm of its appearance.
>
> In comparison with the essentially disjunctive sexual difference, love, in subsuming the object under the being of the subject, constructs the introductory scene in which the non-rapport takes place as counting, the counting-for-two.
>
> As a consequence of an encounter, what is the possibility of a Two which counts neither as one, nor as the sum of one plus one? A Two counted as two in an immanent way? Such is the problem of a scenario in which the Two is neither fusion nor summation. In which, consequently, the Two is in excess of that which composes it, without, for all that, annexing the Three. A real Two, since what composes it is only, by itself or in its being, a non-rapport which agitates the lure of the object.
>
> Thus we have the particular form of two speculative theorems:
>
> Theorem 1: where a non-existence or a lack holds, only an excess can come as a supplement.
>
> Theorem 2: The event constructs the truth of this situation for a situation of being.
>
> Which posits, in the case at hand: it is love which makes the truth of which sex is capable, and not the inverse. ("Scene of Two," 43)

The extreme disjunction of the "two" in Badiou's account of the non-relation of the sexual relation impedes even the construction of "three" that would emerge from a proper synthesis of two. In a properly dialectical process, the "one" in relation to a distinct "one" would combine to make "two" that is a third. As we know from Lacan, however, in courtly love dialectics do not function properly, "there is no synthesis." Rather, we remain with two separate entities who can only construct a "third" as an imaginary, idealized place of unity. Badiou's suggestion that love makes the truth of sex, in light of his first proposition that only excess can supplement lack, demonstrates the way in which love is an attempt to come to terms with the impossible position of desire.

In this scene of love (or lovehate), if sublimation does not enter the picture then we are left circulating in the realm of the abject. This is why it is so important for Lacan to focus on Arnaut Daniel's scatological troubadour poem before turning to Jaufré Rudel's expression of *amor de longh* in the articulation of courtly love as desire. When he shifts from Arnaut Daniel to Jaufré Rudel as an object of inquiry for his discussion of courtly love, Lacan shows how even in the most apparent proper moment, the obstacle represents an obsence moment in the absence of the sexual relationship. Distance as an obstacle serves merely to render palatable the very abjectness that is implied by its imposing solitude and longing for the impossible object.

Foregrounding the history of obscenity within the courtly love poem, Lacan shows how troubadour poetics display desire's anamorphotic nature even while it reveals that instance to be impossible to engage directly. As an example of the scatological quality that some troubadours, starting with the "first troubadour," Guillaume IX, displayed, Arnaut Daniel's poem is often marginalized in studies that seek to render courtly love a decent and proper mode of melancholic longing for the absent object of desire. Because of this lack of focus on the obscene courtly text, the poetic liminality of Daniel's poem has the potential to lead critics to conclude that Lacan quite simply does not know the literary conventions of the medieval text he chooses as his exemplary subject. However, by investigating the complex dynamic of desire within Lacan's analysis of Daniel's text, we begin to perceive the necessity of this generic liminality to Lacan's theory of desire. In so doing, we find that Lacan's medievalism as it is evident in his reference to courtly love is a specific form of postmodern medievalism that allows for play and exploration among generic lines as well as literary conventions. Perhaps more importantly, Lacan's use of the courtly text reveals that medievalism may assume many guises and functions, not the least of which is performed by Lacan when he looks to the Middle Ages to explicate his theory of desire.

In *Seminar VII, The Ethics of Psychoanalysis*, Lacan's seminar entitled "Courtly Love as Anamorphosis" presents courtly love as a grounding point for sublimation and the process of desire. It is here that the apparent binary system of courtly love is inscribed into Lacan's theory of desire. Anamorphosis is a question of style. The artistic representation of an idea, concept, or experience coincides with the structural history of spatial construction in visual forms. Much has been written about this form of dialectical representation in its visual mode. Lacan's reading of courtly love replaces the visual model of structural aesthetic shifting with the linguistic and literary instance of courtly love. Significant about this view of courtly love as a Fort/Da game of expressed desire is the manner in which Lacan addresses courtly love by way of the mediator of an artistic instance. Like desire, courtly love poetry cannot be addressed head-on if one is to perceive the way in which sublimation affects the ethics of desire and its relationship to the signifier. The example of anamorphosis upon which Lacan bases his model of reading courtly love foregrounds the knot bound within the language of the unconscious and desire. That is, to read courtly love precisely as anamorphosis would be to see the way in which it represents, alternately and simultaneously, the dichotomies of spirit and body, sensual and vulgar, expressed and suppressed, lack and fullness, speech and phenomena, etc. When Lacan claims that we must only accept this model "metaphorically," the third instance he adds to the dialectic confounds it such that it can only be perceived askew and by way of language (*Seminar VII*, 142). As such, the dialectical nature of courtly love as anamorphosis is enfolded within the analytical knot. In this formula of desire courtly love is structurally equivalent to the very process of desire.

The knot structure that is created within the system of desire in Arnaut's poem resists dialectical application or definition. This resistance is precisely necessary for Lacan's theory of desire to develop a means of considering sexual difference in a manner that posits polymorphous desire. The role of the signifier as a mediator plays into Lacan's theory of desire on a literal and a metaphorical level. In order to understand the implications of the relationship between the signifier and the sexual relationship as both represent the impossibility of union and full copula or copulation, it is useful to account for the development of Lacan's theory of desire.

Language in general in Lacan's formation is simultaneously obscene and divine, and as such always contains a degree of fictionality.

> In your most ordinary conversations language has a purely fictional character, you give the other the feeling that you are always there, that is to say, that you are capable of producing the expected response, which bears no relation to anything whatsoever that is susceptible to being pursued any further. Nine-tenths of discourses that have effectively taken place are completely fictional in this respect.[35]

The degree to which identification and projection work in the transferential process of speaking to an other renders language itself fictional. Differentiating between direct and indirect language is insignificant if language itself is always subject to interpretation.[36]

Lacan's theory of desire is dependent on representational signs and their concurrent impossibilities. Foregrounding the connection between the linguistic seduction common to courtly love poems and the relationship between the subject and the signifier, he writes:

> [F]or the woman responds for once from her place, and instead of playing along, at the extreme point of his invocation to the signifier, she warns the poet of the form she may take as signifier. I am, she tells him, nothing more than the emptiness to be found in my own internal cesspit, not to say anything worse. Just blow in that for a while and see if your sublimation holds up. (*Seminar VII*, 215)

The necessity of scatology in the challenge to sublimation's defensive walls inserts an apparent dichotomy within courtly love. Desire in its early poetic form asserts sublimation only to attack it with the fantasy of bawdy sexuality. The high and low, spiritual and corporeal expression of desire within troubadour poems strikes Lacan as the limit of the dialectic. Such limits are indeed the philosophical contribution Lacan makes by way of his literary analysis of courtly love and his theory of desire. From the outset of his investigation Lacan's goal was to develop a mode of discussing desire philosophically in the way that it has been sublimated throughout the history of epistemological investigations into Being. The relationship between love and knowledge brings Lacan's theory of desire to the foreground of philosophical readings of Eros that pass under the guise of aesthetics.

Conventions of literary analysis that seek to find a theory at play within a text necessarily render readings that are displaced, even if in a non-disconjunctive form, from the idea at stake. The poetics may work like a theory, and the theory may be revealed therein, but the difference between the theory and the poetics will remain and the contrary may be inserted within that fissure. If that fissure is covered over, it becomes like the mark of the suture within the absence of the desire that emerges from what once was. This is one reason it is crucial to discover the way in which Lacan's theory is based precisely on a text. The text does not reveal the theory; rather, the text enables the theory to be developed. The poetic text houses the theory that must then be elucidated in terms appropriate to theoretical mechanisms.

Recognizing the element of the poetic in the production and recognition of knowledge, Lacan plays with language in a manner that imitates Isidore of Seville's attempt to properly define language at the level of the history of the letter. In *The Etymologies* Isidore's categorization of knowledge and language foregrounds the way in which our sense of the world is partially determined by the terms we use. Inversely, the terms that we coin and their revised definitions are determined by the function of symbolic elements circulating in the world. Isidore, like Boethius, takes up Porphyry's *Isagoge* in order to develop an understanding of the categories in relation to language.[37] Whereas Boethius focuses largely on concepts and topics, however, Isidore is invested in the proper manner in which terms are defined. As definitions of subject, the introduction to the beginning of philosophy represented by the *isagoga* involves terms demonstrating the "fundamental elements of the nature of each thing, making it clear by an unambiguous and substantive definition"[38] ["continens in se demonstrationem primarum rationum de wualibet re quid seit, suaque certa ac substantiali definitione declaretur"]. The presentation of definitions that comprise much of the *Etymologies* reflects, of course, Isidore's investment in the achievement of knowledge of substances by way of linguistic record. Lacan's attempt to "take desire literally" also means to seek the history of language and knowledge about desire at the level of the signifier. His assertion that "we should approach things at the level of the history of each language" plays with the etymological goal pursued by Isidore (*Seminar XX*, 36). Additionally, his willingness to coin neologisms to express concepts for which there is no proper term reflects Lacan's view of ideas as real prior to their lin-

guistic formation, even while he recognizes the importance of employing language to convey ideas as specifically as possible.

In his early piece "Subversion of the Subject and the Dialectic of Desire," Lacan coins the term "*inter-dit*" (the inter-said) to address the
enunciation of the desire of the speaking subject.[39] "Dit" is a word for a
little poem and it is coined by the troubadours. Roger Dragonetti calls
attention to the function of the "dit" and the "inter-dit" with regard to
the level of the letter and the literal in *La Vie de la Lettre au Moyen Age,*
which he dedicates to Lacan. The centrality of the word takes the place
of the empty signifier at the core of the absent cause of desire. This
insistence on the letter suggests that a belief in the potential for categories exists even in light of the limitations of representation and the
holes in signification.

In Lacan's return to courtly love in *Encore,* this treatment-oriented
term "inter-dit" becomes associated with God and the signification of
desire. Playing on the homonym "dit" and "dix," which Dragonetti
shows to signify the redemption of Christ,[40] Lacan formulates the neologism *dit-mension* to assert the relationship between theology and the
explication of the truth of desire.

> To restrict our attention to the first, I enunciated that truth is the "dit-
> mension," the "mension" of what is said *(la mension du dit)*. In this vein,
> you can't say it any better than the Gospels. You can't speak any better
> of the truth. That is why there are the Gospels. You can't even bring
> the dimension of truth into play any better, in other words, push away
> reality in fantasy *(mieux repousser la réalité dans la fantasme)*. *(Seminar
> XX,* 107)

According to the translator's note to this passage, "*Mension* is a neologism, combining the homonyms *mansion* (from the Latin *mansio,*
'dwelling,' which in French was the term for each part of a theater set in
the Middle Ages) and *mention* ('mention,' 'note,' or 'honors,' as in *cum
laude*). It is also the last part of the word 'dimension.'" The prefigura-
tion of the connection between theater and dwelling in the medieval
term *mension* that is carried along in Lacan's neologism calls attention
to ontological performance as it is necessarily combined with the linguistic utterance ("dit"). Lacan's incorporation of the reference to the
troubadour's "dit" into his neologism should not be forgotten. Lacan's
term, then, guides us to the *dit*—the *saying,* of what is being said—the
mension, and carries with both abstract and active forms of enunciation

the mark of the Middle Ages. Such a statement, in the context of the historiography of Christianity, as Lacan places it, presents a constellation whereby desire is encoded. The texts produced and performed by the troubadours provide Lacan with a historical instance wherein ontology and desire coincide.

Illustrating the manner in which desire is embedded with the philosophical history of the search for and production of knowledge within history, as well as the fact that language materializes things in the world, Lacan claims that the "dit-mension" is proof of Freud's existence, since it calls us back to Freud's statements, his "saying." He continues:

> Indeed, that is the proof of Freud's existence — in a certain number of years we will need one. Earlier I associated him with a little friend, Christ. The proof of Christ's existence is obvious: it's Christianity. . . . For the time being, we have the *Three Essays on the Theory of Sexuality* . . . concerning what I call the drive to translate *trieb,* the drift of *jouissance.* All of that, I insist, is precisely what was covered over *(collabé)* during the whole of philosophical antiquity by the idea of knowledge. (*Seminar XX,* 112)

Freud's essays on sexuality have in common the notion of the drives, *das trieb,* which have been concealed beneath a historical investigation into knowledge. Lacan is claiming here that philosophical investigations supplement the investigation of desire. By shifting the ground, placing desire in the fore and knowledge in the back, Lacan develops a concept of philosophical thought that is rooted in his return to Freud, but also takes another step whereby epistemology must account for the concept of desire on which it depends. Choosing the obscene example mimics the project of bringing desire into the foreground in the history of philosophy. Knowledge becomes linked with proper manners, and desire, that which has been repressed and sublimated, becomes linked with the obscene text.

For Lacan, desire as courtly love is best exhibited in the form of obscenity. "I will go so far as to tell you that nowhere more blatantly than in Christianity does the work of art as such show itself as what it has always been in all places — obscenity. The *dit-mension* of obscenity is that by which Christianity revives the religion of men" (*Seminar XX,* 113). The inclusion of obscenity in the scheme of desire, then, brings to the fore the historicity of representation. Thirteenth-century medieval translation theory and practice was fundamentally concerned to differentiate between divine and vulgar languages. High and low were fore-grounded in an attempt to maintain a pure relation of language to divine ideals. Translation *(translatio)* was perceived as a means to convey ideas in another language. The original language was held in higher regard than the vernacular language into which a text was rendered. Dante's *Vita Nuova*, the *Convivio,* and his letter to Can Grande challenged the previous notion that high subjects should be written in Latin. The original production of a text *in vulgari* threatened the notion that Latin was the only proper means of conveying divine ideals. Dante's own work is highly informed by courtly love poets and their texts.

Following other notable medievalists, Lacan observes that in the *Commedia* Dante refers to Arnaut Daniel: "I wouldn't tell all if I didn't add to the file, in case it proves useful, that Dante places Arnaut Daniel in Canto XIV of his Purgatory in the company of sodomites. I haven't been able to pursue the particular genesis of this poem beyond that" *(Seminar XX,* 163). In *De Vulgaria Eloquentia,* Dante discusses the literary effects of the vernacular Provençal, naming and discussing the work of Arnaut Daniel, who also appears in the *Commedia,* and seven other troubadours (Peire d'Alvernha, Guiraut de Bornelh, Bertran de Born, Folquet de Marselh, Aimeric de Peguilhan, Aimeric de Belenoi, and Sordello). Arnaut ranks high among Dante's troubadour predecessors because his subject matter, arms, love, and rectitude are lofty, and Dante would have known Arnaut's poetry by the time he wrote the *Vita Nuova* in 1294. Lacan's own source for his reference to Arnaut seems to be the eight lines of Provençal in canto 26 of *Purgatorio.*

> "Tan m'abellis vostre cortes deman,
> Qu'ieu no me puesc ni voill a vos cobrire.
> Ieu sui Arnaut, que plot e vau cantan;
> Consiros vei la passada floor,
> E vei jausen lo jhoi qu'esper denan.
> Ara vos prec, per aquella valor
> Que vos guida al som de l'escalina,
> Sovenha vos a temps de ma dolor!"

> ["So does your courteous request please me—
> I neither could nor would conceal myself
> From you. I am Arnaut, who, going, weep
> And sing; with grief, I see my former folly;
> With joy, I see the hoped-for day draw near.

Now, by the power that conducts you to
The summit of the stairway, I pray you:
Remember, at time opportune, my pain!"] (XXVI.140–47)[41]

These lines establish Arnaut's signature, providing a link between the signifier and the literary and historical process of *fin amor* for Lacan's theory of desire. Of course, Lacan also would have recognized the reference in Dante to Arnaut's difficult style, and drawn as he is in his seminars to difficult, authoritative, and esoteric texts, this too would have promised a proper notation of a medieval source for his developing theory.

The connection between Dante and Arnaut Daniel provides Lacan with a grounding point for the simultaneous presence of the obscene and the divine. Using the neologism as evidence of the power of vernacular language to contribute to high modes of inquiry, Lacan asserts the divine within his focus on the scatological poetics. The gaze that Dante points toward Beatrice in an attempt to fulfill his desire is one of longing for the projected connection that he perceives Beatrice to have with God. As Lacan said in *Television,* Dante's desire cannot be satisfied, "because from her, he can have only this look, only this object, but of whom he tells us that God fulfills her utterly; it is precisely by receiving the assurance of that from her own mouth that he arouses us."[42] The substitution of the unconscious for God in the scene of desire creates difficulty in understanding precisely where Lacan stands on the issue of the relation between knowledge and the divine, as well as the divine and desire. As his crucial neologism "dit-mension" focuses on the relationship between the obscene and the divine, in Lacan's reading of courtly love, his engagement of Christianity as an example of the secular process of desire is complex.

When he parallels the function of the mystic as the process of erotics, he suggests that we consider the Other as God. Recognizing the problem within his comparison of the experience of *jouissance* with the experience of the mystic, he says, "you are all going to be convinced that I believe in God" (*Seminar XX,* 77). Lacan's resistance to the reading that he in fact does believe in God suggests a self-awareness of the similarity between his articulation of the erotics of the divine and the divine within erotics. Within the realm of the mystic we find the establishment of sexual difference to fall apart. As Dante's envious gaze displaces *jouis-*

sance, precisely as feminine *jouissance*, onto Beatrice in his fantasy of her connection to God, that fantasy is broken down when Lacan considers the mystic. Both men and women can be mystics suggesting that the "not whole" or the "lack" associated with femininity is ultimately about a particular sort of relation between the subject and desire. As Lacan says,

> Mysticism isn't everything that isn't politics. It is something serious, about which several people inform us—most often women, or bright people like Saint John of the Cross, because one is not obliged, when one is male, to situate oneself on the side of $\forall \chi \phi \chi$. One can also situate oneself on the side of the not-whole. There are men who are just as good as women. It happens. And who also feel just fine about it. Despite—I won't say their phallus—despite what encumbers them that goes by that name, they get the idea or sense that there must be a *jouissance* that is beyond. Those are the ones we call mystics. (*Seminar XX, 76*)

This reading of the mystic as a woman or a "bright person" suggests that the entire system that perceives sexual difference to be predicated on *lack*, and *jouissance* to mean *feminine jouissance*, comes unraveled with a consideration of "bright people" who position themselves on the side of the not-whole. The revisionary definition of mystic that Lacan posits plays with sexual difference in a manner that challenges the ecclesiastical understanding of God and the subject. If the male might enter the realm of *jouissance* simply by recognizing his lack of wholeness, then we might call the troubadours mystics according to Lacan's definition. Instead of positioning God as the divine force that separates the subject from knowledge, or that serves as a reminder that our knowledge is always imperfect, the situation of the subject before knowledge, wherein knowledge is conceived of as desire, reflects to the subject the potential for understanding; with that recognition of potential comes the mutual recognition of limitations and imperfection. Nonetheless, Lacan does not believe that this point has yet been made and he focuses his line of inquiry, instead, on the lack within Christ. The ultimate example of the mystic, Christ then represents an instance of the obscene in the context of courtly love, such that any resemblances formerly made between courtly love and the cult of the virgin metamorphosize to foreground the obscenity of the divine.[43] Moving then from Christ's position as the male who experiences *jouissance*, and so the impossible figure, Lacan demonstrates that the issue of *jouissance* (represented as "cunt-torsions" [*conneries*]) is a literary theme, indeed a theme of courtly love that is foundational to the project of psychoanalysis. As such, it is a theme worthy of investigation.

> I've been doing nothing but that since I was twenty, exploring the philosophers on the subject of love. Naturally, I didn't immediately focus on the question of love, but that did dawn on me at one point, with the abbot Rousselot, actually, whom I mentioned earlier, and the whole quarrel about physical love and ecstatic love, as they are called. I understand why Gilson didn't find the opposition to be a very good one. He thought that Rousselot had made a discovery that wasn't really one, because that opposition was part of the problem, and love is just as ecstatic in Aristotle's work as in Saint Bernard's, assuming one knows how to read the chapters regarding φιλία, friendship. Some of you must surely know what literary debauchery occurred around that: Denis de Rougemont—have a look at *Love in the Western World*, it gets red hot!—and then another no stupider than anyone else, named Nygren, a Protestant, [the author of] *Agape and Eros*. Christianity naturally ended up inventing a God such that he is the one who gets off *(jouit)*! *(Seminar XX, 76–77)*

In this condensed, but incomplete, history of his own medievalist background, Lacan gives us a sense of the manner in which he is approaching the theme of courtly love as an instance of desire bound to the articulation of the divine within the secular. The sources that Lacan cites attempt to account for the precise difference between the courtly instance and the divine instance. However, by inventing a God who "gets off," humanity sought to displace the process of desire onto an object that is unknowable, thus cordoning off the problem and projecting it into the hands of the one who knows (God). As such, Christianity itself becomes a symptomatic representation of sublimation and evidence of the unconscious. As Lacan says in the same seminar, "God and ~~Woman's~~ *jouissance*," "by loving God, we love ourselves, and by first loving ourselves—'well-ordered charity,' as it is put—we pay the appropriate homage to God" *(Seminar XX, 71)*. Asserting that he definitely does not believe in God, Lacan pushes his explication to show that God himself is fragmented and not One.

> Why not interpret one face of the Other, the God face, as based on feminine *jouissance*?
>   As all of that is produced thanks to the being of signifiers, and as that being has no other locus than the locus of the Other *(Autre)* that I designate with a capital A, one sees the "cross-sightedness" that results. And as

that is also where the father function is inscribed, insofar as castration is related to the father function, we see that that doesn't make two Gods (*deux Dieu*), but that it doesn't make just one either. (*Seminar XX, 77*)

In the scene of apparent blasphemy, where Lacan shows that the ostensibly monolithic God is fragmented, not merely dual, but utterly fragmentary, we are reminded of his desire to represent the real of universals from *Seminar II*. When he refers his disciples back to the Middle Ages as a moment of articulation of his views on the real, he foregrounds the problems of faith and reason as they engage each other and conflict. The ordinance that he cites from 1277 called attention to the lack of faith in God as the potential for criticism.

> The most severe punishments were decreed for those who played dice at the altar during the Holy Sacrament. Such things seem to me to indicate the existence of a working dimension which is singularly lacking in our time.
>   It is not for nothing that I am telling you about dice and making you play the game of even and odd. Without the shadow of a doubt, there's something rather scandalous about playing a game of dice on the altar, and all the more so during the Holy Sacrament. But I think that the fact that it is possible should restore to you the sense of a capacity which has been far more obliterated than one thinks in the circles we frequent. It is simply what is called the possibility of criticism.[44]

Playing dice at the altar, of course, reflects the belief in Fortune and chance that Lady Philosophy warns against in *The Consolation of Philosophy*. As an expression of the limitations of God's providence, it is offensive to the reason that is based on faith in the church. When Lacan admits the scandalous nature of playing dice on the altar, he is also referring to the euphemistic understanding of "playing dice" as engaging in copulation. In troubadour poetics dice are often referred to (especially by Guillaume IX) in lieu of the more proper term "scrotum" or the more crude term "balls." Guillaume IX's game of chance in love is expressed in his poetics as a game that he sometimes wins and sometimes loses, but always is willing to engage in.[45] In poem six, for instance, he calls himself "perfect master" even though his dice are small. Both critical implications work in this scene where it is important to have the *possibility* of playing dice on the altar. On the one hand, the holy sacrament and place is necessary in order for resistance to occur through criticism. The church must, of course, exist in order for it to be scandalized or betrayed by an expression of skepticism. On the other hand (and these hands are paired, not mutually exclusive), the scene of playing dice on the altar as a euphemism for copulation suggests that the (non)sexual relationship itself represents the potential for criticism. In both cases, the criticism of the singularity of the three-in-one concept of God is called into question. Faith in the order of the cosmos is retained, however, as the challenge of the game of dice is the challenge to the universal system that might determine how one can find meaning.

The history of philosophical, theological, and literary inquiry into universals (both realist and nominalist) represents the triangle as the primary form upon which other shapes, concepts, and ideas are founded and dependent. From Plato's account in the *Timeaus*, to Descartes's meditation on the triangle, through Hegel's use of the tripartite dialectic and Lacan's attempt to adhere to the dialectical process, the triangular structure of essences, knowledge, desire, courtly love, the trinity, and faith, the triangle reveals the formalist and classical tendencies of medieval and Lacanian investigations of these subjects. Focusing here on the Trinity as defined by Nicholas of Cusa, we perceive the manner in which the triangle is employed to reveal infinity, thus explicating the manner in which the Father, the Son, and the Holy Spirit are a unity of three-in-one.

> Dico igitur si esset linea infinita, illa esset recta, illa esset triangulus, illa esset circulus et esset sphaera; et pariformiter, si esset sphaera infinita, illa esset circulus, triangulus, et linea; et its de traingulo infinito atque circulo infinito idem dicemdum est.

> [If there were an infinite line, I maintain that it would be at once a straight line, a triangle, a circle, a sphere; similarly, if there were an infinite sphere, it would at once be a circle, a triangle and a line, and it would be likewise with the infinite triangle and infinite circle.][46]

Additionally, the three-fold triangle becomes the infinite circle by way of continuity.

> Nam sit triangulus ABC causatus per positionem, per circumductionem lineae AB, quousque B venit in C, A fixo remanente: Non habet dubium, quando linea AB esset infinita et penitus circumduceretur B, quosque rediret ad initium, circulum maximum causari, curus BC est portio. Et quia est portio arcus infiniti, tunc est linea recta BC. Et quoniam omnis pars infiniti est infinita, igitur BC non est minor itegro arcu circumferentiae infinitae. Erit igitur BC non tantum portio sed completissima curcumferentia. Quare necessarium est triangulum ABC esse circulum maximum.

[Let us suppose that the triangle A-B-C is described by the line A-B moving from the fixed point A until it falls on C; were the line infinite and were it to continue till it returned to its initial position, there is no doubt we would have the infinite circle of which B-C is a part. Being a part of an infinite arc, B-C is then a straight line. Now as every part of the infinite is infinite, therefore B-C is not smaller than the entire, infinite circumference; B-C, therefore, is not only a part, but is, in the fullest sense, the circumference. Necessarily we must conclude that the triangle A-B-C is the infinite circle.][47]

As a representation of infinity, the triangle is the perfection of the trinity. The three points transfer to the mode of circularity that is necessary for the understanding of the infinite.[48] Lacan refers to Nicholas of Cusa several times in the course of his lectures. At times, he is in fact discussing the triangle, but when challenged on his point, he, like Cusa, interchanges the sphere with the triangle.[49] He resists the notion of triangularity because it does not reflect the geometric play necessary to understand desire. In *Seminar II, The Ego in Freud's Theory and in the Technique of Psychoanalysis*, Lacan's use of triangularity is challenged by the realist Jean-Paul Valabrega:

> You spoke of triangularity. . . . Does this notion then belong to the imaginary or to the symbolic order? Since you spoke of ignorance just now, I thought of Nicholas de Cusa, who, thoughout the whole of the first part of the *De Docta Ignorantia* engages in a formal analysis of the notion of triangularity, and ties it, it seems to me, to the symbol. (*Seminar II*, 315)

Lacan corrects the understanding of his previous lecture on cybernetics and language saying, "I didn't take the triangle as my example, but the circle, and that's not the same thing" (*Seminar II*, 315). Attempting to distinguish himself from Cusa in this case, he says that the triangle and the circle are different. However, his actual articulation of the Imaginary, Symbolic, Real connection suggests that in fact they are engaged in a circular process akin to the understanding of the three elements of the Trinity. Valabrega perceives this dissonance or contradiction in Lacan's teaching and says, "we no longer knew whether, for you, the circularity or triangularity pertains to the symbolic or the imaginary order in these experiments" (*Seminar II*, 315). Supplementing the circle for the triangle, Lacan actually skips over the expression of the triangularity at stake in the infinite play of the baroque motion of the desire of the unconscious in the three orders. As individual orders, the Imaginary, the Symbolic, and the Real are ultimately bound together and not discrete as the structuralist understanding of Lacan would support them to be. Though he remains in a structuralist phase in this early text, he already points toward the post-structuralist play with knots that will consume his attention in the latter part of his career. The limitations of the ostensibly perfect formalism of the triangular system are evident in Lacan's move from the tripartite structure of the dialectics of desire to a more complex version of it in the form of the knot. As a mode of understanding the way in which the real is bound up with the symbolic and the imaginary, as well as the way in which the structure of desire exceeds the limits of the dialectical system, the theory of knots represents a form of universal that is like a nucleus—alone, bare, and pure as universal categories.

In his "Glosses on Porphyry" from his *Logica "ingredientibus,"* Peter Abelard explains that the universals are "alone," "bare," and "pure." Although Lacan would certainly oppose Abelard's claim that understanding precisely means understanding with reference to God because nothing can be conceived of as distinct from God, what he could take (or might have taken) from Abelard is the ternary application of solitude, bareness, and purity to the universals. According to Abelard,

> [T]he understanding of universals is deservedly called the "alone" and "bare" and "pure." "Alone," apart from sensation, because it does not perceive the thing as sensible. "Bare," with respect to the abstraction of forms, either all or some of them. "Pure" of everything, as far as being discrete is concerned, because no thing, whether matter or form, is picked out in it.[50]

The universal of desire manifests itself in Lacan's theory as the locus of the "alone" because there is no unification in the sexual relationship, the "bare" because it is a linguistic striptease exposing the innermost quality of desire, and the "pure" because it is bound to an understanding of the potential for the material instantiation of the immaterial of desire. This trinity is bound to Lacan's articulation of the way in which God exists as a sublimated instance of desire. As he says, the "pure" of philosophy is the material connected to the spiritual by way of the understanding of love vis-à-vis God (*Seminar XX*, 68). This connection between obscenity and divinity thus imposes a view of desire as a universal that is abstract and physical despite its physical limitations. The fantasy of the properly abstract woman, supplemented as she is by the all too real, real woman, reflects the search for desire within the awareness of its impossibility.[51] Placing the woman as object and cause of desire in the position of the divine, we see the way in which unconscious desire supplements the position of God.

The representation of the Real as fantasmatic object of desire in Marie de France's *Lanval* foregrounds the manner in which desire seeks its absent object. The appearance of the supernatural Queen A, seen as a group hallucination dependent upon the hope of the barons to perceive the ideal object of their desire, creates a rupture in the properly hidden status of woman.[52] As an instance of the supernatural presence of the divine fantasmatic presence, Queen A is precisely opposed to the horror of the presence of *real* women, and as such, she renders a limit case for the cause of desire as that which is suspended in the illusory realm of desire's fantasy. This difference between the absent object of desire as it materializes in *Lanval* and the all too present woman who supplements the cause of desire is reflected in Lacan's anamorphotic institution of the naked female in repose that he hung on his wall. The potential for aesthetic representation finds its limits in the "realism" of Arnaut Daniel's scatological troubadour poem as well as in Courbet's painting *The Origin of the World*.[53]

In the study of his country home in Guitrancourt, called "La Prévôté" (the provost's house), Lacan had Gustave Courbet's 1866 painting *L'Origine du monde (The Origin of the World)*.[54] The painting was initially composed for Khalil Bey, a Turkish diplomat. The picture is a nude with a direct view of the genitals of a woman whose legs are spread as if she is waiting to be touched, or as if she has just finished having sex. Roudinesco recounts its full and fascinating history: it was taken by the Nazis, then transferred to Russia by way of various controlling hands as well as various ideological state apparatuses, and its historical trace patterns the traces of desire as a visible object. Lacan found the picture in 1955 and hung it in his study presumably as a representation of the impossibility of representing desire; or perhaps just as art on the wall. After his wife Sylvia Bataille requested that he conceal the picture or take it down because she was worried about offending the neighbors and the cleaning lady, he then installed a sliding wooden panel, on which he hung André Masson's abstract painting of the erotic elements of Courbet's original. So, hanging on the wall, concealed, not behind a veil or a curtain, but rather a wooden panel with another painting on it, then, is the "horror" of the female genitalia in sexual repose. This visual representation of anamorphosis serves as an analogy of Lacan's medievalism, the process of desire, and the absence of causality. The initial representation by Courbet must be seen as no more direct or literal than the abstract version by Masson. Rather, both versions display the absence of the image as properly represented.

The knot that emerges even in a scene whereby an attempt is made to represent, linearly or flatly, feminine sexuality takes on the status of the baroque. The crucial shift in the dialectic occurs when we distinguish between the notion of a dialectical process on the level of interaction or concepts and the process on the level of language. Courtly love enacts a dialectical process in Idea form to render a literary moment that defines desire as something outside of the process of that dialectic. Lacan's claim to the difference between courtly love and the Hegelian dialectical system of thesis, antithesis, and synthesis is based on the premise that no synthesis occurs within courtly love. The employment of the dialectical system in his definition of desire articulates concepts that are not precisely dialectical in form. Since his theory of desire is based on a reading of courtly love poetry, and since Lacan claims that courtly love poetry is not dialectical, the logical conclusion to the syllogism would be that desire is not dialectical.

> [I]n Hegel it is desire *(Begierde)* that is given the responsibility for that minimum connexion with ancient knowledge *(connaissance)* that the subject must retain if truth is to be immanent in the realization of knowledge *(savoir)* [sic]. Hegel's "cunning of reason" means that, from beginning to end, the subject knows what he wants.... It is here that Freud reopens the junction between truth and knowledge to the mobility out of which revolutions come.... In this respect: that desire becomes bound up with the desire of the Other, but that in this loop lies the desire to know. (*Écrits,* 301)

The "desire to know" continually turns the dialectic into a loop. Does this mean, however, that it takes on the form of a knot? Or is this precisely the definition of a dialectical system? The answer seems to lie in Lacan's statement that, in contrast to Hegel's notion of history, the subject's relationship to ancient knowledge confounds the ability to know the face of truth when s/he sees it.

The absent object or object as absence, and the desire that is necessitated, promoted, and recognized in such a scene, is precisely the symptom, regardless of the form it assumes. In 1975–76 during his "knot" phase, Lacan gave his seminar "Le Sinthome," which, based on the Bloch and Warburg etymological dictionary, Lacan discovered was an earlier form of the contemporary term "symptome." Homonymically the word *sinthome* calls forth many other layers of significance. Two of these various possible meanings are (1) the word sounds like "saint homme" in French, which means of course, holy man in English; (2) the word can be extended to "sinthomas-aquinas." By focusing on wordplay and the way in which Lacan turns the sign into a symptom of the knot, we therefore move from perceiving language as metaphorical to desire, or the unconscious as structured like a language, to a metonymical structure wherein all three aspects are concurrently available. This is a strange and multiply dialectical concept to conceive, let alone to articulate; when language ultimately was exhausted for him, Lacan turned to his play with knots.

CHAPTER FOUR

The Quadrangle, the Hard Sciences, and Nonclassical Thinking

Science is indeed never other than an explanatory fiction that derives, as if a condition of our intellectual processes, from an act of faith in the tendency of reality to form itself into meaningful systems. At least the models proposed by science provide a context in which the meaning of individual forms can take shape.

—Paul Zumthor, *Toward a Medieval Poetics*

When the dialectics of desire have arrived at a limit and we are left with a knot, we begin to approach the moment when Lacan turns to the *matheme* in his attempts to understand the navel of the unconscious.[1] As the knot of desire unfolds in the resistance to the (non)dialectics of courtly love, the real of the unconscious emerges as a universal category. Instead of three, we find four elements at play in the unconscious dimension of desire and language.

Invested in making his point as clear as possible (despite opinion to the contrary), Lacan searched for the properly universal language in which to convey his ideas to his disciples. His idealization of mathematics, the hard sciences, and the physical manifestation of the search for the singular solution to the knots of the unconscious, language, and desire reflect an appeal to a mode of expression that is not limited to an abstract form of language.[2] With a concern toward proper pedagogical models, Lacan coins and develops the four discourses of the university, the master, the hysteric, and the analyst in his attempt to demonstrate his point about desire and courtly love. In so doing, he also appeals to

Plato's *Meno* to illustrate the limits of pedagogy. As an instance of a classical model by which we find the boundaries of knowledge, the question of the possibility of teaching virtue addressed in the *Meno* urges an awareness of a higher order, a divine force, that establishes virtue as an unknowable yet universal category. Taking into account the cosmological understanding that seeks a divine or unknowable quality as a response to the aporia of knowledge, Lacan's obsession with the proper *matheme* that might best convey his ideas parallels the idealization of the hard sciences in the history of the discourse of the university.

Chaucer's *A Treatise on the Astrolabe* exemplifies the element of the nonclassical model of thinking that emerges from within the classical to call into question the notion of epistemological cuts as bound to epochal difference.[3] Further, the obsessive interest of scholars in *Antigone* demonstrates the challenge to the laws and order of the natural world in favor of a faith in the unknowable reflects a properly didactic pedagogical moment in Lacan's work that ultimately asserts the universal categories of desire and the unconscious.

Before embarking on the trajectory of this argument, a word about the four discourses of psychoanalysis will be of assistance in an understanding of the epistemological and metaphysical knot at play here. The four discourses, including the discourse of the master, the discourse of the university, the discourse of the hysteric, and the discourse of the analyst, are all geared toward an articulation of the signification of love. As Lacan says, "love is the sign that one is changing discourses."[4] The structure of these discourses reveals the circulation of power within the scene of the speaking subject in relation to an other. Lacan's four discourses are mapped in Figure 5, and they include the discourses of the master, the university, the hysteric, and the psychoanalyst. The chart shows the play of language, agency, and desire within these different discourses. Each of the four discourses has four elements of articulation where we find signification moving among alternate systems of power.

In the master's discourse, the master signifier seeks impossible knowledge and the element of unknowability returns to the subject with the element of *jouissance*. Although he does not possess full knowledge and often expresses uncertainty, the master's discourse presumes to speak as if he is certain. The discourse of the university presumes to speak from a place of knowledge and aims to locate *jouissance* to produce a subject who is often powerless in the face of the master signifier but who, if a

The Master's Discourse

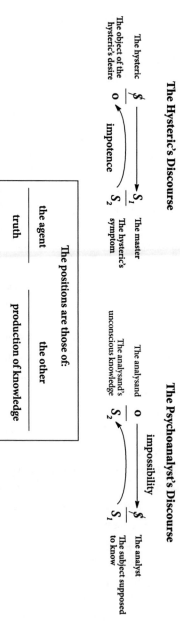

The master $\dfrac{S_1}{\$}$ $\xrightarrow{\text{impossibility}}$ $\dfrac{S_2}{O}$ The slave
The slave's production
of knowledge

is enlightened by its regression from:

The Hysteric's Discourse

The hysteric $\dfrac{\$}{O}$ $\xrightarrow{}$ $\dfrac{S_1}{S_2}$ The master

The object of the   impotence   The hysteric's
hysteric's desire   symptom

The University's Discourse

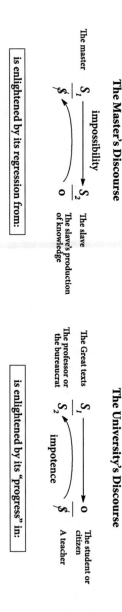

The Great texts $\dfrac{S_1}{S_2}$ $\xrightarrow{}$ $\dfrac{O}{\$}$ The student or
The professor or   impotence   citizen
the bureaucrat   A teacher

is enlightened by its "progress" in:

The Psychoanalyst's Discourse

The analysand $\dfrac{O}{S_2}$ $\xrightarrow{\text{impossibility}}$ $\dfrac{\$}{S_1}$ The analyst

The analysand's   The subject supposed
unconscious knowledge   to know

The positions are those of:

$$\frac{\text{the agent}}{\text{truth}} \qquad \frac{\text{the other}}{\text{production of knowledge}}$$

The terms are:

S_1 The master signifier
S_2 Knowledge
$\$$ The Subject
O Extra *jouissance* (the object o)

Figure 5

good student, can move into the place of the master signifier. The discourse of the hysteric seeks to put mastery in the place where there is only the subject and believes that *jouissance* is the truth of the product of knowledge. In an overdetermined manner, the hysteric speaks from an impossible place and so cannot reach the *jouissance* that is the goal. The analyst's discourse puts the analyst in the position of surplus *jouissance* in relation to the subject in order to attempt to produce the master signifier, which can assist in the location or development of knowledge. The juxtaposition of these discursive spaces further complicates the position of the subject so that the hysteric in discourse with the analyst will engage in a transferential relationship that likely foregrounds *jouissance,* the overlapping element in the movement of desire. Or, alternatively, the discourse of the university will often conflict with the discourse of the master because the position of knowledge differs so vastly in the two systems.

Throughout his seminars Lacan shifts among the four discourses and often attempts to use language pedagogically and transferentially, allowing the auditor to locate him in whichever discursive space is most useful to him at the time. When possible, he conflates the different discursive registers showing their overlap and interdependency. As a speaking subject, Lacan is all of the above: master, hysteric, analyst, and the university. As a teacher, Lacan refuses to speak from the position of the master, yet he often finds himself requiring that space. As an analyst, Lacan seeks knowledge from the position of the hysteric, and when he is in the position of the university discourse, he shifts to the discourse of the analyst, ever resisting the proper application of the system that he establishes precisely because, in that resistance, he reflects the sign of love that is, above all, crucial to the analyst and the teacher.

In performing this mutability, Lacan imitates Socrates who also refuses to allow his discursive position to be pinned down. In the *Meno,* a dialogue that Lacan refers to incessantly in *Seminar II, The Ego in Freud's Theory and in the Technique of Psychoanalysis,* we find Socrates engaged in a metapedagogical analysis of the potential for virtue to be taught. Meno asks Socrates, "can virtue be taught?" And Socrates begins responding by requiring a definition of virtue that illustrates the manner in which the very question attempts to position virtue as a universal category. Virtue, says Socrates (like Boethius's version of happiness after him), cannot be defined by its parts because it is a unity whose fragmentation would eliminate its character. The crucial elements of the dialogue for the purposes of this discussion are found in Socrates' approach to teaching the possibility of teaching an unknowable element, the representation of the irrational quality of the diagonal of the square, and the appeal to the divine at the limits of understanding in the definition of a universal category. These points shall be addressed in the course of this chapter.

Lacan employs the equations in the *Meno* to display the function of truth as it is driven by an internal power rendering it incomplete when we try to teach it: "the knowledge to which truth comes to be knotted must actually be endowed with its own inertia, which makes it lose something of the virtue which initiated its deposition as such, since it exhibits an obvious propensity to misrecognize its own meaning."[5] If language fails, it is due to the failure of scientific modes of inquiry, and not, in this case, to the limitations of language. Strangely, despite the precedence that language takes in the question at stake, this desire forwards a more *realist* view of knowledge than it does a *nominalist* one.

Lacan displays a certain resistance to Socrates' understanding of virtue as a unity when he says that we "lose something of the virtue" and suggests that virtue is not whole. If virtue were whole, as Socrates suggests it is, it could not lose any element of its being. Indeed, this universal quality means that, according to Socrates, virtue cannot be taught. He says:

> Can you name any other subject, in which the professed teachers are not only not recognized as teachers of others, but are thought to have no understanding of it themselves, and to be no good at the very subject they profess to teach, whereas those who are acknowledged to be the best at it are in two minds whether it can be taught or not? When people are so confused about a subject, can you say that they are in a true sense teachers?
>
> MENO: Certainly not.
>
> SOCRATES: And we have also agreed that a subject of which there were neither teachers nor students was not one which could be taught.
>
> MENO: That is so.
>
> SOCRATES: Now there turn out to be neither teachers nor students of virtue, so it would appear that virtue could not be taught.[6]

Following this passage we find a discussion on the unknowability of virtue and the fact that that which is not knowledge cannot be taught. When Lacan misinterprets this passage to say that virtue cannot be taught because we lose something in the process of teaching, he detours from the focus on the unknowability of virtue to engage the limitations of language in the communication of a universal.

Although Lacan says that the "ambiguity of knowledge and truth" are at the core of the problem, he focuses on the problems of the modes of knowing rather than the limitations of knowledge in the face of the universal (*Seminar II*, 5). This is because Lacan has an investment in considering the scientific element of language as a means of achieving and communicating knowledge. He therefore posits Socrates' skeptical view of science in the pursuit of virtue: "at the very moment when Socrates inaugurates this new being-in-the-world which here I call subjectivity, he realizes that science will not be able to transmit the means to achieve the most precious thing, the *arête*, the excellence of the human being" (*Seminar II*, 5). This is a critique of science familiar to the history of philosophy—at the limits of inquiry, science fails to account for human emotions or attributes. Two seemingly contradictory points emerge from this opening discussion of the ego by way of the *Meno* in Lacan's second seminar. First, Lacan points out the limitations of science for the investigation of universal categories like "virtue," even while he continues to idealize the hard sciences. Second, Lacan, perhaps because he is speaking from the position of one who considers himself to be a scientist at this moment, suggests the universality of the unconscious (here in the form of the ego).

> What has happened since Socrates? A lot of things, and in particular the concept of the ego has seen the light of day.
>   When something comes to light, something which we are forced to consider as new, when another structural order emerges, well then, it creates its own perspective within the past, and we say—*This can never not have been there, this has existed from the beginning.* Besides, isn't that a property which our experience demonstrates? (*Seminar II*, 5)

Thus, at the beginning of this seminar on the development of the ego, Lacan insists that the ego has always already been in existence, making it a real category. In case it is not clear, this "concept of the ego" is also of course synonymous with the unconscious. Therefore the unconscious is presented as a transhistorical, transepochal entity that *exists*.

The quadrangle, with its potential multiplicity of trajectories, reveals complications of realism and nominalism with regard to the drive for singularity within the diversity of universality. As Arkady Plotnitsky notes in his essay "Difference," the diagonal of the square addressed in Plato's *Meno* and analyzed by Deleuze and Guattari in *A Thousand Plateaus*, and by Deleuze in *Logic and Sense*, is the "first irrational quality ever discovered."[7] The consideration of the diagonal of the square inspired "a crisis of Greek mathematics and philosophy alike, . . . establishing the insufficiency of a given system of axioms to ascertain either truth or falsity of all proportions derivable from these axioms."[8] Similarly, the square as a mathematical unit and one that represents love and desire in Lacan's scheme displays impossibility, the limits of knowledge, and the various discursive realms in which the struggle for certainty plays. The implications of the quadrangle for mathematics, science, and pedagogy, as well as the process of desire, will be more thoroughly addressed in the final section of this chapter. Initially, its significance reflects the movement from classical to nonclassical (or postclassical) thinking as that which explodes the limitations of classical triangular formalization with regard to distinguishing the emergence of modernity and its relation to the hard sciences as a means of understanding natural laws.

Lacan's drive to uncover the absolute subject and the truth of desire led to his adherence to the dialectical system and, paradoxically, to his refusal to allow that system to limit his theory of desire. Lacan's reliance on Kojève's theory of the cut between antiquity and modernity articulated clearly by Jean-Claude Milner reveals the historiographical play at stake in Lacan's movement from the dialectic to the knot. If, for Kojève, "the index of the major cut between the world of Antiquity and the modern world was the appearance of Christianity,"[9] then his Hegelianism leads to a view of history that exceeds particular paradigm shifts and accounts for broad ones. Empirical events have little effect on the modes of thinking popular to different historical epochs. Indeed, according to Kojève's system, the epoch itself would be redefined in vast terms distinguishing moments like antiquity and modernity, but refusing any more discrete taxonomy ("Lacan and the Ideal of Science," 28). Milner also summarizes Koyré's theses, which resemble Kojève's on the level of Hegelianism but focus more specifically on the effects that scientific discoveries have on epistemological changes. For Koyré, the difference between antiquity and modernity is marked by the scientific changes made by Galileo. Antiquity is distinct from modernity because it lacks scientific awareness and consideration; all science is modern science ("Lacan and the Ideal of Science," 29). Both Kojève and Koyré base their theses on the notion that a *cut* exists between two historical epochs whose epistemes differ because of a revolution in reason or faith.

The history of theories about the cut involves a mode of thinking about epochs as they form subjectivity.[10] From these theories, Lacan derives the beginnings of his exploration into knots. Since the knots that Lacan studies are characterized by the ability to cut one string and undo the knot, the cut is fundamental to his knot theories. Further, it is important to remember that the graph of desire revolves around the cut in which desire emerges. Milner summarizes Lacan's thesis on the cut in this way:

1. There are major cuts.
2. Koyré's thesis is but a special case of Kojève's thesis; in other words, modern science is a major cut in Kojève's sense.
3. Psychoanalysis is intrinsically modern. ("Lacan and the Ideal of Science," 31)

Despite the attention that Koyré places on the presence of mathematics in antiquity, he states that these (pre)scientific explorations depended on finding an eternal or universal cause and effect. Modern science (the only science) is based on particular empirical results.[11] In a profound essay also collected in *Lacan and the Human Sciences* entitled "Lacan and Experience," François Regnault states that "Lacan's method consists in keeping together the level of absolute singularity of the case and the level of universality, which is an equation, or what he calls a *matheme*."[12] Given this definition of science as particularly modern due to its resistance to universality and absolute findings, a summary of Lacan's thesis of the cut that finds psychoanalysis to be intrinsically modern must be questioned.

The precise extent to which science is modern, as well as the corresponding extent to which psychoanalysis is modern, relies on the distinction of scientific method as classical or nonclassical, methodologies of mathematical proofs and their relation to desire, as well as modes of cosmological understanding. A close study of Chaucer's approach to the sciences "valid" or "quasi" in his *A Treatise on the Astrolabe* reveals a key to unlocking the safe in which the unconscious of the "medieval mind" is held. I put "medieval mind" in warning quotation marks here because it is not my goal to universalize the mind, nor do I want to suggest in any way that generalizations about "the mind" may be asserted. On the contrary, this approach to epochal shifts marks the precise particularity of each subject's psyche. The specific examples of the quasi sciences put forth by Chaucer and Lacan place their work within the medieval quarrel over the universals such that each arrives at a singular understanding of the overlaps and boundaries between realism and nominalism. Lacan's graph of desire, his idealization of mathematics, the *matheme* as the perfect signifier, and the hard sciences, are abutted by his concomitant awareness of the impossibility of the formalism he seeks. Similarly, Chaucer's endeavor to write a scientific treatise, witnessed in the incomplete translation known as *A Treatise on the Astrolabe*, combines with a myriad of references to astronomy, astrology, mathematics, and alchemy throughout his work to present a complex struggle with the potential for science to solve or to create human problems.

Before engaging this complex issue, the drive to define scientificity requires some mapping. Prior to postclassical awareness (as it is expressed most thoroughly by Plotnitsky) of the "quasi" or "pseudo" nature of science itself, science was broken down into the "hard" and the "soft" sciences, or valid sciences contrary to the "quasi" or "wretched" sciences (which were not considered science at all).[13] Mathematics and physics, for instance, were considered "hard" sciences while biology was considered a "soft" science (which holds true today in many arenas). Similarly, modern scientists call astronomy a valid science while astrology and alchemy are quasi sciences if they merit the label "science" at all; psychoanalysis fears falling into the category of quasi and so it seeks to use methods affiliated with the hard sciences (but this is only one potential explanation for Lacan's obsession with mathematics and knot theory). This value judgment is utterly dependent upon historical context, however, and the categories of the sciences themselves are constantly shifting. Scholarship on the history of the sciences reveals a concern with the "quasi" nature of all science including the most apparently objective, mathematics.[14]

The particular instances of the psychoanalytical experience and exploration may not be applicable to a universal mode of explaining what used to be called human identity. However, the drive for a means of conveying a theory universally reveals a resistance to the discrete ways in which psychoanalysis defines the subject. Lacan's play with knots aims at the discovery of a universal, eternal response to the problem of articulating psychoanalysis, which itself is based on particular instances and cannot be universally applied.

In "The Critique of the Foundations of the Hegelian Dialectic" Georges Bataille reads Hartmann's "Révue de metaphysique et de morale."[15] The result of this short piece is a view of psychoanalysis as the answer to dialectical confusion among Marxist practices. Following Hartmann, Bataille urges a reading of Hegel's writings on the dialectic that sets aside the universality of dialectics. Affirming the difference between the presence of a concept in language and the presence of a concept in experience (fiction vs. reality, concept vs. practice, idea vs. form, fantasy vs. desire, etc.), Bataille argues that the same concepts may be dialectical in one arena but not necessarily in both at the same time. The result is a particularity of dialectical experience whose practice must be considered case-by-case, moment-by-moment, concept-by-concept, and word-by-word.

Bataille uses the example of the "hard" sciences to exemplify this argument. Mathematics, for instance, was distinguished from dialectical thought during the nineteenth century in order to account for a "more rigorous" science of knowledge; eliminating the linguistic element of mathematical symbols, mathematicians asserted that their language was a more pure and ideal form of communication than other semiotic systems. But that distinction, as Bataille explains, does not eliminate elements of dialectical thinking from mathematical formulae or procedures.

> If, in its origins, a mathematical theory can present a certain "floating" in its principles and can lack rigor in its demonstrations, that is a weakness—isn't it superfluous to say?—and not the proof of the dialectical character of the object of science. It is true that mathematics is constructed through the denial of the degeneracies and weaknesses that its development introduces. But quite different are the completed domain of science and the detours that were necessary in order for the human mind to arrive at the point where this structure is found. The dialectic does not express the nature of mathematics; it applies to the agent and not to the object of scientific activity. . . . It is not a question of setting aside dialectical thought; one must instead try to know the limit beyond which its application in this direction is fruitful. ("Critique of the Foundations," 111)

Bataille then employs psychoanalysis as a marker of the difference between spiritualism and the philosophical investigation of concepts in nature. Psychoanalysis becomes the answer to the question of the limits of the dialectic. And in this answer, we find Lacan's study of knots. At the end of his career Lacan spent most of his time attempting to locate a mathematical explanation for the knot-like process of unconscious desire. Working from Gödel's theorem of incompleteness, Lacan articulates the way in which lack resides at the center of language.[16] Having become frustrated with the limits to which phonetic language could convey psychoanalysis, he sought refuge in the symbolic language of the *matheme.* Lacan's belief in the absolute power of mathematical symbols to convey ideas without confusion is one motivating force behind his play with knot formations. Early in *Encore* Lacan claims:

> [N]othing seems to better constitute the horizon of analytical discourse than the use made of the letter by mathematics. The letter reveals in discourse what is called, not by chance or without necessity — grammar. Grammar is that aspect of language that is revealed only in writing *(a l'écrit).*
>
> Beyond language, this effect, which is produced by being based only on writing, is certainly the ideal of mathematics. Now to refuse to refer to writing *(l'écrit)* is to forbid oneself what can actually be articulated using *(de)* all effects of language. This articulation occurs in what results from language regardless of what we do — namely, a presumed shy of and beyond *(en deçà et au-delà).* (*Seminar XX*, 44)

Part of his investment in finding the perfect knot to demonstrate desire and its role within psychoanalysis is due to his determination to maintain its scientificity.[17] In his introduction to *Lacan and the Human Sciences* Alexandre Leupin lucidly summarizes this drive.

> If psychoanalysis is to attain the status of a science, it will have to be formalized in a mathematical way in order to put the accent not on meaning and quantity but on relation (structure) and quality. This requirement is inseparable from a mathematization of space (a topology), which will find its most elaborate development in Lacan's later work. Lacan therefore renews Freud's ambition of scientificity, but at the same time he radically transforms the modalities of legitimization of this rationality: We know well enough that Freud drew upon medicine and biology to ensure the scientific consistency of his ideas. These two fields are replaced, in Lacan, by mathematics and topology. (2)

Leupin associates Lacan's interest in the scientificity of psychoanalysis with his desire to eliminate transference from the articulation of the theories on which it is founded. His search for the *matheme,* Leupin says, is part of his attempt to remove the proper name from psychoanalytic explication.

The scientificity of psychoanalysis lies in its capacity of being transmissible without reference to a person: that is, without being affected by transference. The introduction of the *matheme* is intended to allow psychoanalysis to approach the status granted, for example, to the theory of relativity, which is pertinent without any reference to Einstein's biography and desires. (*Lacan and the Human Sciences,* 3)

Leupin states that the difficulty of completing the project to eliminate transference and the symptom from the transmission of psychoanalysis is founded in its need to discover a common language, therefore reintroducing problems of signification and interpretation (however [quasi-] mathematical) into the formula of psychoanalysis.

Lacan's awareness of the impossibility of transmitting an idea without transference leads to the dissembling of science itself. "Psychoanalysis is privileged in the sense that in it symbolism is reduced to the effect of truth which, whether extracted or not from its pathetical forms, is isolated in its knot as the counterpart without which nothing can be conceived about science."[18] The central function played by the knot reveals that despite Lacan's insistence on the discovery of a mode of communicating without transference, the search is futile. His own play with knots and his work on the *matheme* and topology are the result of his transferential relationship with the mathematician Georges-Th. Guilbaud. Elizabeth Roudinesco describes Lacan's relationship with Guilbaud as one of profound connection and identification that was based on mutual respect and adoration. During the 1950s Lacan and Guilbaud spent time together "in their shared passion, forever tying knots in bits of string, inflating children's swimming belts, braiding and cutting things out."[19] The masturbatory processes of tying knots, braiding, and cutting things, combined with the oral fixation of inflating swimming belts, calls attention to the homoeroticism of the friendship between Lacan and the mathematician. The desire between the two men, however, was to remain sublimated in their play with knots.[20]

It was not until the same messenger appeared to Lacan in the form of a young female mathematician that he was able to engage the topological connection between the knot and desire (transference) on a level other than the expository. As Roudinesco reports, Valérie Marchande told Lacan about the Borromeos arms of the Milanese dynasty that were made up of a "clover leaf or trefoil and standing for a triple alliance"

(*Jacques Lacan,* 363). This correspondence, which occurred in 1972, reinitiated Lacan's old relationship with Guilbaud by way of the female mediator. Heteronormativity of the endeavor having been confirmed through the appearance of Marchande, Lacan was then able to join a group consisting of young mathematicians who shared his interest in finding a proper topology for psychoanalysis. He began his research into the Borromean knot and entered the group of mathematicians who were highly aware of the parallel between their analytical investments in knots and the corresponding knot of desire. According to Roudinesco, the group's rejection of society "was reflected in a determination to hold together the three components of a knot representing the minimal form of the social link" (*Jacques Lacan,* 365). One of the group's members and a favorite student of Lacan's, Pierre Soury, said, "Life in small groups makes for stability in individuals. It's like marriage. . . . A small group is born and dies, but you don't enter or leave it. The ideal small group is a Borromean one, based on a comparison between small groups and the Borromean chains" (*Jacques Lacan,* 365). Soury's awareness of the circulation of desire within the small group and within the knot was resisted by Lacan, who sought to sublimate his desire through his attempts at the scientific answer to the question of desire. He defends himself against accusations of transference, antifeminism, and homoerotic desire when he states in "Rings of String" that he is interested in the "discordance between knowledge and being" (*Seminar XX,* 120).

> I don't know how to approach, why not say it, the truth—no more
> than woman.[21] I have said that the one and the other are the same thing,
> at least to man. They constitute the same conundrum (*embarras*). As
> it turns out, I relish the one and the other, despite what people say.
> (*Seminar XX,* 120)

Lacan's equivocation heightens the defensive nature of this statement. He claims that his investment in truth is the crux of his exploration. Yet his insistence on his desire for truth and women foregrounds his desire to be seen as a heterosexual man who is nonetheless sympathetic to the cause of women. Instead, he appears to look for women's cause as a symptom of her existence. The parallel structure of the knot as a quasi-mathematical theoretical model, and of the graphs of desire as diagrammatic and topological explications for the impossibility of the sexual relation, binds scientific inquiry to a perverse form of realism that seeks a universal answer to the questions of the *matheme* and desire.

Lacan continued to investigate feminine sexuality and hysteria by playing with knots as a means, perhaps, of avoiding turning his gaze on his own desire. His fascination with knots became an obsession as he attempted to understand the "monstrosity" of desire (*Jacques Lacan*, 366–67). Roudinesco employs the metaphor of Lacan's correspondence with other members of the "planet Borromeo" (Soury, Michel Thomé, and Christian Léger) stating that "there were fifty letters from Lacan, a hundred and fifty from his colleagues: a veritable epic made up of suffering and melancholy, in which everyone involved exhausted themselves in the attempt to solve the riddle of the unconscious by means of telegrams, *pneumatiques,* and ordinary letters" (*Jacques Lacan*, 367). The sheer number of correspondences among the group testifies to the obsessive approach they took to the study of knots. It also reveals the powerful transference circulating among the group, wherein each member constantly shared ideas and sought reaction from the others. When verbal communication failed them, the members of the group would often gather to congratulate each other on their progress. Roudinesco's description of the investigation into knots resembles that of a case study of hysteria. "Often, after spending hours drawing surfaces, twisting the inner tubes that they had delivered in large quantities, or filling baskets with bits of string and cutouts of colored paper, the others would get a message from Lacan asking them for the solution of a problem. Neither they nor he could find it, and the search went on" (*Jacques Lacan*, 367). Lacan's insistence on personal contact appeared in the form of messages that said, "I'm going crazy, do please phone or come and see me" (*Jacques Lacan*, 367). The transference among the members of the group grew as the difficulty of their endeavor and its infinite progression increased. The limit that Lacan searched for in order to begin to put the theory of *mathemes* into practice and convey it to members of the mathematics community who were not associated with psychoanalysis came to be realized in the form of transference itself.

> In this experimentation with limits, the work on knots abolished the frontiers between analytic practice and theory, turning psychoanalysis itself into a kind of Borromean space in which the transferential

relationship took on literal form and enabled those concerned to re-discover their childhood: the childhood of play, of nursing, of empti-ness, of lack, of *béance*, and of the *not whole*. (*Jacques Lacan*, 368)

The symptom cannot be eliminated despite attempts to eliminate lan-guage from the scene of psychoanalysis. Transference, the instance of psychoanalytical investigation that Lacan was determined to eliminate from its expression, became the driving force behind his study of knots.

In *Representing the Holocaust* Dominick LaCapra addresses the prob-lem of transference in historiography and among theoretical critics.[22] Two of his chapters investigate the way in which criticism is affected by transferential relationships, first to Paul de Man in "Paul de Man as Object of Transference," and second with regard to the uses of psycho-analysis within medieval studies in "The Return of the Historically Repressed." LaCapra's conclusions in those chapters aid in an under-standing of the significance of Lacan's transference with his mathemati-cal group as he sought to uncover the secret behind the knot of desire.

"Paul de Man as Object of Transference" focuses on the paradox of De Man's Nazism and the love that was shown to him by theorists such as Derrida, Felman, and Jameson (all of whom write about the Holo-caust and its traumatic effects on the twentieth century as well as De Man's participation in fascism). LaCapra aptly notes that for these scholars the "difficulty is that the transferential problem plays itself out without being thematized" (*Representing the Holocaust*, 135). The differ-ence between his study of recent scholars mourning the death of Paul de Man and the transferential relationship between Lacan and the members of his knot-group is that Lacan does thematize the problem of transference; he simply does not look at himself as a participant in its dy-namic. Lacan's willingness to ignore his own role in the process of trans-ference is limited, however, to a consideration of his desire. He is highly aware of the presence of transference in others directed toward him. He does not consider his own desire as a part of the problem to articulate desire. This failure to consider his own desire in the process of his analy-sis of the subject of desire leads him to cathect his drives around the possibility for a scientific discourse. What emerges from Lacan's play with knots is more evidently a semiotic system whereby the visual graph dis-plays and supplements the abstract idea than it is evidence of a scientific system. The argument transfers to the study of the Middle Ages where we find that psychoanalysis is not "mobilized" as an applicative "tool" for the study of distant historical contexts, but rather that it is always already within the text by way of internal repetition. Mathematically, this internal repetition and the notion that the "original" point is always a duplication of itself takes on the form of a knot.

In *Seminar XX*, Lacan's seminar on "Rings of String" articulates his findings that relate the knot to the unconscious processes of desire and the limits to which language may convey them.

> Since what is at stake for us is to take language as *(comme)* that which functions in order to make up for the absence of the sole part of the real that cannot manage to be formed from being *(se former de l'être)*— namely, the sexual relationship—what basis can we find in merely reading letters? It is in the very play of mathematical writing *(l'écrit)* that we must find the compass reading toward which to head in order to draw from this practice—from this new social link, analytic discourse, that emerges and spreads in such a singular fashion—what can be drawn from it regarding the function of language. (*Seminar XX*, 48)

The central function of mathematical knowledge and language in determining the direction and reading of the compass points toward the history of the astrolabe, in some senses a multifaceted and complex, dynamic compass dependent upon mathematical processes and methods.

Love and knowledge are bound to textuality or a nominalist awareness of imperfection despite Lacan's desire to find solutions within the realist approach to universality, demonstrating Lacan's own struggle with the elements of the debate over the existence of real universals. Lacan's claim that "knowledge, which structures the being who speaks on the basis of a specific cohabitation, is closely related to love. All love is based on a certain relationship between two unconscious knowledges," reveals the extent to which that love and that knowledge may remain unconscious despite attempts to analyze it within the conscious realm of language (*Seminar XX*, 144). Although Lacan's statement following this one centers on transference, he (frustratingly) continues to foreclose his own relationship to his desire.

> If I have enunciated that the subject supposed to know is what motivates transference, that is but a particular, specific application of what we find in our experience. I'll ask you to look at the text of what I enunciated here, in the middle of this year, regarding the choice of love. I spoke ultimately, of recognition, recognition—via signs that are always punctuated enigmatically—of the way in which being is affected qua subject of unconscious knowledge. (*Seminar XX*, 144)

Lacan is referring his audience back to his lectures on courtly love. The "choice of love" is the nonchoice wherein the enigma of desire infiltrates knowledge and the ability to know oneself. Lacan's refusal to admit his unconscious desire into the realm of consciousness causes him to persist in his play with knots and leads him to invest his energies on the instance of courtly love.[23]

Despite, or because of, his willingness to criticize Lacan, François Roustang is the most insightful reader of Lacan's struggle to identify his work in psychoanalysis with the hard sciences. Roustang's *Le Réel de Lacan*, translated into English as *The Lacanian Delusion*, associates our desire to follow Lacan with his promise of a type of knowledge that transcends disciplinary boundaries. In addition to his careful critique of Lacan's faltering attempts to find a universal language in psychoanalysis, Roustang shows how Lacan's work continually returns to the question of desire.[24] He records: "Psychology is said to be a science because it is based on the energetic concept of the libido, which is 'merely the symbolic notation for the equivalence between the dynamisms that such images invest in behavior.'"[25] The passage that Roustang cites to support his point is from *Écrits* and reads:

> Through this notation the efficacy of such images, without yet being amenable to a single form of measurement, but already equipped with either a plus or a minus sign, can be expressed through the equilibrium that they set up, and by employing, as it were, a method of *double weighing (double pesée)*. As used here, the notion of libido is no longer metapsychological: *it is the instrument of psychology's progress towards a form of positive knowledge (savoir)* [emphasis added]. For example, combining this notion of libidinal investment with a structure as concretely defined as the super-ego represents—over the idealizing definition of moral conscience, as well as the functional abstraction of those reactions known as *opposition or imitation*—progress of a kind comparable only to the introduction into the physical sciences of the *weight over volume ratio*, when it replaced the quantitative categories of heavy and light. The rudiments of a positive determination have thus been introduced into psychical realities which a relativist definition has made it possible to objectify. This determination is dynamic, or relative to the facts of desire. (*Écrits*, 91)

Quite rightly, Roustang demolishes the supposition that psychoanalysis can possibly become like a science. One danger of admitting that psychoanalysis is a hard science is that it would become a "second rate" science

(*Lacanian Delusion*, 23); better to be a first-rate, unclassifiable, questionably systematic approach to knowledge than to be a second-rate science. Roustang walks through the ways in which Lacan's attempt to find Kantian universal objectivity in psychoanalysis fails according to the above statement, saying that "universality" here means only commonality, and that mathematical language is highly specific and cannot be approached in the willy-nilly way that Lacan perceives it. Indeed. Yet, there are two aspects of Lacan's attempt to render desire scientific that Roustang does not address: (1) the transference that Lacan engages in with his contemporaries working within the hard sciences, and, notably, with his own teachers, and (2) the limitations of science itself. This would enable the categorization or scientificity of desire and psychoanalysis if it indeed does discover a mathematical proof that works.

Lacanian scholars generally assume and assert that Lacan's followers engage in transference with him. What is overlooked in idealizations or persecutions of Lacan's work is his own desire to engage with his interlocutors—the countertransference. We have just seen the way in which Lacan's play with knots situates him within a system of transference with mathematicians and topologists. A brief exploration of Lacan's transferential relationship with Freud will aid in an understanding of his verbal adherence to, but practical refusal of, scientificity.

In the passage cited above, although Roustang criticizes Lacan's use of Einsteinian relativity, what is left out of his analysis is the way in which Lacan's idealization of that scientific method reveals his desire to carry out Freud's project and institute it within his theory of desire. The passage performs a movement from Freudian discourse to Lacan's own language that provides a crystallization of his overarching work to "return to Freud" while asserting his own ideas. This conflict between transference and the desire for independence accounts, at least partly, for the obvious contradictions and impossibilities in Lacan's attention to "the facts of desire." Reading the passage slowly, we find the following.

1. Lacan seeks a proper notation for desire, ultimately in the form of his *mathemes* and graphs.
2. He complicates the propriety of notation by adding a "double weighing."
3. He completed Freud's desire for scientificity by moving the libido from the realm of metapsychology to a form of positive knowledge.
4. He provides an example, using the terms of high science, that nonetheless shows point three to be impossible.

5. He concludes by undoing his statement in point three when he says that the determination is *dynamic* and *relative* to the "facts" of desire.

A different way of outlining this passage would be simply to state that Lacan wants to have his Freud and beat him too. First, Lacan seeks to follow and assert Freud's theory and raise it to an ideal level of science; but then he shows that such an ideal is impossible, even though he maintains the use of scientific language, thereby exhibiting a debt to Freud. Such a complex conflagration of desire to adhere to the father's system and refuse it reveals the problems at stake in Lacan's attempt to find a universal or mathematical language to describe desire. This drive to please and punish the father will be returned to in the final section of this chapter as it reveals much about pedagogy within psychoanalysis, the discourse of the master, and the desire of the disciple.

Chaucer's awareness of the disciple's struggle with identification and alterity is copiously displayed in his work. The pedagogical and scientific (or quasi-scientific) *A Treatise on the Astrolabe* asserts a premodern response to the struggle for scientific definition that provides insight into the potential answers to questions regarding Lacan's investment in the *matheme* and knot theory, his transference with mathematicians, and his idealization of the hard sciences, as well as his pedagogical exhibitionism. In the context of analysis of the split between antiquity and modernity that Kojève and Koyré attribute to the scientific method of inquiry, Chaucer's text illuminates an approach to science as an art in a manner that accepts its flaws while documenting its validity and recognizing its status as a science that is necessarily, by virtue of its human production, imperfect.

Throughout his oeuvre, Chaucer demonstrates an interest in articulating the differences among the sciences and in understanding the valid or quasi characteristics of various forms of scientific inquiry and its linguistic performance. In *The Miller's Tale,* for instance, Nicholas (likely named as a reference to Nicholas of Lynn, the author of the *Kalendarium,* one primary source for Chaucer's *A Treatise on the Astrolabe*) abuses his knowledge of astronomy and astrology to trick John the carpenter so that he may be alone with Alisoun. During the Middle Ages the sciences of astronomy and astrology were bound together.[26] Some Chaucerians as well as some historians of science seek to distinguish between them in an effort to maintain the difference between proper science and pseudoscience. However, those Chaucerians and historians of science who rely on the etymology and teachings of the two disciplines recognize their overlap, supplementarity, and occasional similitude.[27] In *The Canon's Yeoman's Tale* the "slidynge science" of alchemy is used to trick the priest and even the honest alchemist tricks himself with his own knowledge.[28] The difference between the sciences as valid or quasi emerges as a subjective determination of the knowledge, method, and intention of the subject as a scientist. "Proper" science is that which is learned and employed in a systematic manner and intended for "good" use. However, the determination of "good" use is a value judgment that alters contextually; it has ultimate validity for Chaucer when it reveals an alignment of human understanding with faith in a divine cosmological system or plan. Astronomy and astrology are fit scientific methods when they are employed as a means of understanding the cosmos; however, when they are used to attempt to control or manipulate earthly actions, they mutate into false sciences akin to alchemy, which is invalid since it reveals the subject's hubris and seeks to interfere with God's realm or, as stated in *The Second Nun's Tale*, His "privetee."

Additionally, as Larry D. Benson says, Chaucer's translation of Boethius reveals the balance between scientific knowledge and faith to be one that is determined by an idealization of realism balanced by an investigation into the potential for pure linguistic communication.[29] (It should be noted that this is strikingly similar to the characterization of Lacan's realism in the Introduction.) Accordingly, both scientists and artists seek a universal language that is free of potential misinterpretation and can achieve proper symbolization. For Chaucer, translating Latin and Old French texts into English reveals the simultaneous impossibility of such a universal symbolic order and the drive to communicate directly to the largest possible audience. The introduction to *A Treatise on the Astrolabe* illustrates Chaucer's self-conscious decision to translate the astronomical treatises into English as a means of determining the difference between particular and universal forms of knowledge as well as between reason and the drives.

Historian of science Otto Neugebauer begins his 1968 essay, "On the Planetary Theory of Copernicus," with reference to Koyré's lecture on Copernicus, revealing that Koyré's idealization of Copernicus's method and mathematical genius asserts a false distinction between "real" science and "quasi" or "pseudo" science when it employs Copernicus as the marker of the difference between antiquity and modernity.[30] Commenting also on Vieta's account of periodicity and chance within science, which disparages Copernicus's method, Neugebauer shows how both idealization and refusal of method render the technicalization of science, or its scientificity, utterly dependent upon the mathematical proofs at hand.

> Both pronouncements are quite characteristic of their times: on the one
> hand, the ever increasing modern tendency toward hero worship on the
> basis of "ideas" and disrespect for technicalities; on the other hand, the
> aggressiveness of Renaissance scholarship, which did not hesitate to
> point out weaknesses wherever they could be found. But the reader will
> notice that neither one of the above-mentioned statements is concerned
> with the alternative geocentric versus heliocentric universe but with the
> mathematical achievements and abilities of Copernicus.[31]

Neugebauer's work calls into question the potential for periodization of scientific history based on the nonlinear history of scientific and mathematical methods and proofs, as well as the particularity of the narratives that dilute the potential for pure knowledge. In short, Neugebauer believes in the potential for realism but perceives its impossibility due to nominalism and the historical records whose narratives alter the concept of the event, preventing it from being known. For him, as for Barbara Herrnstein Smith, Arkady Plotnitsky, and other thinkers of postclassicism and nonclassicism, the distinction between quasi or pseudoscience and "real" or "valid" science is indeterminable.[32] As such, the best that a scientist can do is to record and account for the differences and similarities among scientific methods and operations throughout history. In doing this work, Neugebauer shows that premodern science, or the science of antiquity, is precisely akin to modern science, dethroning Koyré's widely followed assertion that "all science is modern science" and demonstrating instead how the history of science is utterly dependent upon the investigations and methods established in all documents seeking to explain mathematically, empirically, or qualitatively enigmas of nature and the cosmos. Such a desire to construct a verifiable history of science itself leads Neugebauer to study the ostensibly "quasi," "pseudo," or "wretched" sciences of astronomy and astrology and to show how they are sound sciences even in their necessary permutations of "proper" science.

In sum, distinguishing between the proper sciences and those that are called pseudosciences (like alchemy, astrology, and magic) is a struggle not only for Chaucer and Lacan, but also for historians of science and scientists working in all fields. The effort to find differences among proper or pseudosciences fails when confronted with the issue of universality and scientific method. Rather than claim that some sciences are valid and others invalid, the goal of the mathematization of concepts and drives is to render universal particular modes of understanding and expression.

As Walter Skeat notes in his preface to *A Treatise on the Astrolabe*, Zedler's *Universal Lexicon* states that astrolabes are either "universal" or "particular."[33] This distinction reveals the variations of the method and its use and gestures toward a differential structure of the universal and the particular as one wherein "particularity" may also include multiplicity. Such variability can be read as either codifying the scientific method or as revealing its potential inconsistencies and uncertainty with regard to the goals or expectations of its application. Skeat's mention of the vagueness of the term *astrolabe* ("It should be observed here that the term 'astrolabe' alone is vague" [*Treatise*, xxxi]) supports this uncertainty. The term was ascribed to "any circular instrument used for observation of the stars" until the sixteenth and seventeenth centuries when it was used to designate the "Astrolabe Planisphere," meaning the astrolabe on a flat surface (*Treatise*, xxxii). These uncertainties and variations between the particular and the universal are foregrounded in Chaucer's introductory address to Lewis where he qualifies the number of conclusions that may be gained from the lesson of *A Treatise on the Astrolabe* in three ways. First, he states that the lesson is particular, "therfore haue I geuen the a suffisaunt astralabie as for owre orisonte, compowned after the latitude of Oxenford" (*Treatise*, 6). Second, he limits the lesson to a "certain nombre of conclusions apertenyng to the same instrument" (*Treatise*, 8). Such a limitation to the particular instrument is significant since it further restricts the particularity of the knowledge gained through the lesson itself while simultaneously providing Lewis with the foundations for knowledge that he might then apply more broadly on his own. The pedagogical moment is then particular in order to have more general potential. His third limitation explains the rationale for this particularity, and the repetition of "certain" is indicative of the precise uncertainty of the lesson.

I seye a certain of conclusions, for thre causes. The furste cause is this:
trust wel þat alle the conclusiouns that had ben fownde, or elles possibli
myhten be fownde in so noble an instrument as an astralabie, be vn-
knowe perfitly to any mortal man in the regioun, as I suppose. A-nother
cause is this; þat sothly, in any tretis of the astrlabie þat I haue seyn,
there ben some conclusions þat wole nat in alle thines performen hir
byhests; & some of hem ben to harde to thy tender age of .x. yer to
conseyue. (*Treatise*, 9–18)

Skeat puts this quite simply, "I say *some,* for three reasons; 1. because
some of them are unknown in this land; 2. because some are uncertain;
or else 3. are too hard" (*Treatise*, 1–2). The unknowability and uncertainty (or the third presumption that the knowledge is out of reach or
too difficult—another form of unknowability) regarding the elements
of the lesson limits its particularity while providing an illusion of general
applicability. The incompleteness of the text itself, however, further particularizes the lesson since the full tables of latitudes and longitudes of
stars, declinations of the sun, and the longitudes of certain towns
planned for part three, the universal elements and the motions of the
heavenly bodies planned for part four, and the general rules of astronomical theory planned for part five are not given. What we *do* find is
the element of knowledge that will allow Lewis to use his particular instrument to determine singular knowledge from his own location. In a
manner of speaking, then, Chaucer is teaching his son to find his way
home, or giving him the knowledge to understand his home so that he
may recognize its particularity among the external variations of time
and space.[34] The use of English, the mother tongue, further supports
this pedagogical approach from a domestic perspective of a father teaching his son in an unofficial mode that seeks to sediment its significance
in the child's mind.

Among the scholarship on Chaucer's *Treatise,* there is an investment
on the part of those working in the fields of literary history and literary
theory to uncover the accuracy of Chaucer's numbers and findings in
order to decode *The Canterbury Tales.* Alternately, debates ensue regarding the accuracy of textual transmission and translation issues. Scientific
historians, as well, seek to delineate where Chaucer is right and where
he is wrong in his premises, computation, and use of the astrolabe; their
conclusions rarely take *A Treatise on the Astrolabe* seriously in its own
right and use it instead to comment on the accuracy or quasi science of

The Canterbury Tales. Exceptions exist, of course; Sigmund Eisner and J. D. North as well as Marijane Osborn state that Chaucer may be considered a contributor to the fields of both literary and scientific history. In general though, *A Treatise on the Astrolabe,* perhaps because it presents itself and is considered in scholarship to be a translation derived primarily from Massahalla's *De receptione,* Nicholas of Lynn's *Kalendarium,* John Sumor's *Kalendarium,* and John of Sacrobosco's *de Sphera (On the Sphere)* and is written in prose, merits less attention to literary detail than *The Canterbury Tales.* The decoding that is so central to literary analysis leads scholars to use the *Treatise* as if it is a self-authored guide to Chaucer's poetry, rather than a text worthy of critical reading in its own literariness. Analysis of the explicit goal of the *Treatise,* "to slay envy," then, leads to a potential fusion of forms of literary and scientific analysis that often remain distinct or seek to distinguish disciplinary lines in scholarship on the *Treatise.*[35] Chaucer's use of a scientific text as "bread and milk for children" and as a means to cure his son of potential experience or expression of envy clearly binds the process of scientific knowledge and personal drives in a manner that contributes to an understanding of his role in the quarrel of the universals with a consideration of theological problems of free will and predestination.

Chaucer states that his goal in writing the *Treatise* for his ten-year-old son, Lewis, is to teach him some of the conclusions of the astrolabe precisely in order to "slay envy." He states in the final lines of the preface, "I nam but a lewd compilator of the labour of olde Astrologiens, and haue his translated in myn Englissh only for thi doctrine; & with this swerd shal I slen envie" (*Treatise,* 42–44) (Skeat's gloss records, "I have done no more than compile from old writers on the subject, and I have translated it into English solely for thine instruction; and with this sword shall I slay envy" [2].) Whether Chaucer means by "this swerd" the lessons of the astrolabe and its science or the language of English (or the pen that he uses to record his translation, or perhaps the process of instruction itself), the presentation of *A Treatise on the Astrolabe* in English is designed to foreclose *envy,* an uncontainable, immeasurable, and sometimes unconscious emotion or sin. Of course, the link between envy and mathematics may be seen in the desire for balance of commodity possessions or qualities that are quantifiable. The link between scientific teachings and the drive to prevent or thwart a form of desire (envy is above all a form of desire for that which one does not have or believes one does not or cannot have, and as such reflects the lack of Lacanian sexual difference) reveals that Chaucer's foray into the scientific realm is much like Lacan's in its motivation to discover a universal language and episteme and one that will link the material with the spiritual and phenomenal modes of being and expression. Indeed, Chaucer's gift of the *Treatise* itself is an expression of love for Lewis.

The distinction between astronomy and astrology such as it existed at all during the Middle Ages was founded on the element of the passions within the mathematical sciences. Astronomy gains status as a more pure or valid science than astrology because it dealt solely with mathematics, while astrology also addressed the passions. I want to emphasize that even this distinction is a precarious one, as the debate over categories of science itself is active and fraught throughout scientific history. Most scholars agree with Eisner, North, and Neugebauer that there was little if any distinction between the sciences at all. Nonetheless, since many scholars also attempt to clarify a crucial difference between astronomy and astrology, Chaucer's focus on the passions within his astronomical text is worthy of consideration. What is clear from his introduction to the *Treatise* is that Chaucer himself either does not hold astronomy as separate from the passions or he is attempting to assert that it should not remain separate in a consideration of the relationship between mathematics and envy. His scientific tract, then, also contributes in a complicated manner to a view of forms of desire.

Significantly, Chaucer's approach to the *Treatise* as a cure for the passion of envy does not have precedent in the original sources that he translates when he produces the *Treatise*. Though there is some debate about the extent to which Chaucer relies on various sources including treatises by Nicholas of Lynn, John Sumor, and John Sacrobosco as well as Ptolomy, Aristotle, Plato, and Robert Grosseteste, he certainly imitates them even if he does not directly translate their language. Chaucer shifts the genre of the *Treatise,* however, when he adds that its goal is to "slay envy." Other source materials provide prologues and prefaces to their technical material that situate the study of astronomy and astrology within a divine, hierarchical understanding of cosmology. Nicholas of Lynn, for example, dedicates his *Kalendarium* to Jesus Christ, describing himself to be "unworthy" and "least among readers of sacred theology."[36] The conventional quality apparent in Nicholas of Lynn's prologue marks the calendar as a tool for determining the cosmological order so that ecclesiastical, lay, and medical decisions regarding the body and its spirit might succeed in their appropriate manners. Lynn's *Kalendarium* is descriptive and derived from a view of the universe as something that subjects might seek to exist in, but not understand or control. In contrast, we find that Chaucer's presentation of the *Treatise* aims toward an understanding of the workings of the universe so that the desire to control it may be assuaged.

This contribution takes on further significance when it is remembered that Chaucer's text participates in a broad history of scientific, philosophical, and theological texts about the relation between the singular human will and the universal cosmos, generally seen as divine. The uncertainty of Chaucer's sources, leading most scholars to debate the origin of the *Treatise,* is logical given the abundant textual context and history that contributes to its shaping. Each of the following litany of contextual sources that enable intertextual understanding of Chaucer's *Treatise* is debated as a valid or pseudoscientific text in its own right, or as a literary text that seeks to solve questions of causality between humans and the cosmos, or to determine the extent to which knowledge can lead to free will and self-determination. From Ptolomy's *Almageste* to Cicero's *Somnium (The Dream of Scipio)* and Aristotle's *De Caelo* and his *Metaphysics* to the work of Boethius, Martianus Capella, Alan de Lille, Macrobius, and many others, what we find is a distinction between the pure mathematics of astronomy and the more convoluted version of it that considers the passions in the science of astrology. When there is a distinction between the two fields of astronomy and astrology among ancient and medieval texts, the passions are precisely the differentiating point. The texts that Chaucer most overtly imitates or translates in his *Treatise* do not address the passions. Rather, his most evidently primary sources adhere to a more pure mathematical form of investment in the knowledge of the cosmos.

Since Chaucer alters this lineage of treatise, first by stating that his goal is to "slay envy" (probably with the aid of Orion's sword), and second by halting his work before writing or inserting the mathematical tables of which his primary sources are composed, he varies the concept of the treatise itself, therefore asserting a different relationship between mathematics and the passions. The precise absence of the promised charts and tables from the *Treatise* reflects a statement regarding the significance of the form of knowledge and the ability to use the instrument of the astrolabe as more crucial than the display or potential memorization of the mathematical knowledge that can be charted. This absence suggests that even mathematical structures are imperfect, mutable, and particular. The form of knowledge that is most significant to the understanding of the cosmos is that which enables one to employ the astrolabe at one's will, rather than to determine one's will by virtue of complete mathematical formulae. This perspectival approach to knowledge particularizes it such that the subject may participate in a singular way within a broader and universal play in the cosmos. Universality itself is an abstraction that depends largely upon the way in which one uses the knowledge given and with the recognition of the imperfection and uncertainty inherent in that knowledge. Thus, when Chaucer discusses the difficulty of some topics and the unknowability of others, he contributes to the production of further knowledge, which is driven by a desire to know the unknown, but with an awareness of the limitations on knowledge.

What remains unclear is how Chaucer's *A Treatise on the Astrolabe*—in its incomplete form—succeeds or fails in offering the lesson that is intended to "slay envy." Does the absence of the universal forms of knowledge and the applications of the astrolabe to the broader cosmos solidify an understanding of the particular such that the universal is perceptible within the particular, therefore satisfying epistemophilia and sating desire for the external or universal? Or does the singularity of the lesson make a promise that is unfulfilled either because it is impossible to attain universal knowledge, because the teacher chooses not to provide it, or because the child, Lewis, is incapable of understanding it? In this latter case, do the limits of knowledge provided in the text further envy rather than foreclose it? In other words, does the absence of universality lead to an acceptance of uncertainty or strengthen the desire for knowledge and motivate envy?[37]

In "Arithmetic and the Mentality of Chaucer," Derek Brewer states that the value of mathematical language is that it can convey ideas that are incommunicable in other forms of language, including, most dominantly, linguistic efforts.[38] Mathematics cannot, however, convey the statement "I love you." According to Brewer,

Arithmetic is never thought of as an intrinsic element in a poet's mentality, and naturally so. The nature of arithmetic is to be impersonal, systematic, but empirical, independent of values and feelings. If number is a "language" as a modern view has it, because it is symbolic, it is not a language in which one can say "I love you." To think of arithmetic, and the associated activities of measurement and calculation, as a language is in this case, at least, misleading. It is a tool for manipulation and control, without intrinsic purpose or intention. ("Arithmetic," 156)

Since Brewer's point is that arithmetic is precisely an "intrinsic element in the poet's mentality," it is clear that he is distinguishing *mentality* from *drives* or *personality*. Chaucer's *mentality* contains certain forms of knowledge that he uses in his poetry to manipulate and control his meaning, to insert (according to Brewer's argument) intentionality into his poetry. Therefore, they are used to attain a certainty about observable events, but lack the potential for predication. This is one crucial limit of mathematics and the *matheme* against which Lacan struggles in his search for universals. Without paying what might be considered cynical attention to the moments and scenes of seduction when the phrase "I love you" could be described in the same words that Brewer gives to math ("measurement . . . calculation . . . manipulation . . . control, without [or even with] intrinsic purpose or intention"), one might consider instead the way in which "I love you" is as much a symbolic statement as the mathematical symbols that may or may not be able to characterize it. Since the phrase "I love you" is mutable and simultaneously particular and universalizing, it is also always already symbolic in nature as it captures that which cannot be signified — love. The potential for mathematical symbolization of the phrase, then, is an attempt to more accurately give meaning to the vagueness and uncertainty of the three elements of the statement itself, "I," "love," and "you." For Lacan, the *matheme* would potentially achieve the universal form of the statement "I love you," if only he could find the proper form in which this occurs. Many of Lacan's graphs are in fact attempts to display his progress toward this goal. They do not, however, document a finite achievement on his part.

Illustrating that Lacan does in fact achieve the mathematicization of the statement "I love you," in "The Scene of Two" Alain Badiou remathematizes Lacan's theory of desire, rendering possible the supplement of the statement "I *matheme* you" for "I love you."[39] Through his mathematization of the process of love and the impossibility of the sexual relationship *(rapport)*, Badiou suggests in the order of reflexivity that "all living singularity is related to itself; for transitivity, that all rapport goes through what Sartre named phenomena of seriality; for anti-symmetry, that there is never indifference of a singularity to its place in a rapport" ("Scene of Two," 47). What Badiou claims to be the "crucial thesis" here is that the relation between humans is precisely not one of relation at all. The *rapport* is always already necessarily particular, singular, and segregative or disjunctive—it is always already a *nonrapport*. Rather than take this as a limiting, negative view, however, what Badiou's mathematization of love reveals is the movement from singularity and apparent insularity to universality (much like the same move made by Kierkegaard when he claims that proper ethics become universal only when they are absolutely singular), is a movement that concretizes love by enabling its universalization. Love is then "the alternating movement of an external expansion of the Two, which constructs the scene, and of a return of the atomic object, which erases the two as such, but not exactly the virtual outline of its expansion" ("Scene of Two," 53). In other words, and in Badiou's concluding words, "Love is a thought" ("Scene of Two," 55).

If love is indeed a "thought," then its mathematization is certainly possible if mathematical notation accounts for the irrational qualities such as the square root of negative one. The *matheme* does not eliminate the element of passion from astronomy any more than it enables a universalization of love, desire, or knowledge. To return then to Lacan's pronouncement in *Encore* that mathematical writing provides a *compass* by which we can determine an understanding of desire, we find his approach to resemble that displayed by Chaucer in the *Treatise*. Recall, if you will, Lacan's statement:

> Since what is at stake for us is to take language as *(comme)* that which functions in order to make up for the absence of the sole part of the real that cannot manage to be formed from being *(se former de l'être)*— namely, the sexual relationship—what basis can we find in merely reading letters? It is in the very play of mathematical writing *(l'écrit)* that we must find the compass reading toward which to head in order to draw from this practice—from this new social link, analytic discourse, that emerges and spreads in such a singular fashion—what can be drawn from it regarding the function of language. (*Seminar XX*, 48)

To properly schematize desire and its process reveals a belief in the realism of the concept of desire. The awareness of the limitations of linguistic, semiotic, or mathematization of the abstract concept of desire coincides with the drive to continually represent it and pin it down in proper notation in a manner that reveals the impossibility of science to the realism that Lacan and Chaucer seek to achieve.

The apparently irreconcilable problems of historical epochs, the distinction of science as ancient or modern, and the potential for recognizing the unconscious within the "medieval mind" have solutions in the astrolabe itself, which can determine the *retrograde* effects of time and planetary influences as well as the parallel *retrograde* effect of desire in Lacan's graph. It is important to note here that this is not to say that these effects are empirically sound in a positivist manner; rather, the textual evidence of their roles as hinges upon which these arguments turn merits focus and provides evidence in their own presence.

Two potential responses to these questions of history and desire emerge from the juxtaposition of Chaucer's *A Treatise on the Astrolabe* with Lacan's theory of desire. First, one may foreground Chaucer's poetics. Second, one may examine the graph of desire in relation to the structures of the astrolabe and the process of retrograde significance. The first approach leads to a unique reading of *A Treatise on the Astrolabe* in that it takes the *Treatise* as its primary subject and uses the poetics to decode its pedagogical and moral goal of slaying envy in Lewis. This inverts the typical reading of the *Treatise* in conjunction with Chaucer's poetics, wherein the *Treatise* is employed to determine the accuracy or deficiencies of the astronomical and astrological references within the poetry. Since most readers of the *Treatise* who also consider *The Canterbury Tales,* or other Chaucerian texts, use it as a key to understanding the poetics, when that project is inverted and the poetics aid in an understanding of the prose *Treatise* we find that the idealization of science is replete with a concern for narrative.

The disciplinary lines that are clearly challenged by Chaucer's foray into the science of the astrolabe are maintained when one uses the *Treatise* as a key for understanding the map of the poetics. However, such boundaries are called into question if one considers the literariness of the scientific or pseudoscientific text. The second approach to these questions, one that rereads Lacan's graphs of desire against the *Treatise* and the history of the astrolabe, provides insight into the questions of periodicity and nonclassical thinking that are at stake in this chapter. Additionally, the juxtaposition of Lacan's idealization of the *matheme* with Chaucer's text illustrates an uncanny similarity between the structures of the cosmology described and determined by the astrolabe and the process of desire itself.

The retrograde effect is significant in both astronomical theory and Lacan's theory of desire. In astronomical theory, it refers to the movement of the planets out of their proscribed orbits as the proper trajectories would project them to move. In the moment of retrogression, the planet shifts an eastward trajectory and moves westward, returning after a quick loop to its eastward direction. In the process, the planet appears to slow its movement, stop, and then reverse its path.[40] Plato's contemporary Eudoxus was the first to define and detail the retrograde effect as he accounted for the way in which the same stars sometimes appeared brighter and sometimes more dim. When the planet is in its retrogressive moment, it appears brighter than when it is on a forward trajectory. Especially of interest as we compare this planetary retrogression to the process of desire and an approach to historiography is this phrase of Kuhn's: "a planet can retrogress only when its motion brings it nearest to the earth and that is the position in which the planet should and does appear brightest" (*Copernican Revolution*, 62).

In Lacanian theory, the retrograde occurs at the crucial turning point of desire, when the subject seeks to position himself in the world with respect to the signifier. The retrograde or retroversion allows the subject to announce himself as becoming what he will have been, asserting an interplay between the future, the past, and the present that displaces temporality and calls into question any linear form of subjective recognition. Further, desire is always already a retrograde effect as it is in response to the imagined voice of the other. As the subject asks of the other, within him or the external other, *Che vuoi?* "what do you want?" "what do you want *of me?*" the process of desire is always in response to a call and therefore always returning to the subject as an instantiation of the future within the present that is affected by the past; indeed, often the process of desire feels as though it is constructed by the past because it makes sense of its actions by way of the historical narrative of its subjective being. Such a play with temporality, combined with the real of the unconscious as a universal category, posits a nonclassical notion of the damage that periodicity or the imposition of epistemic breaks based on falsely determined epistemological cuts can do to forms of knowledge.

As Neugebauer points out in "On the Planetary Theory of Copernicus," with respect to scientific knowledge these epochal distinctions are based on the faulty recognition of difference in some scientific systems because the focus is limited to the level of symbolic notation. "Modern historians, making ample use of the advantage of hindsight, stress the revolutionary significance of the heliocentric system and the simplifications it had introduced. In fact, the actual computation of planetary positions follows exactly the ancient pattern and the results are the same" ("Planetary Theory," 505). Even more emphatically, he warns against false and hasty periodization of epistemological cuts in "Aspects of Early Greek Astronomy."

> That we could use sources from the Roman imperial period until deep into the Middle Ages is due to more than a lucky accident of preservation of antiquated material. The extreme simplicity of the arithmetical methods, their entanglement with *a priori* speculations of numerological character (politely called "pythagorean"), the lack of observational accuracy, all this makes early Greek astronomy ideally suited to the mental climate of the Middle Ages.
> Our results imply a strong warning against periodization of cultural history. (369) [41]

To consider the limits of the hard sciences in the articulation of desire, and to recognize the real that emerges from this fall from grace that the sciences experience in Lacan's system and in nonclassical thinking, is to begin to understand what it means to "take desire literally." The problem of a cosmological order that does not account for a divine presence, like God, but does admit the real of universals repeatedly hits the wall of reason and requires an element of faith. This all must occur, nonetheless, without an appeal to an Absolute Spirit, Unity, or Totality.

Aware of the pitfalls of Hegelian historiography (absolutism, tyranny, eschatology, etc.), Lacan reasserts his project to uncover the history of desire as it has been sublated within the history of knowledge. He defies the notion that history is universal and calls attention to the particularities of language in its narrative of the emotions and desire that drive actions. His pejorative use of the capitalized H in history associates absolutist history with the imposition of false meaning on narratives of the past.

> People do History precisely in order to make us believe that it has some sort of meaning. On the contrary, the first thing we must do is begin

from the following: we are confronted with a saying *(dire)*, the saying
(dire) of another person who recounts his stupidities, embarrassments,
inhibitions, and emotions *(émois)*. What is it that we must read therein?
Nothing but the effects of those instances of saying *(dires)*. We see in
what sense these effects agitate, stir things up, and bother speaking
beings. Of course, for that to lead to something, it must serve them,
and it does serve them, by God, in working things out, accommodating
themselves, and managing all the same — in a bumbling, stumbling
sort of way — to give a shadow of life to the feeling known as love.
(Seminar XX, 46)

The goal of a good history in Lacan's terms is clearly imbricated with a
linguistic account (written or spoken) of desire and love. His refusal to
find "meaning" in the historical narratives that present themselves as
accounts of events displaces signification onto the moment of desire.
The attention Lacan calls to the struggle to articulate desire reflects the
textual process that constructs his historiographical ideas.

In her reading of Lacan's historiography, Teresa Brennan finds in his
writings a master/slave dialogue between the subject and its culture.
In *History after Lacan* she claims that although Lacan does not adhere
strictly to Hegelianism, he does rely on the dialectic to determine the
effects of historical events on the subject.[42] She finds in Lacan's reading
of history and subjectivity a difference between the psychical fantasy as
it is narrated and the event itself.

Despite his almost postmodern aspersions on grand theories of history,
Lacan has a fledgling one nestling in his work. It builds on the Hegelian
master-slave dialectic. Like Marx, Lacan reverses some of Hegel's implications. But he does not stand Hegel on his head. Rather, he turns him
back to front. If history led anywhere, it was to the "ego's era." Lacan
discards any Hegelian optimism about progress to higher moments as
history unfolds, or the "appeal to any tomorrow" (Lacan 1953b, 80). For
Lacan, "the problem is knowing whether the Master-Slave conflict will
find its resolution in the service of the machine." *(History after Lacan, 8)*

Brennan's insistence that Lacan's historiography follows the dialectical
model accounts for only one aspect of his view of history. By revealing
the limits of the dialectic in his outline of desire, Lacan also implicitly
proposes a consideration of history that, like desire and signification,
assumes the form of a knot.

The function of signification and desire in any historiographical process must be considered on the level of historical narrative. Joan Copjec

places the import of Lacan's historiography on the literary event. In *Read My Desire* Copjec sets out to find the cause of desire and to distinguish Lacan's historiography from Foucault's in order to call attention to the way in which Lacan's theory aids in cultural analysis.[43] Her notion that the literary event is as powerful within the culture industry as the "historical" event calls attention to the textual quality of history. "For if it is desire rather than words that we are to take literally...This is a truth that cannot be tolerated by historicism, which refuses to believe in repression and proudly professes to be illiterate in desire" (*Read My Desire*, 14). The question Copjec raises inserts desire into the process of writing history. To take desire "literally" means to engage the symptoms it renders within the process of signification and to account for historical narrative with the knowledge that gaps in explication will always undermine the attempt at coherence and meaning. From Copjec's reading of Lacan's historiography, we perceive how desire is imbricated with historical narrative. The literary event, as such, constructs the historicity of desire while simultaneously calling it into question.

Lacan's medievalism is dependent upon the relationship between the history of language and the impossibility of writing categorical reals. His assertion that "we should approach things at the level of the history of each language" (*Seminar XX*, 36) grants import to the diverse histories behind cultural paradigms and their impact on the conceptions and practices of sexuality. At the level of the limit, the history of the French language finds its views of sexuality most explicitly in courtly love poetics. The early use of various vernacular languages to articulate desire distinguishes courtly love from divine forms of love addressed to God and stated in Latin. Lacan's historiography, depending on the vernacular performance of desire, vacillates between perceiving History as monumental or absolute and as contingent upon discourses of desire.[44]

> To raise such questions is the habitual function of History. One should say — above all, don't touch that H, the initial of History. That would be a fine way of bringing people back to the first of the letters, the one to which I confine my attention, the letter A. The Bible begins, by the way, only with the letter B — it left behind the letter A so that I could take charge of it. (*Seminar XX*, 46)

The "charge" that Lacan takes over the letter "A" is, of course, his play with the *objet a*, the cause and limit of desire. Here, Lacan's use of the capital "H" in History shifts away from monumental or Hegelian absolutist history and implies the excess involved in any historiographical process. The insertion of the "A" simultaneously referring to the *autre* and the *object a* of Lacan's theory of desire reveals the imbrication of his historiographical process with the articulation of desire. The surplus that the letter insists upon with the fields of historiography and desire leaves the H intact but alters its function. This view of history is inflected by Lacan's medievalism, which takes on the form of constructing a view of love that enables the subject to express polymorphous desire and sexuality. The idealization of mathematics takes Lacan closer to an articulation of his object of desire; however it also reflects the limits of signification on any level.

In a properly classical system, an analysis of *Antigone* and Lacan's reading of the tragedy find the appeal to the divine order to conflict with, supercede, or untie the laws of humans. As the play has been the topic of numerous critiques that display much about the relationship between politics and desire, subjectivity, kinship, and the moral order, I am going to limit this analysis to show the way in which *Antigone,* as a pedagogical example of the zone between the two deaths, functions in Lacan's work as an example of nonclassical in the classical.

A crucial aspect of Lacan's medievalism central to the development and articulation of his theory of desire is presented textually through his pedagogical analogies. Lacan often refers to texts from the Middle Ages as a means of teaching his theories. Throughout the course of his seminars, Lacan's use of analogy, wherein he states that a particular theory works like a specific text, performs an application of the theory to the text he mentions. The moment between the two deaths functions within Lacan's general formulation of desire as a concept that relies on particular readings of premodern texts, rendering his pedagogy and historiography intricately related to the theory of desire.

Put briefly and reductively, the two deaths are a mode of existing in relation to the self that perceives the self as already dead, such that physical death is an end to a life of fragmented subjectivity. The two deaths provide a conceptual intersection for Lacan's discussion of desire and tragedy. They also reveal a temporal play among abstract methods of viewing the subject that lend significance to Lacan's medievalism. Forms of historiography that persist without the conceptual framework of the two deaths will maintain a view, however limited, of history as potentially real. The two deaths contribute to historiography a sense that the past is always already impossible to represent, not simply because it is irretrievable, but also because subjectivity itself exists in a zone of phantasmatic relation to itself. Lived experiences that recognize the disjunction between coherence and fragmentation defined by the two deaths also accept that what is called real is the limit of desire. The retrograde effect so significant to the astronomical system and to the system of desire is also at play in the moment between the two deaths and Lacan's approach to *Antigone*.

Since Lacan's own theory is worked out by way of application, it is important in this chapter to examine the possibilities of the move between analogy and application, a dynamic that imitates the moment between the two deaths. Pedagogical analogy and the application of a theoretical concept to a text reinforce an interlocutor's understanding of an abstract concept. Outside of the pedagogical arena, analogy and application provide a methodological means of engaging disciplines and ideas that seem otherwise distinct and unrelated. Since Lacan's work is usually focused on an abstract subject but often digresses in the forms of examples that reveal or demonstrate that subject, application and analogy are crucial aspects of his methodology. Whereas Lacan's explication of desire as a broad concept (and aspects of it including sublimation and *jouissance*) focuses on medieval texts and their literary and philosophical contexts, his pedagogical example for the concept of between the two deaths extends further back in history to a classical text — *Antigone*.

If, as I argue throughout this project, Lacan's theory of desire is intricately woven into his implicit medievalism, why then does a crucial aspect of desire require an example from the classical period? Does Lacan's medievalism lose a form of systematicity that would be required to make this argument complete and persuasive? Are Lacan's other examples from the Middle Ages then simply convenient for him? Or are they symptomatic of his debt to Freud such that he, as the child, studies what comes after the subject of the father? Are the medieval and the classical periods conflated in Lacan's theory of desire? Or is there something fundamental to the concept of between the two deaths that requires a classical example where other aspects of desire require examples from the Middle Ages? Once Lacan has used an example of a classical text, is he not paving the way for applications of the theory to other texts, produced later in history? Would another text, and a medieval one at that, have provided a clearer example of what has been one of the more confounding psychoanalytical concepts within academic discourse? Or is there a crucial feature of a medievalist project that gains integrity by referring to the classical period?[45] Even further, is there an inherent non-classical element within the appropriation of the classical within medieval ideological and textual systems?

These questions begin to address the difference between Lacan's systematic medievalism and a project that simply refers to medieval texts as moments of textual and conceptual exemplification. They lead, of course, to many other questions regarding periodization and the location of authority and clarity in the distant past. They are questions that arise from a consideration of the very concept of the space and time between the two deaths as it is articulated in the context of Lacan's reading of Sophocles' *Antigone*.[46]

Lacan devoted the spring of 1960 to studying *Antigone* and the question of tragedy. His three seminars "The Splendor of Antigone," "The Articulations of the Play," and "Antigone Between the Two Deaths" are sandwiched between his seminar on *jouissance* ("The Paradox of *Jouissance*") and a consideration of the role of ethics within the praxis of psychoanalysis ("The Tragic Dimension of Analytical Experience"). The organization of these seminars is significant because it reveals the placement of the classical age between Lacan's consideration of desire, the Middle Ages, and the movement from the abstract to the practical. According to this organizational pattern, one must move from a reading of desire that takes place in the literary context of the Middle Ages to a reading of the praxis of the psychoanalytical treatment by way of the classical period. The distant past (the classical) stands between the premodern and the modern (or postmodern) as a necessary detour.

A second view of this organizational pattern would suggest that Lacan's reading of desire must travel from the Middle Ages to the classical period as a means of gaining the authority necessary to formulate his own theory of treatment. Since Freud relied heavily on classical texts for his development of a treatment methodology, in order to contribute his thoughts Lacan must demonstrate his ability to perform a similar textual analysis. This second view is also in line with medievalist methodology as well as historiographical practice during the Middle Ages, both of which depend largely on an ability to refer to the distant past as authoritative.

The desire to display knowledge of texts considered valuable because they are ancient is displayed by Lacan's choice of a textual example that has been the object of interrogation by others whom he seeks to emulate — including, most obviously, Hegel and Freud. Lacan begins his discussion of *Antigone* by indirectly invoking those with whom he wants to be considered an intellectual peer.

> I am not the one who has decreed that *Antigone* is to be a turning point in the field that interests us, namely ethics. People have been aware of that for a long time. And even those who haven't realized this are not unaware of the fact that there are scholarly debates on the topic. Is there anyone who doesn't evoke *Antigone* whenever there is a question of a law that causes conflict in us even though it is acknowledged by the community to be a just law?
>
> And what is one to think of the scholars' contribution to the discussion of *Antigone*? What is one to think of it when one has, like me, gone over the ground for one's own interest and for the interest of those one is speaking to?[47]

The generality of references to *Antigone* places Lacan's discussion within a broad historical framework of analyses of ethics. Knowledge of the text is limited not only to those auditors familiar with scholarly discourse on the subject, but extends to any person who has considered the role of ethics within daily life. Lacan employs the authority of Sophocles' text to reach a broad audience of auditors. The conflict addressed by a reading of *Antigone* extends his argument to any auditor who has felt a sense of rebellion against the laws of society. This rebellious instinct presages Lacan's own commentary on the vast array of scholarship on the play. Lacan invokes a subject that brings authority to his topic by means of association, simultaneously inserting a question into the precise authoritative possibility of that association.

Lacan's answer to this problem of historical authority is to provide a genealogy of criticism on *Antigone* and ethics.

> Well now, while I have tried to omit nothing that seemed important in all that has been said on the question, so as not to deprive either you or me of this help that I might derive from this lengthy historical survey, I have nevertheless often had the impression that I was lost in quite extraordinary byways. One learns that the opinions formulated by the pens of our great thinkers over the centuries are strange indeed. (*Seminar VII*, 243)

To state that the thoughts of those he is employing as a means of authority are "strange" is to insert a criticism of those thoughts as well as of their position as authoritative. Lacan looks to the authorities (past scholars) for assistance and guidance in his foray into the field of ethics and finds, like Dante guided by Virgil, that his sources further confound him rather than provide a direct response to his questions. His own response is to rebel against the vast scholarly discourse on the subject and to inaugurate his own reading of the play.

Notably, within the first few moments of his summary of the criticism about *Antigone*, Lacan returns to a medievalist position. Moving from the word *catharsis*, Lacan invokes the Cathars, the medieval group central to his articulation of *jouissance*.[48] "What are the Cathars? They are the pure. Catharsis is a pure person. And the word in its original sense doesn't mean illumination or discharge, but purification" (*Seminar VII*, 245). More than a mere homonym, the transition from *catharsis* to *Cathars* signifies the movement from the classical period back to the Middle Ages, the primary locale for Lacan's articulation of his theory of desire. Its reinsertion into his discussion of a classical text marks a return to the Middle Ages as he approaches a discussion of between the two deaths and its relevance to desire. Further, Lacan finds the medieval aspect of the classical elements of tragedy when he extends his homonymic connection to affect his reading of the classical play.

> Doubtless in classical antiquity, too, the term "catharsis" was already used in a medical context, in Hippocrates, for example, with a specifically medical meaning; it is linked to forms of elimination, to discharge, to a return to normality. But, on the other hand, in other contexts it is linked to purification and especially to ritual purification. Hence the ambiguity which we, as you might suspect, are far from the first to discover. (*Seminar VII*, 245)

Eliminating the classical period in general as an authoritative source, Lacan in turn invokes the authority of the "science" of medicine and, again, a group of scholars whose knowledge of etymology would support his observation. The unique quality of this passage, instead, lies in its vacillation between classical antiquity and the Middle Ages. He alters the pattern of authoritative systems by invoking the Cathars as a citational source in a context that would require further discussion of the classical period. The movement within this introductory seminar on *Antigone* from classical to medieval, and then back to the classical, reveals the power of the Middle Ages in Lacan's theory of desire as well as his need to maintain a difference as an author who discusses the past in a manner that defies and confounds strict periodization. The classical need not influence the medieval in a linear manner; rather, the medieval can also remind us of aspects of the classical period that have been overlooked or forgotten. Perhaps even more significantly, intersecting both discussions of the tragedy of *Antigone* is the formulation of Lacan's theory of desire.

From the question of tragedy and ethics, Lacan quickly moves back to the topic of desire. He states, "In effect, *Antigone* reveals to us the line of sight that defines desire" (*Seminar VII*, 247). Lacan continues this hypothesis by addressing the tragedy of *Antigone* by way of the character Antigone's beauty and the beauty associated with the terror of the uncanny.[49] This "zone" between horror and beauty is central to the genre of tragedy; it is also representative of the sublime as the link between Lacan's discussions of tragedy and desire.

> It is when passing through that zone that the beam of desire is both reflected and refracted till it ends up giving us that most strange and most profound of effects, which is the effect of beauty on desire.
>
> It seems to split desire strangely as it continues on its way, for one cannot say that it is completely extinguished by the apprehension of beauty. It continues on its way, but now more than elsewhere, it has a sense of being taken in, and this is manifested by the splendor and magnificence of the zone that draws it on. On the other hand, since its excitement is not refracted but reflected, rejected, it knows it to be most real. But there is no longer any object. (*Seminar VII*, 248)[50]

The "zone" being invoked here is the space and time between the two deaths. Lacan does not state this until *Seminar XX* when he discusses "Antigone Between the Two Deaths." However, his explication of the "zone" in which desire is the plaything of beauty and an object (real or imaginary, present or absent) mirrors his explication of the concept of between the two deaths. Most succinctly, this articulation appears thus: "from Antigone's point of view life can only be approached, can only be lived or thought about, from the place of that limit where her life is already lost, where she is already on the other side. But from that place she can see it and live it in the form of something already lost" (*Seminar VII*, 280). This "zone" between life and death requires the acceptance of the self as already dead, as observing the self from a distant place, indeed, from a place that is most real and from which place the object itself disappears. Therein lies the connection between tragedy and desire for Lacan's theory. Or, as Lacan puts it, "In effect, Antigone herself has been declaring from the beginning: 'I am dead and I desire death'" (*Seminar VII*, 281). This latter statement, however, is the sort that leads to misinterpretation of the state of Being between the two deaths.

Common readings of the psychoanalytic concept of the space and time between the two deaths, as formulated by Freud and clarified by Lacan, rely on various images popular to our late twentieth-century cultural medievalism. A few of these tropes are

- Gothic figures speaking as phantoms from beyond the grave.[51]
- The warrior reminiscent of the Green Knight in *Sir Gawain and the Green Knight,* whose physicality seems to be disconnected from the continuity of his life and can be damaged, broken, dismembered, and severed without causing death to the subject.
- The rampant Dracula figures representing the "undead," who commodify the living and must be killed with the spiritual aid of God.[52]

These readings of the two deaths involve interesting concepts and may effectively problematize notions of history, capitalism, religion, and repetition. However, their adherence to a notion of dialectical play between the two deaths leads to a definition that is perhaps better marked by the uncanny than the moment between the two deaths that involves a knot-like temporality more labyrinthine and inarticulable than the dialectical form of the uncanny.[53]

For Lacan, the inability to express oneself in language during a state of mourning leads the subject in question to feel as though time has stopped. The space between the two deaths emerges as difficult to convey precisely because it relies on a concept for which one has no words, and for which time does not progress. In Lacan's formulation, "This relationship to being (the second death) suspends everything that has to do with transformation, with the cycle of generation and decay or with history itself, and it places us on a level that is more extreme than any other insofar as it is directly attached to language as such" (*Seminar VII*, 285). The suspension and sublation of being is necessary to the focus on language and signification as a beginning point from which to explore gaps in meaning and desire. Brought specifically to the crucial realm of language, the analyst becomes a literary critic who reads the words of the patient sifting out the fictional from the real, the legible from the illegible, and striving to comprehend the way in which the most apparently superfluous words contribute to significance. Clearly, Lacan as analyst is also Lacan as literary critic.

The centrality of *Antigone* to philosophical and psychoanalytical history makes it a logical example for Lacan to employ when discussing the concept of between the two deaths. As he states, however, other examples perhaps demonstrate the idea more clearly than the highly charged classical play by Sophocles. "The dimension involved here is not unique to *Antigone*. I could suggest that you look in a number of places and you will find something analogous without having to search too hard. The zone defined in that way has a strange function in tragedy" (*Seminar VII*, 248). Often, Lacan's statements do suggest other texts wherein the student may find an analogous text for the concept being explicated. Here, Lacan's silence indicates his apparent reluctance to extend his application of theory to a medieval text. For, as is indicated by his reference to the Middle Ages so early on in this seminar, examples of the "zone" between the two deaths abound in medieval literature.

To repeat Lacan's words at the beginning of his use of *Antigone* as a pedagogical example for the concept of between the two deaths, "The dimension involved here is not unique to *Antigone*. I could suggest that you look in a number of places and you find something analogous without having to search too hard. The zone defined in that way has a strange function in tragedy" (*Seminar VII*, 248). Although elsewhere Lacan provides alternative examples for his students to uncover, here he remains silent and leaves the process of search and discovery to the student. The concept of between the two deaths links Lacan's historiographical, literary, theoretical, and treatment-oriented ideas. To remain on the level of the historico-literary for the time being, Lacan's seminar "Antigone Between the Two Deaths" is perhaps the most overtly classically oriented among those published.[54] The movement from medievalism to classicism within this discussion of the "zone" between the two deaths imitates Lacan's approach to history that resists linear eschatology. Between the two deaths and a historiography of desire that depends largely on a reading of medieval texts require a metacritical approach to pedagogical analogy and the forms of application that accompany it.

This framework of application serves to remind the scholar of the imbrication between tragedy and desire. In both cases, sublimation is at work.

Lacan's dependence on the Middle Ages for his articulation of desire reveals that despite the "discovery" of the unconscious in the nineteenth century, its persistence was already embedded in the medieval mind. Subjectivity in the Middle Ages has been denied a complex psychological framework due to its overt dependence upon God and a Christian cosmology. Lacan's theory of desire reveals that these dependencies assert and attest to an awareness of the unconscious. As Lacan works through the history of courtly love, his focus on sublimation and the limits of desire and language presents a new reading of courtly love as a philosophical phenomenon that, due to its inconsistencies and paradoxes, resists generalities of purity and barbarity typically associated with the Middle Ages. Certainly *Antigone* holds more weight in the general scheme of the history of knowledge among those who do not specialize in studying the Middle Ages. Additionally, the study of *Antigone* places Lacan's discussion within an ostensibly "global" discussion of desire. Nonetheless, at its kernel, Lacan's reading of *Antigone* coalesces around his concern with the desire that is evident in texts that are precisely medieval, and not classical.

What then is the difference between desire as it appears in the Middle Ages and desire as it appears in the classical? The topics of love and sexuality have been the source of much discussion among scholars in the past thirty years (and indeed, throughout history). The topic of desire, however, is often folded into those two topics that lend themselves to speculation about practice. To maintain a separate category for desire means of course to claim that love and sexuality can often exist without desire. Though this claim may hold up only for an instance, it is within that instance that Lacan seeks to investigate desire. The interstices in which the moment or instance of desire can occur are limited to the ability to thwart or limit sublimation. Once sublimation occurs within the process of desire, that desire is occluded by the secondary impulse that emanates from it.

The classical element present in the medieval system of knowledge about the order of the cosmos and desire does not preclude nonclassical thinking. The very indeterminacy of the astrolabe that Chaucer gives to Lewis as a pseudoscientific means for controlling his passion of envy, for satisfying his *envie*, his desire, reflects a nonclassical moment. The retrograde effect of the planets and desire cause creases in the fabric of knowledge that reveal its status as baroque.[55] Additionally, Lacan's seemingly interminable and certainly obsessive play with knots in his attempt to untie the knots of language, the unconscious, and desire reflect the nonclassical elements in his thought. All of this points to the difficulty of determining meaning and the centrality that language and the symbolic order play in the pedagogical process, taking us back to Lacan's problem with Socrates and showing how, in the real of virtue (like the real of the unconscious) something is lost when we try to explain it.

CHAPTER FIVE

The Pentangle and the Resistant Knot

> Poetry is a sort of inspired mathematics, which gives us equations, not for abstract figures, triangles, spheres, and the like, but equations for human emotions.
>
> —Ezra Pound, *The Spirit of Romance*

The perfect circle of the five-pointed pentangle shares the knot-like structure of the unconscious and its resistance. Resistance is in psychoanalysis and it is necessary to the function of the psyche and the knot of language. The pentangle and the knot additionally resist cutting or untying, and analysis will remain a symptom of the navel of the real of the unconscious.[1] As Elizabeth Scala has shown, resistance among medievalists to psychoanalysis is yet another symptomatic example of the fact that psychoanalysis is in textual criticism.[2] In teaching and in writing about theory and literature the questions always return: Why read? Why write? Regardless of our analytical approaches to texts and the ideological agendas that we bring to our work, we read and write to get beyond the limits of the navel of the text; we seek to untie and analyze the resistant core of textuality.

Reminding us as theorists to return to poetry, Avital Ronell suggests that the mathematization and logical analytics of theory have overtaken the focus of theory, which initially began with an understanding of the very relationship between poetry and philosophy. She warns, "the misery of theory without poetry is an event whose measure still has to be taken."[3]

By calling for a return to poetry and the richness offered by poetic language, Ronell opens a discussion within the state of critical theory. In this sense, medievalists are already leading innovative scholarship even as we bemoan our belated status with regard to our object of inquiry. The work done by medievalists (including that of Lacan) has always remained within the realm of the poetic, even as it has become increasingly engaged in contributing new ideas to theoretical discussions. Perhaps this is largely due to the focus on the word, etymology, and repetition that are equally important in the study of medieval literature and theoretical texts.[4] It is also, however, due to the persistent perception that language both approaches and resists the boundaries of knowledge. As medievalists, theory is embedded in the work of reading poetics.

In chapter 4 I distinguished between Lacan's concept of the zone between the two deaths and the representation of the uncanny often associated with the Green Knight's decapitation in the beginning of *Sir Gawain and the Green Knight*.[5] Gawain's resistance to courtly love and the sovereign law of the double contract that he makes with the Green Knight/Bercilak reflect his desire to defend himself against split consciousness. When he feigns sleep in the bedroom he creates distance and an obstacle central to courtly love and he simultaneously puts up a barrier against the play of the courtly love dynamic; when he lies to Bercilak and does not give him the garter, he asserts resistance to the proper order of the game. His resistance to the demands of the two court systems of Arthur and Bercilak give way to his search for solace in the value of his own life; it is in this sense that Gawain exists between the two deaths. The perfect infinity displayed by the pentangle that he wears on his shield does not provide the mathematical proof necessary for his understanding of his own existence in relation to others. Neither does the garter, which supplements the pentangle and seems to replace the perfect knot with a more complex knot fabricated of holiness as well as desire, solve the search for his whole identity. Rather, what both of these knot-like objects represent is that the knot itself is merely a symbol, a symptomatic representation of the fact that the navel of the unconscious cannot be known in any manner other than through the symptom.

Similarly, this concluding chapter will investigate the overlapping structure of the desire to resist desire seen in *Sir Gawain and the Green*

Knight and the memoirs of Daniel Paul Schreber. Both texts work under the retrograde signification of the motto, "Honi soi qui mal y pense."[6] The textual cases of Gawain and Schreber reflect the way in which the unconscious symptomatically emerges as a real; they also show how hysteria, paranoia, and mysticism are discursive forces that are bound together in the discourse of analysis. Most importantly, these two cases of overt resistance to the dynamics of courtly love demonstrate the impenetrability of the navel at the core of the analytical knot. It is no wonder that Lacan drove himself crazy attempting to find the proper cut in the knot; in fact, he was pursuing a detour that would never quite get him to the unanalyzable element of the real. He was, in a sense, unconsciously fooling himself into believing that he could properly represent what he consciously knew to be the limits of knowability, effability, and analysis. And this is the paradox of the real: it is, on some fundamental level, taken in faith even while it denies belief.

Beyond the name given to it or as defined by Freud and Lacan, the unconscious exists as a real. As Lacan argues in *Television,* the hysteric's discourse is a limit case wherein we find the unconscious displayed overtly; as a limit case, it also serves to call attention to that which is less overt, less obvious, and more difficult to discern, but nonetheless still present, textually and in the real. As Amy Hollywood notes, "The real is also tied to the symptom and hence to hysteria. From Charcot to Irigaray, hysteria and mysticism are linked by this convergence in the real."[7] Structured like a knot, the unconscious also displays a potential for a geometric understanding. However, within the paranoid subject, the unconscious is not merely a knot, but a knot with a "resistant nucleus" as Lacan says in the "Introduction to the Question of the Psychoses" in *Seminar III, The Psychoses.*[8] As a limit case of the expression and repression of the unconscious, paranoia is the inversion of hysteria, suggesting that an understanding of hysteria is important to the articulation of paranoia. Freud even went so far as to mark a sexual difference between the two categories when he said that only men could be paranoid psychotics and only women could be hysterics. This false categorization of the attribution of disease to humans based on an anatomical mode of determining sexual difference falls apart in the face of the human subject seeking to make sense of the order of the world. The limits of analysis are confronted in the hysteric and the paranoid psychotic subject, illustrating the manner in which the unconscious escapes proper articulation.

Scientific discourse, as a mode of attempting to articulate the ineffable, is central to an understanding of the limits of analysis; however, even scientific and mathematical systems have proven to be inadequate to the location of certainty with regard to the unconscious or other unknowable systems. The question of scientific discourse, language as mathematical, calculable, measurable, and determinate, is also a limit case wherein the conceptual real is approached through an impossibly and overdetermined play with signifiers. To the self-addressed question, "what distinguishes scientific discourse from the hysteric's discourse?" Lacan says, "I conclude that scientific discourse and the hysteric's discourse have *almost* the same structure."[9] The *almost* is significant as a mode of difference in the established parallel, but it appears to fall out of the remainder of the statement that explains why we cannot signify the unconscious: "which explains our error, induced by Freud himself, in hoping that one day there would be a thermodynamic able to provide—within the future of science—the unconscious with its posthumous explanation" (*Television*, 23).

The obstacle to the articulation of the unconscious is fundamentally based on the fact that the unconscious is comprised of energy, which is not a substance, but a "numerical constant that a physicist has to find in his calculations to be able to work.... Without this constant, which is merely a combination of calculations . . . you have no more physics . . . energy is nothing other than the numerical value *(chiffre)* of a constant" (*Television*, 22). In terms of the potential to *signify* energy, Lacan is being direct with regard to the ultimate failure of language and mathematics; however, his awareness of this failure also points to the way in which the energy of the drives, and their transformation and processing that occur in and create the unconscious, is precisely inarticulable. As such, the unconscious is evident in the various forms of language, mathematical, logical, or poetic, hysterical, scientific, or psychotic, that display the textuality of the psyche.

The discourse of the psychotic is the inverse of the discourse of the hysteric.[10] Where the psychotic projects symptoms onto the Other, the hysteric internalizes symptoms into the self. The hyperrational language of the psychotic does not appear to reveal the unconscious at all.

Everything is conscious and rational, and language is precisely logical and ordered when spoken or written by the psychotic; yet, psychotic speech takes on a fictional quality because the signifier does not properly refer to the thing itself. In this sense, all language has an element of psychosis that does not admit for the possibility of the real.

We have seen how, despite his awareness that the knot of the unconscious cannot be cut in a singular place and so rectified into a properly organized string, Lacan struggled to untie the knot to the point of his symptomatic call to his friend, "Please come to see me, I'm going crazy." The irony, of course, of the moment of going crazy while attempting to solve the riddle of the unconscious should not be lost, nor should it be minimized. The sacrifice that Lacan makes of his own conscious knowledge of the limits of knowledge in his attempt to uncover the secret of the unconscious reveals his precise determination to locate the real in reality.

This chapter seeks to address the question of the obviousness of the presence of the unconscious during the Middle Ages by way of *Sir Gawain and the Green Knight* and the problem of lovesickness. Gawain's refusal to play into the system of courtly love and its expectations reveals that, like the letter in Lacan's "Seminar on the Purloined Letter," the unconscious always arrives.[11] Whether the conscious decision to allow desire into its realm is made or not, desire seeks to display and perform its self-perpetuation in the subject. In this sense, *Sir Gawain and the Green Knight* is an exemplary text of the presence of the unconscious in medieval literature. The representation of the knot of desire, illustrated primarily by the significance of the pentangle in the tale, but also by Gawain's feigned sleep and his ultimate lie to Bercilak, displays the symptomatic longing to play a game that will allow him access to an understanding of the order of the world. The distrust of the very notion that the letter will always arrive leads Gawain to play at the hide-and-seek of the Fort/Da game. Of course, one will always simultaneously lose and win this game for the effort, since the effort itself proves the point that is being tested, revealing the extent to which the unconscious is present even when it is in hiding. In contrast to these revelations of the unconscious, the hysteric's fear that the unconscious will certainly be revealed leads to perversions that seek to hide its failings, laying bare the rawness of the unconscious in that process. In the interest of desexualizing hysteria and psychosis, we can then reconsider Gawain as a figure who is evidence of both disorders in one character, therefore degendering, or double-gendering Gawain.[12]

The Endless Knot

The "endeles knot" of the pentangle presented on Sir Gawain's shield ("þerfore on his schene schelde shapen watz þe knot")[13] in the history of criticism on *Sir Gawain and the Green Knight* has long represented Sir Gawain's connection with the divine and honor. As a symbol of infinity, the pentangle also represents the importance of the number five, which was shown in Boethius's *De Arithmetica* to be one of a few "circular numbers."[14] In his award-winning essay "The Gödel in *Gawain*," David Baker points to the pentangle and the girdle as the two symbols of paradox in the text, and rightly sees that paradox is ultimately an interwoven knot.[15] Baker follows Ross Arthur's work on medieval sign theory to reproduce the ways in which the pentangle is an image of "endless self-replication" in order to show how the pentangle is central to the display of paradox in the poem, and with reference to understanding the world order, he states that "the pentangle is the closest any 'real-world' shape comes to being paradoxical. For it is also symbolically, although not technically, infinite since its numerical and geometrical self-replication could be continued 'usque in infinitum'" ("Gödel in *Gawain*," 358). Baker also suggests that the pentangle is then similar to the description of the triangle so central to Nicholas of Cusa's concept of God and infinity. "For in the Christian tradition, Christ must be both entirely human and entirely divine, just as Nicholas of Cusa points out that an infinite circle must also be an infinite triangle simultaneously" ("Gödel in *Gawain*," 359). We are returned, then, to a discussion of dialectics — the pentangle, like the triangle, is a representation of the spherical manner in which dialectics give way to a knot-like structure.

The pentangle represents the geometric possibility of infinity, pointing implicitly toward a connection between the human and divine orders. Boethius explains the significance of the number five as a circular number in *De Arithmetica:*

> Nam quinquies quinque, qui fit 25, ab 5 progressus, in eosdem 5 desinit. Et si hos rersum quinquies ducas, in eosdem 5 eorum terminus veniet. Quinquies 25 fiunt 125, et si hoc rursis quinquies ducas, in quinarium numerum extremitas terminabitur. Atque hoc usque in infinitum idem semper evenit.[16]

[For 5 times 5, which makes 25, starts from 5 and ends in the same number, 5. And if you multiply that by 5 again, the end turns out to be 5
again. For 5 times 25 makes 125, and if you multiply by 5 again, the answer
will end with the number 5. And this always happens up to infinity.]

The question at stake with regard to a discussion of the presence of universal categories without the simultaneous presence of a divine power
leads us to wonder how it is possible to conceive of infinity without
conceiving of God. It is not possible to conceive of God without the concept of infinity, and this is one of the reasons that the medieval scholastics worked so diligently to produce a proof of infinity; however, it is
possible to conceive of infinity without a conception of a God that would
be thought to have caused or enabled this infinity. If infinity simply
exists, then it does not owe a debt to a creator and so potentially exists
ex nihilo. In this sense, the significance of the number as a referent for
symbolic infinity might be transferred to a process by which we consider
the unconscious in the order of the world.

As Lacan struggles to articulate the unconscious he demonstrates
that we must not be satisfied by recognizing a paradox; we must struggle
to make sense of it even if we encounter obstacles, aporias, and impossibilities. Therefore, we must *begin* with the paradox and move toward
an articulation of its knotted structure. Baker recognizes this necessity
when he says, "the shield's image is not the sign of Sir Gawain himself,
but rather the symbol of the paradoxical quest he is undertaking. So the
pentangle naturally disappears when the quest is completed: another
symbol is found" ("Gödel in *Gawain*," 359). Identifying this "paradoxical quest" as evidence of the struggle of the Gawain poet to display the
unconscious as real foregrounds the significance as well as the arbitrari-
ness of the image of the pentangle. In the quest for an articulation of
the unconscious, we shift from the mathematical and theological knot
to the textuality of the sexual knot symbolized by the girdle.

The girdle, illustrated as another form of a knot, braided and materially woven to construct the combination of material and spiritual connection, of course, serves in *Sir Gawain and the Green Knight* as another
symbol of Gawain's knotted unconscious.[17] Its difference from the pentangle is evident in its status as a gift that is to be hidden rather than
worn or flaunted on the shield. It is also the symbol of sexuality and, as
in Marie de France's *Guigemar*, recalls the love-knot that binds two lovers.
Rather than reflect a strong connection to the Lady in *Sir Gawain and*

the Green Knight, however, the implication of the love-knot in this case gestures toward a representation of Gawain's understanding that desire is embedded in the unconscious, which is structured like a knot and like language. The textuality or texturality of the braided girdle, then, calls attention to the multiplicity of the poem's narratives in a manner that Baker attributes to Gawain's recognition of paradox as he cites Helen Cooper's discussion of the changing perspectives in the poem. Cooper writes that "The poet plays games with points of view throughout the poem, sometimes, as here, insisting that the poem is no more than a story that he has heard or read, at other times placing himself within the narrative as if he were present, or indeed within the protagonist's mind."[18] Despite arguments that we can perceive the thoughts within Gawain's mind at times in the poem, the perception of this as evidence of the unconscious during the Middle Ages has not been forwarded.[19] Even more crucial than the symbols of the knot and the girdle themselves is their role in demonstrating the knot-like structure of the unconscious and the manner in which the courtly text reflects the tethering of the unconscious to desire.

The order of the pentangle symbolizes the divine order of the world that marks Gawain's epistemological and ontological systems. The multiple fives on his shield reflect the play with the number as an infinite system that Boethius has shown. His five senses and five fingers are faultless as is his faith (*Sir Gawain,* II.640–45). The circularity of the pentangle is perfect:

> Now all of these five pentads favorably pertained to this knight,
> And each one united with the other so that none had an end,
> And fixed upon five points that never failed,
> Or never settled the same on any side, or severed either,
> Without an end at any corner, anywhere to be found,
> Wherever the design started or proceeded to a point.
> Therefore, on his shiny shield, shaped was the knot,
> Royally, with red gold upon red gules;
> It is proclaimed the perfect pentangle by the people
> With lore. (*Sir Gawain,* II.656–65)

Perfection is indeed a high order to fulfill, and the fact that Gawain has the image on his shield reflects both his desire to achieve perfection and his awareness of the distance between his own actions and those of the one who might deserve to wear the pentangle. Or perhaps, eliminating this split, Gawain's adherence to the order of perfection represented by the pentangle actually reveals the imperfection that is found in the knot. Infinite circularity is often more confusing than it is symbolic of order, especially if we, like Lacan, attempt to work from outside of or against Catholic ideology. As the bearer of the knot of imperfection finally approaches Bercilak's castle, after much Hamlet-like procrastination, he finds in its turrets "good-looking loopholes that locked together well" (*Sir Gawain*, II.792), reflecting the strength and fortification, but also the web of solid fabric that can contain the knot. The baroque description of the castle with its interwoven stones, harmonic pinnacles, and "chalk-white chimneys" and their gothic complexity demonstrate the folds of the strength of the unconscious realm of desire that Gawain is about to enter (*Sir Gawain*, II.798). The perfect order of the pentangle becomes simplistic when confronted by the complexity of the scene that is foreign to Gawain. As such, having been welcomed into the castle, Gawain attempts to protect himself with sleep.

The most overt example of Gawain's unconscious at work, his feigned sleep, will aid in the understanding of his symptomatic display in which we find him attempting to hide his unconscious from others. Gawain's sleep has often been read as his passivity, his refusal to engage the Lady because he cannot decide how to respond to her, or because he is fearful of what the encounter will signify. Perceived as emasculating, this passivity also contributes to Carolyn Dinshaw's brilliant reading of the polymorphous sexuality within the poem.[20] The fact that Gawain feigns sleep is indeed testament to a desire to appear as if he is not engaged in the moment. The process of performing the image of sleep, however, also reflects an understanding on his part of the significance of sleep as well as his ability to lie, which will be so important later in the poem.

Engaging in the unconscious realm that is pure sleep, he hides his feelings. When confronted by the Lady, his feigned sleep conceals his shame. The representation of Gawain as "embarrassed" is enigmatic given his ostensible perfection and stability. The scene is a familiar one as Gawain sleeps while Bercilak rides out to hunt.

> Gawain, the brave courtier, in a good bed rests,
> Lies snug, while the daylight illumined the walls,
> Under coverlet so comfortable, curtained about;
> And as he slid into slumbering, suddenly he heard
> A little sound at his door, steadily drawn open;

And he heaves up his head from his haven in bed,
A corner of the curtain he caught up a little,
And gazes warily forward for what it might be.
It was the lady, loveliest to behold,
Who drew the door after her discreetly and quietly,
And moved toward the bed; and the man was embarrassed,
And lay down listlessly, making believe he slept. (*Sir Gawain*, II.1179–90)

The Middle English term that is here replaced by "embarrassed" is "schamed," reflecting a more pure feeling of shame than the word "embarrassed" suggests. As an internal projection of hatred toward the self for one's own feelings, shame is alternately a form of modesty and aggression.[21] That Gawain feels shame is representative of either his feelings of desire that he wishes to repress, his precise lack of feeling of desire, or his sense that he is doing something wrong by sleeping. The latter response makes sense in light of his procrastinated pursuit of the promise that he made to the Green Knight. He should be ashamed that, as one who seeks to be the knight of perfection, he fails to keep his word, thus placing himself further from the possibility of attaining his goal. But Gawain does not consciously recognize his feelings; rather, they emerge symptomatically as he performs passivity, feigning sleep while the Lady sits on his bed gazing at him. At this moment Gawain is simultaneously a child, pretending to his mother that he is asleep, as well as prey and hunter. As such, Gawain carves out the time he needs to rationalize his emotive drives, searching his "conscience" for a rational and potentially ethical response to the Lady's inquiry (also presented as a demand or a request akin to that of the Other in the scene of desire) that is silently uttered by her appearance in his room. However, Gawain's conscience does not complete a successful internal dialogue and Gawain must relinquish his attempts to hermeticize his psyche in order to discover what the Other wants. Of course, his conscience reflects his intellectual curiosity as well as his desire to know (or to resist knowing) what brings her to his chambers. Having bought some time for himself, Gawain decides that the answer will be found in "conversation" and so he opens his eyes to confront the Lady. What happens between the time when he decides to feign sleep and when he opens his eyes is as interesting as the scene that follows during which the Lady begins the game of courtship, challenging Gawain to a beheading contest parallel to the one in which he is already engaged (or avoiding).

Placing the Lady in the position of God, Gawain attempts to protect himself from her advances. In his attempt to shut down his emotive responses to phenomenal stimulants, and to the Lady, Gawain foregrounds his fear of his own desire such that the shame that he feels determines the manner in which he hides himself in order to hide his unconscious desires, which, rather than come forth as real, manifest themselves in a paranoid fashion as their own inversion, hatred toward the self.

The structure of paranoia alters emotions in such a manner that feeling is inverted and then projected. As Freud defines paranoia in his case study of Daniel Paul Schreber, whom he reads as a subject by way of his memoirs (Freud is a literary critic here focusing on the text), the paranoid turns the statement "I love him" into "He hates me."

> The proposition "I (a man) love him" is contradicted by:
> a) Delusions of persecution; for it loudly asserts: "I do not *love* him —
> I *hate* him."
>   This contradiction, which could be expressed in no other way in the unconscious, cannot, however, become conscious to a paranoiac in this form. The mechanism of symptom-formation in paranoia requires that internal perceptions, or feelings, shall be replaced by external perceptions. Consequently, the proposition "I hate him" becomes transformed by *projection* into another one: "*He hates* (persecutes) *me,*" which will justify me in hating him. And thus the unconscious feeling, which is in fact the motive force, makes its appearance as though it were the consequence of an external perception:
>   "I do not *love* him — I *hate* him, because HE PERSECUTES ME" [i.e., he hates me].[22]

Freud also notes that the cause of paranoia is often associated with humiliation, akin to shame.[23] What is unique to the system in Gawain's scene, however, is the heterosexual display of paranoia with regard to the Lady. If, as Carolyn Dinshaw has shown, there is no certainty that Gawain's desire is for the Lady, that the Lady is precisely a mediator for the affection or desire between Gawain and Bercilak, then paranoia would not function here in this way because Gawain would feel desire for the Lady as sublimated desire for the man.[24] In Freud's view, this paranoid "erotomania" often shifts to "I do not love *him* —I love her" (*Three Case Histories,* 166). However, Gawain never addresses his love to the Lady; he acts as the passive recipient of her love. This scene in which paranoia displays itself between a man and a woman suggests that Freud's view of the homosexual nature of paranoia is broken down in *Sir Gawain and the Green Knight*. If Freud were right, then Gawain would be paranoid with regard to Bercilak. Instead, he is paranoid with regard to the Lady. Remembering that along with the pentangle, Gawain also has an image of the Virgin Mary on his shield, however, we might transfer this situation to suggest that Gawain is in fact paranoid with regard to God.

Read as a metatale about the telling of a tale that is interrupted on Christmas Eve, the tale itself has been shown to foreground the Christian elements of the text. Gawain's faith leads him to place his life in the hands of God's will, but his faltering faith makes him fear that God will not protect him, hence the need for the girdle. As the Green Knight invokes God's will at the scene of the beheading match, saying, "Gawain . . . may God protect you!" he challenges Gawain's faith (*Sir Gawain*, IV.2239). Although Gawain, by accepting the girdle, has already called into question the extent to which God, in fact, will protect him, that he has faith neither in God nor the supernatural power of the girdle is demonstrated by his ducking away from the first blow. The great faith of the shield does not stand up to the fear that God is out to persecute him.

The fragility of this order that is so revered in critics of Gawain is reflected further by his refusal of the knot of the girdle. Again feeling shame at the use of the girdle (a mechanism by which he is perceived to cheat at the beheading game), Gawain reacts with anger this time, tossing away the girdle and its knot.

> All the blood in his breast blended in his face,
> So that he shrank with shame when the stalwart one spoke.
> The first words formed by the knight in the field were:
> "Accursed be cowardice and covetousness also;
> In you are villainy and vice that virtue destroy."
> Then he took the neat knot, and unties the contrivance,
> Hurled the belt angrily toward the green man himself.
> "There is the false favor; may misfortune befall it!" (*Sir Gawain*, IV.2371–78)

If it illustrates a conversion into proper faith, then this disregard of the knot serves to uphold a properly Christian reading of the poem. However, if we consider the role of the knot as that which has reflected the mathematical structure of the world, the order of the universe, then Gawain's tossing aside of the knot also represents his refusal of that order as it is bound to a divine presence; whether that presence is embodied by God or by a supernatural force, Gawain is refusing the element of the unknowable in an attempt to control his actions in the future, and, therefore, refusing his unconscious. In this active refusal, he also calls attention to the status of the unconscious as real. The knotting and unknotting of the pentangle and the belt illustrate the process by which Gawain seeks to conceal that which he must recognize as real.

> What Freud discovers in the unconscious . . . is something utterly different from realizing that broadly speaking one can give a sexual meaning to everything one knows, for the reason that knowing has always been open to the famous metaphor (the side of meaning Jung exploited). It is the real that permits the effective unknotting of what makes the symptom hold together, namely a knot of signifiers. Where here knotting and unknotting are not metaphors, but real reality to be taken as those knots that in fact are built up through developing chains of the signifying material. (*Television*, 14)

What Gawain cannot realize is that even through a conscious decision to repress his unconscious, he is exhibiting a means by which the unconscious emerges. He proclaims that his "nature" is to be loyal and liberal as a knight and refuses to acknowledge the reasons for his actions that have then gone against his "nature." Gawain's "nature" is a conscious version of himself that he seeks to enact because the other version, the one in which his unconscious acts out and displays itself in his actions, leads to sorrow. In search of happiness, then, Gawain makes a decision to repress his desire toward "treachery and untruth." Truth, however, or "trothe" is a conscious activity that is not-whole because it is an instance of repression. An alternate and more hopeful reading here would be to suggest that Bercilak "cures" Gawain of his paranoia; he no longer suffers at the end of the tale, and so perhaps he has successfully integrated his desire into his subjectivity by confronting his utter shame. In this case, the text represents the psychoanalytical cure at work in the tale. And, as Lacan says, we do not need the active articulation of the process to know that it has existed.

> The cure is a demand that originates in the voice of the sufferer, of someone who suffers from his body or his thought. The astonishing thing is that there be a response, and that through time medicine, using words, has hit the bull's-eye.
>
> How did this happen before the unconscious was located? In order to work, a practice doesn't have to be elucidated; this is what can be deduced from that. (*Television*, 11)

Lacan's view is that the precise location of the unconscious is not significant to an understanding of its functioning. Similarly, whether Gawain represses his unconscious or integrates it into a new system, his rejection of the knot suggests that he has untied the order by which he lived. The rejection of the unconscious as a mode of knowledge for Gawain is further supported by the misogynist reference to Solomon that critics often find to be out of place in the poem. The projection of evil onto women and the suggestion that "it would be a big gain / To love them, but not believe them, and to stay levelheaded" (*Sir Gawain*, IV.2421–22) is as much a lament over the need to control and repress desire as it is a comment on the way in which masculinity is derived from repression. As such, the final statement added to the manuscript during the nineteenth century and reflecting the order of the garter, "Honi soi qui mal y pense" (translated as "shame be to the man who has evil in his mind," or alternately, "evil be to him who evil thinks"), becomes significant of a challenge to the reader to attempt to find goodness *and* desire, rather than to simply give over desire such that a false or flat sense of nobility might be achieved.

Elizabeth Scala sees evidence of the unconscious at work in the lack of storytelling and the repetition in *Sir Gawain and the Green Knight,* arguing that, "The *figure* of the absent narrative provides both an emblem of and a visible locus for a 'repressed' of the poem, marking the place from which the plot-through-repetition emerges."[25] And, like the subject's actions in a scene of repetition automatism, Gawain's actions are necessarily "doomed to fail" (*Absent Narratives,* 51). The inexorable trajectory of the energy of desire in the scene of acting-out the unconscious, however, does not stop the subject from proceeding to attempt to alter the outcome of a scene in which the conscious character of desire masquerades as the figure in control.

Scala's thesis echoes that of Jean-Louis Baudry whose "Freud and 'Literary Creation'" analyzes the way in which the unconscious contributes to the structure of the "lost text." "The 'unconscious,' a functional concept linked to a certain state of the text, serves to define both the site of the lost text's recuperation and the transformative mechanisms to which the text is subjected."[26] These mechanisms include time, cultural specificity, historical context, as well as the process by which the unconscious affects the conscious process of reading and interpretation. Even more central to the conception of realism in Lacan's thought and in relation to medieval literature is Baudry's interrogation of Freud's reading of the real. Giving voice to Freud, Baudry asks, "How is it that fictional characters are described in such a way that they seem to be subject to the same psychical forces as real people?" ("Freud and 'Literary Creation,'" 71). His answer, which emerges throughout the essay, relies on Freud's representation of the "'scene of writing' as metaphor for the psychical apparatus" ("Freud and 'Literary Creation,'" 91), and this parallel is bound to the way in which desire enables and prohibits representation:

> Unsatisfied desires, said Freud, promote phantasms, and every phantasm is the realization of a desire. Is desire then linked, or should it be linked, to representations? Or is representation that which undoes desire, turns it away from being the desire for that practice, textual production, within which the term "desire" may itself be improper or useless. Is representation not, in the end, in its opposition to such practice, that which keeps intact the closed and repetitive cycle of meaning, of the sign, of presences, of the subject, of neurosis? Could we not say that desire itself is an effect of representation, of the bringing-to-presence, and that insofar as desire is always desire for something (something that would be God or a representation thereof), it is bound up with the teleological thought of meaning? This would allow us to understand the complicity between neurosis itself and a system founded on representation; and to understand how neurosis is obliged to block and occult writing for the same reason that makes neurosis a defense-mechanism against sex. (*Television*, 90)

Gawain projects his own resistance in the form of sleep and in his refusal to give up the garter in the repetition of the beheading scene as a means of attempting to block the sexual encounter. This symptomatic expression reflects that his unconscious is acting out in the scene of desire.

As Gawain's plight to come to terms with the unconscious as a real within the world leads him to seek a functioning repression of his unconscious, Daniel Paul Schreber's attempt to produce a world order and to deceive God reflects a paranoid system that attempts to control the world by controlling his unconscious. Like the reader of *Sir Gawain and the Green Knight* who added the phrase "honi soi qui mal y pense," Schreber employs this phrase in the course of his memoirs as a warning against criticism. For Gawain, the attempt to control his actions becomes linked with a recognition that he cannot know the universe. He does, nonetheless, seek to gain goodness by sacrificing his desire. For

Schreber, the proper place of knowledge is that which is hidden from God so that it cannot be removed from his mind. In both cases, the actual sensation of knowledge is limited by the play of the unconscious within the conscious.

The Sacred Real

An examination of universal knowledge rightly begins with a consideration of nonknowledge, as defined by Bataille. In *The Unfinished System of Non-knowledge* we find a collection of various texts in which Bataille sought to understand the relationship between the poetic and the sacred.[27] At the core of this mottled text is Bataille's investigation of Nietzsche, which is useful in the context of a discussion of the impossibility of courting or seducing God as is the case with Schreber's desire to be "fucked" by God. For a good part of *The Unfinished System of Non-knowledge* we are presented with a transcript of a seminar on "sin" at which Bataille presented his lecture *On Nietzsche* to an audience composed of Christian clergy and secular philosophers, presented at Mr. Marcel Moré's home on 5 March 1944.[28] Among those present at the meeting were Arthur Adanmov, Maurice Blanchot, Bolin, Simone de Beauvoir, Jean Bruno, Pierre Burgelin, Albert Camus, Courturier, Father Jean Danliélou, Father Henri Dubarle, Maurice de Gandillac, Jean Hyppolite, Pierre Klossowski, Lahay, Michel Leiris, Pierre Lescure, Jacques Madaule, Gabriel Marcel Louis Massignon, Father Augustin, Maydieu, Maurice Merleau-Ponty, Marcel Morém Niunir Hafex, Jean Paulhan, Pierre Prévost, and Jean-Paul Sartre (*Unfinished System*, 26–27). In his speech, Bataille's second fundamental proposition is that "In 'communication,' in love, desire has nothingness as its object. It is like this with any 'sacrifice'" (*Unfinished System*, 28). Because communication "happens only between two beings at risk," the sacrificial gift has the potential to unite the human subject with the divine. However, immediately following this statement, Bataille proposes his third claim: "More often than the sacred object, desire has the flesh as its object and in carnal desire the game of 'communication' appears rigorously in its complexity. In the carnal act, in desecration—and in desecrating himself—man crosses the limit of beings" (*Unfinished System*, 29). Therefore, desire is attracted not by the body itself, but by the wound, lack, rupture, or gap in the body. How closely this resembles Lacan's theory of desire as it is worked out in "Subversion of the Subject and the Dialectic of Desire in the Freudian Unconscious."[29] Indeed the links between Lacan and Bataille are profound. The discussion of the limits of desire, sacrifice, and the potential for communicating with the divine performed by the unlikely combination of lay philosophers and clergy members turns mostly around the problem of communication itself and a definition of sin. L. O. Aranye Fradenburg's book *Sacrifice Your Love* demonstrates how this process is crucial to an understanding of psychoanalysis for medievalists, and in "The Institution of Rot" Michel de Certeau outlines the similarities between the processes of mystical writing and psychoanalysis.[30] Situating his discussion of Schreber's mysticism within the context of sixteenth- and seventeenth-century mystics such as Meister Eckhart, Hadewijch of Anvers, St. Teresa,[31] and Angelus Silesius, de Certeau argues that the fundamental commonality between their writings and Schreber's memoirs lies in the power of the death drive. In this essay de Certeau claims that the mystic's goal is one of erasure and dispossession—a "will to be done with" ("Institution of Rot," 89). The clear persecutory desire is involved in a psychical process that is perhaps less clear; the will to achieve one's own nonexistence. Potentially, the mystical or nonmystical subject who seeks to establish her/his own nonexistence understands, whether cognitively or instinctively, that the process of desire requires a rupture for it to work dialectically. What is astonishing about the difference between the mystics and the psychotic Schreber, however, is the way in which those ruptures or gaps are characterized and the role that communication plays in the attempt to render the self one with God.

In a fundamental manner Gawain and Schreber both perceive that they are playing a game with God or an alternate sovereign power and both refuse to play according to the rules.[32] Their resistance to the proper approach to the expectations set forth for them reflects their investment in thwarting the process of desire. They exhibit the death drive at work, even as they seek their own immortality. This confusion with regard to the goal of the game and their own power to make things right in it reflects their symptomatic display of the unconscious. They are both constantly acting out against the power that they have determined will castrate/decapitate or copulate with them. In both cases, Gawain and Schreber manifest a refusal of the scene of courtly love. In the case of Gawain, his refusal of the Lady and Bercilak impedes the inherent obstacles within courtly love and asserts artificial obstacles such that sublimation cannot work. In the case of Schreber, his confusion regarding his desire simultaneously to court and thwart God interferes with the process of desire and the ability to repress the unconscious. Resistance in these cases causes the navel of the unconscious to be perverted into a projected fetish onto the knot-like apparati of the pentangle, the garter, and in the case of Schreber, ribbons and his writing.

The knot is a symptom of desire and of the navel and it reflects the real of the unconscious. The play with knots is a detour or a distraction from the navel and will never be solved. Even the concern with castration that pervades much scholarship within psychoanalysis and on *Sir Gawain and the Green Knight* is a form of resistance to the limits of analysis. As we saw in chapter 4, Lacan's obsession with tying and untying knots led to a certain degree of hysteria about the proper center of signification. Knowing already that he could not achieve the proper cut that would solve the riddle of the unconscious, Lacan nonetheless was driven to attempt to find it. Similarly, in *Sir Gawain and the Green Knight* Gawain's repetition and his refusal to properly participate in the games of courtly love and knightly duty that are set forth for him by Bercilak and the Lady reflect that his plight cannot arrive at its center. The split between the material and the spiritual in Gawain's search reflects that Bercilak forgives him, despite his breach of contract, because he knows that Gawain is always already repeating the attempt to be (and not to be) honorable.[33] This is precisely the structure of the knot and the limits of analysis wherein the subject is driven by repetition to attempt to understand the navel of the unconscious. And this is precisely the moment when we arrive at the real. As Lacan says, "the real is beyond the automaton, the return, the coming-back, the insistence of the signs, by which we see ourselves governed by the pleasure principle. The real is that which always lies behind the automaton."[34]

In this moment of arrival at the real, we also find the intersections of hysteria, psychosis, neurosis, and the four discourses. Elizabeth Grosz's analysis of the hysteric shows how this is related to a particular form of self-mutilation:

> The hysteric's symptom is a response to her annihilation as active subject, a resistance or refusal to confirm what is expected of her. Not able to take up an active position by will alone . . . she lives out and uses her passivity in an active defiance of her social position. She (psychically) mutilates herself in order to prevent her brutalisation at the hands of others.[35]

The psychic self-mutilation recognized here is highly significant to an investigation of dispossession and disavowal of self and desire in Gawain and Schreber. Despite the clarity and astuteness of Grosz's formulation, her vision of the annihilators of the active subject remains external. The motivation behind the self-mutilation and disavowal that engages and drives Gawain and Schreber is not merely fear of "the hands of others," but, rather, dread of the hands of God.

The early thirteenth-century instructional text *Hali Meiðheð* promotes chastity by claiming that it prepares a woman for the splendor of immortality: "þis mihte is þet an þet I pos deadliche lif schaweð in hire an estat of þe blisse undeadlich I þet eadi lond as brude ne nimð ne brudgume brude."[36] Additionally, in the hyperbolic warning against lechery, the reader learns that the act of sexual intercourse causes death: "þet dreoir dede on ende eueð þet deaðes dunt" (*Hali Meiðheð*, 14). The rhetoric here is psychologically powerful, suggesting that the sex act leads to death. The correlative to this statement is, of course, that if one refrains from sex one has the power to foreclose the impact of the final death-blow, that is, to avoid death and achieve immortality. This connection between chastity and immortality superimposes one form of dispossession of the body and the self (the will to chastity) onto an infinite possession of self achieved through immortality of the spirit. Although sex can cause death, chastity will ensure a life beyond death, therefore promising a death that does not kill. It is in this sense that the death drive, or the drive toward dispossession, is evident.

Schreber's desire is to become a woman in order to have intercourse with God. Schreber's desire to "be f——ked by God" is often associated with his vision of himself as a whore submitting to male aggression in the primal scene.[37] However, despite its overt focus on the body, Schreber's famous statement, "it really must be rather pleasant (lovely) to be a woman succumbing to intercourse," signifies his desire to be united with God.[38] This desire is so strong that he wishes "God would never attempt to withdraw ... but would follow [his] attraction without resistance permanently and uninterruptedly" (*Memoirs*, 210). When God *withdraws* from Schreber it causes him great psychic and somatic stress. He relies on a union with God in order to affirm his rationality. Yet, he is willing to dispossess himself of his male body, to kill part of himself, in hopes of preserving that rationality and evading his conception of a delusional state.

God is not necessarily always ready to approach Schreber. Rather, Schreber must make himself ready *just in case* God chooses finally to advance toward him in an erotic manner. In effect, then, he seduces God and convinces himself that he seeks to ward off God's advances. Schreber records: "as soon as I am alone with God, if I may so express myself, I must continually or at least at certain times, strive to give divine rays the impression of a woman at the height of sexual delight" (*Memoirs,* 208). Further, to remain engaged in the sexual scenario with Schreber, and therefore to act as a constant witness to his rationality, God demands "constant enjoyment" from him (*Memoirs,* 209). As soon as God draws away, Schreber is rendered delusional. He needs constantly to prove himself, and this proof may best be exhibited through the mysticism of the sexual act with God.

Significantly, however, this erotic connection to God exists in a binary opposition to any earthly promiscuity. Schreber testifies that, "low sensuousness is not a motive in [his] case" (*Memoirs,* 208). In fact, Schreber contests that his self-eroticization is enacted only in order to achieve unity with God. Despite his constant references to his "soul-voluptuousness," his body remains chaste:

> I *never mean any sexual desires towards other human beings (females) least of all sexual intercourse,* but that I have to imagine myself as man and woman in one person having certain sexual excitement etc—which perhaps under other circumstances might be considered immoral— but which has nothing whatever to do with any idea of masturbation or anything like it. (*Memoirs,* 208)

Schreber's insistence on the transcendental aspects of his sexual eroticism foregrounds the desire for physical chastity while engaging in the unifying act of copulation with God. To imagine himself as man and woman releases Schreber of tangible sexual desire, rendering him a spiritual being in communion with God. Schreber's celibate sexuality, then, is enacted in the name of achieving immortality. He needs to be a woman submitting to the act of intercourse in order to fill the role of eternal mother and virgin.

Schreber's transvestitism and transsexualism protect him from his own mortality while, paradoxically, killing his existence as a man. As a transsexual, he is neither man nor woman; rather, he thinks that he is a being involved in a mystical act. Outside of his body, dispossessed of his limitations as male, Schreber is not vulnerable to death; he enacts one form of dispossession of self in order to gain transcendence. The desire to become a woman in order to copulate with God is one way of assuming the soul of another, and transcending his own death. As Freud notes, Schreber's "mission" of redeeming and repopulating the world could only be brought about through his transvestitism and transsexualism.[39] Toward the end of the text, Schreber reveals that his fetishization of self-emasculation is a form of achieving immortality: "It is therefore possible, indeed probable, that to the end of my days there will be strong indications of femaleness, but that I shall die as a man.... This raises the further question, whether I am at all mortal and what could possibly cause my death" (*Memoirs*, 212). Though he will die as a man, the thought that immediately occurs to him after imagining his death is that he cannot possibly die.

The voluntary assumption of one's own "nonexistence" may be read as a projection of what remains a "solipsistic" Cartesian statement that "I can only be certain of the ideas in my own mind." In this case, "nonexistence" is determined by the cessation of thinking, significantly one of Schreber's greatest and most constant fears and desires. However, this concept of "nonexistence" that logically follows from Žižek's formulation is a literal and somewhat simplistic one that would claim "madness" as a state of being that does not count. On the other hand, as it gestures toward a conception of the self as Other, the Cartesian system submits itself as anything but solipsistic and, therefore, requires a more complex analysis of the "nonexistence" of subjectivity.[40] In attempting to perceive the self as Other, Descartes distinguishes between his projected self and the self-censoring aspect of subjectivity that keeps vigilance over projection. Thus, he already introduces a concept of alterity that distinguishes what may be perceived as theological, mystical, or hagiographic accounts of subjectivity (in this case those accounts that attempt to find sameness within difference) from a concept of subjectivity that perceives differences and *différance* within the subject. Within this alterity emerges an interstice wherein "nonexistence" is situated. In the process of projecting an image of the self as Other, a process that is enacted partly in order to overcome that very distance between self and Other, the subject becomes a performance seeking to authenticate its own "reality."

Specifically, Schreber's specular performance of femininity on which the self is literally projected as a sexually (anatomically) determined Other demonstrates this practice of exposing alterity in the attempt to achieve homogeneity. If projection may be perceived as a weapon, not only a defense, but also a *projectile* displacement of the "mental projection of the surface of the body" (to recite Freud's words), then Schreber's process of "becoming-woman" and phantasmatically engaging in intercourse with God must be read as a means of projecting his *imago* in order to eliminate the disparity between that *imago* and the image of him externally perceived by the world.[41] Schreber's weapon of his female *imago* serves not only as a defense against admitting to his homosexual desire, but also as one that engages him directly with God, allowing him to remain outside of the technological status of automaton through the experience of an overwhelming and overdetermined sense of soul-voluptuousness and bodily feeling. His "becoming-woman," externally, psychically, and bodily, provides a barrier against an absence of feeling, thus protecting him in his movement toward "pure exteriority" from becoming the purely exterior *technē*. This performance of "becoming-woman" is situated within Schreber's attempt to gauge his mental stability and insure his presence within "reality."

Schreber's suspicion of this fragile state between sleeping and waking is also evident in his confessional moment during which he reveals his desire to become a woman in order to copulate with God. Again, concerned with distinguishing between his own conscious thoughts and those thoughts that occur to him without the aid of his self-censoring apparatus, Schreber is careful to note the liminal time during which his fantasy of womanhood arises:

> One morning while still in bed (whether still half asleep or already awake I cannot remember), I had a feeling which, thinking about it later when fully awake, struck me as highly peculiar. It was the idea that it really must be rather pleasant to be a woman succumbing to intercourse. This idea was so foreign to my whole nature that I may say I would have rejected it with indignation if fully awake; from what I have experienced since I cannot exclude the possibility that some external influences were at work to implant this idea in me. (*Memoirs,* 63)

Considered in light of the remainder of the sentence, which separates the moment in which the feeling occurred from his subsequent fully conscious recollection, Schreber's parenthetical aside that blurs the lines between the psychical states of "half asleep" and "already awake" is self-contradictory. On the one hand, his inability to determine whether his fantasy of being a woman occurred while he was still half asleep or already awake suggests that the difference is relatively insignificant. Yet, on the other hand, Schreber's insistence that the idea must have arisen during a liminal space, since he would have rejected it if fully awake, demonstrates his extreme investment in differentiating between ideas over which he has control and those which are "implanted" in his mind.

Schreber's attempt to discriminate between his own thoughts and those that are imposed on him corresponds to the significance he places upon rationality, and his sense that he is expected by the rays, and by God, to be constantly engaged in compulsive thinking. Liminal states are tormenting for Schreber because their fragility and ambiguity prevent him from taxonomizing his thoughts. For Schreber, a cessation of thinking will lead to his dementia and, hence, an erasure of his existence: "cessation of thinking, however temporary, and the resulting state in which definite thoughts formulated in words do not echo from the nerves of a human being in a form appreciable to the rays, implies that this person's mental capacities are extinct, or to use a common though obviously misunderstood human expression, the advent of dementia" (*Memoirs*, 153). In his flight from dementia, Schreber employs the Cartesian logic of the relationship between thinking and subjectivity. Schreber believes that if his constant thinking pauses, God disregards, disinherits, or *withdraws from* him.[42]

Schreber's sense that he is vulnerable to external influences demonstrates his correlative fear of becoming a mechanized technological apparatus. In order to preserve what he perceives to be his independent motivations and desires, he "pictures" himself as a woman. Through the act of "picturing" Schreber creates stable images and evades the persecution of the rays. " 'Picturing' in this sense may therefore be called a reversed miracle. In the same way as rays throw on to my nerves pictures they would like to see especially in dreams, I in turn produce pictures for the rays which I want them to see" (*Memoirs*, 181). He overcomes his submission to the rays by uniting his interior and exterior and, therefore, appearing to fulfill their desires by giving them something that will occupy their scopic drives. His symptomatic disavowal of his perceived authority through self-emasculation enables Schreber to gain another form of power when he aligns his self-image with his projected image. "Picturing" enables Schreber to transform his imagined images into memories whose reality is verified by the shared vision between himself and the rays. Although he is aware of the role his imagination plays in this exercise of "picturing" he nevertheless employs it as a test of his reality. Re-calling detailed impressions he creates his own sense of the past, thus placing himself outside of his confined situation within the institutions of the asylum and his male body.

Schreber's "picturing" is fundamental to his creation of his female identity. As he aligns and manipulates both his projected self and his *imago*, Schreber asserts a dispossession of self and an overdetermined identification with "woman." Picturing enables him to become a woman, inculcating his female *imago* within his memory and incorporating nonexistence as a prevention against his own disappearance into dementia.[43] In other words, through "picturing" he projects and, like the projectile of the weapon, he literally inscribes ("draws") an ideal image of chaste female voluptuousness, akin to what he imagines to have been expressed by the Virgin Mary in his mind so that he might not be a victim of uncontrolled thoughts. In his formulation, the fantasmatic female body armors him against being perceived or accused of allowing his thoughts to relax. In this sense, the female body and image he constructs serves as metallic armor against his notion of the persecutory aural forces barraging him with orders and expectations.

In addition to the mystical and technological associations that are inherent in Schreber's "picturing" (chastity, soul-voluptuousness, a transcendent ideal, on the one hand; photography, cinematography, ideological-state surveillance, etc. on the other—images that are all parallel to the voices and the sounds of the birds), his external self-representation unites his bodily ego with a metallic suit of armor; the shimmering reflection of the metal mimics the tain of the mirror in which Schreber sees himself. He literally becomes his own mirror image when his body externally reflects its interiority. His ability to confirm the image others would have of his body, were they to witness his trans-formation, is rooted in his production of himself as his own external witness.

Indeed, the hypothetical witness is integral to Schreber's revisionary mirror scene: "I venture to assert flatly that anybody who sees me stand-ing in front of a mirror with the upper part of my body naked would get the undoubted *impression of a female trunk*—especially when the illusion is strengthened by some feminine adornments" (*Memoirs*, 207). These feminine adornments are ribbons that Schreber ties in his hair and around parts of his body. Like the garter that Gawain bears as a protective measure and a defense against his own death, Schreber finds solace in the textuality of the woven fabric.

Schreber's conception of himself as a woman depends upon this vision of himself before the mirror. He must visually perceive himself as he would appear to others in order to affirm continuity between his imagined self-perception and his real presence.[44] The focus on the "trunk" in Schreber's mirror scene recalls Victor Tausk's discussion of Nataljia A, who perceived her "trunk," or her torso, to be a different sort of trunk — a coffin — and a mechanized object. The external perception of the body renders the body contingently external to that very vision, alienating the subject from the body, and the possibility of confusing the body with a mechanical or technological object; this mode of self-perception also foregrounds the notion of the subject as automaton. Therefore, even as he attempts to shield himself from such a concept of subjectivity, Schreber enacts a process that renders possible such a scene. Yet, it must also be recalled that the act of "picturing" is a direct response to the badgering voices. Schreber mediates the persecutory potential of the voices by giving the rays something to look at, and thus disarming them of their purely auratic sovereign power.

In the effort to naturalize his constructed female body, Schreber risks falling into the category of pure construct, and thus becoming that from which he seeks to protect himself. Schreber's transsexuality is causally linked to his desire to stop his unbearable compulsive thinking. When he pictures himself as a woman, he claims to "use up all his imaginative and cognitive powers." Since all of his mental energies are involved in the creation of his femininity, he protects himself against the hyperbolic thinking instigated by the rays and by his own desire to protect himself from their influence. By dispossessing himself of his perception of his maleness, and traveling into nonexistence through an overdetermined identification with "woman," he embodies nonexistence. In this sense he achieves the death that transcends death.

This is the imposition of the state between the two deaths, wherein the real of the universal unconscious becomes evident. What is clear from the relationship between excess, decadence, and the desire to be one with God in body and language is that the idealization of universal forms is in fact impossible. Regardless of the manipulations imposed onto the body, and the imaginative formation of a "root language," the particular instance of Schreber's psychosis is in fact particular. Any application made by Freud or Lacan of the primary base case for paranoid schizophrenia, or psychosis, is linked back to Schreber carefully by way of linguistic investigations and considerations of fragmented subjectivity. In fact, the only universal idea that arises from psychoanalysis is the paradoxically sustaining notion that each subject is fragmented and that each experience manifests itself differently within each subject.

Gawain and Schreber, the neurotic, the hysteric, and the psychotic all seek to construct their own nonexistence, while psychoanalysis reveals that through sublimation the subject is always already accomplishing this, and the trick is not to push it further, but rather to become aware of it.

Refrain: Materiality and Spirituality/Lacan a Thomist?

Finally, in response to Kristeva's question and assertion "Lacan a Thomist?" we can respond by saying that indeed, to the extent that Lacan's concept of the real relies on a scholastic belief in universals as it is also bound to a sense of the materiality of language, Lacan is a Thomist.

The question of the extent to which psychoanalysis is or is not materialist is central to an understanding of Lacan's realism. As I was writing this book, among the many perplexing questions and apparent contradictions that pervade Lacan's work, one question stands out as having been unavailable to discussion until the understanding of Lacan's position as a realist was available. Why does Lacan invoke Maimonides in *Seminar I, Freud's Papers on Technique,* and not merely invoke him in a citational manner, but promise to study, analyze, and discuss him, only to fail to fulfill that promise? This question comes from the position of a reader of Lacan who finds curious his consistent engagement and rejection of Catholicism. Not willing to allow this to limit a reading of his work to a psychobiography (by which we might say that his family system and his education within the traditions and ideology of Catholicism led him to rebel, but not to push that rebellion far enough, or perhaps to push it too far emulating an atheistic Jew [e.g., Freud] and thus leading to his overdetermined supplementation of God with the unconscious), I continued to seek an alternate answer in his work or in the conception of the Middle Ages. This led me to presume for a moment that Lacan's medievalism meant that he was bound within the Christian system that continues to dominate an understanding of the Middle Ages, despite attempts to "open the doors" to non-Christian and non-Western texts, ideas, and methods in the discipline of medieval studies. Why, for instance, after promising to take up Maimonides, and therefore suggesting an alternative to the Catholic history that influences his work so profoundly, does he fail to keep his word? In the seminar immediately following his promise, he returns instead to a discussion of Augustine, after which he references Maimonides occasionally alone, and sometimes in conjunction with Spinoza; but he never fulfills the promise to *study* Maimonides. Why is this? Lacan's promise to study Maimonides comes at the end of "The Creative Function of Speech" where he says:

> Next time I will tell you about *The Guide of the Perplexed* by Maimonides, which is an esoteric work. You'll see the extent to which he deliberately organizes his discourse in such a way that what he wants to say, which is not sayable — it is him who says this — can nonetheless be revealed. He says what cannot or must not be said by means of a certain disorder, certain ruptures, certain intentional discordances. Well, the slips, the holes, the disputes, the repetitions of the subject also express, but here spontaneously, innocently, the manner in which his discourse is organized. And that is what we have to read. We will come back to this, because the texts are worth the trouble of being brought together.[45]

"The texts" here refers to Freud's work on transference *(Übertragung)* found in the seventh section of the *Tramdeutung (The Interpretation of Dreams),* "The Psychology of the Dream-processes." At stake in this discussion is the way in which desire exceeds articulation. *Übertragung* (transference) is

> the phenomenon constituted by the fact that it is not possible to give a direct translation for a given desire repressed by the subject. This desire of the subject is forbidden to his mode of discourse, and cannot get itself recognized. Why? Because amongst the elements of the repression there is something which partakes of the ineffable. There are essential relations which no discourse can express adequately, except in what I called just now the interlineation. (*Seminar I,* 245)

One possible answer to this enigma is that Lacan's need to articulate the way in which universals are real, and the way that this is precariously bound to an understanding of the Real, leads him to employ the language of Christianity as a bouncing board from which to spring his arguments. A second answer is that he in fact prefers to study the history that he seeks to reject than to positively site the history that he seeks to uphold. A third possibility is that, in fact, having studied Maimonides on his own after invoking him, he has decided that Maimonides is not who he thought he was and that he prefers to leave him alone. A fourth possibility is that the study of Maimonides would contradict his focus on courtly love as a phenomenon of Provence, since Maimonides was persecuted by the Provençals.

I prefer a fifth possibility, which is that, without paying explicit attention to Maimonides, he does ultimately return to him throughout the course of his seminars. As Maimonides was so central to the work of Leo Strauss (Strauss introduces the standard edition of *The Guide of the Perplexed* and discusses him in *Persecution and the Art of Writing*), when Lacan references Strauss in the context of his discussion of the reality principle (as we saw in chapter 1), he invokes Maimonides' shadow. Even more importantly, as he introduces Maimonides in *Seminar I* as a philosopher who focuses on the gaps, slippages, and failures of language to state the ineffable real, he articulates the manner in which he will approach language *consistently* throughout his work. The position that Maimonides earns is one of a figurehead to the seminars, and, although he does not study him overtly, as he does Freud, he implicitly engages the history of non-Christian philosophy as it applies to psychoanalysis by way of a consideration of Maimonides' medieval approach to language, knowledge, and desire. The full articulation of this argument belongs to a different text, and for now must remain a gesture in the direction of the non-Christian nature of Lacan's medievalism *despite* the prominence that Catholicism plays in his work (and thus, I imitate Lacan in promising that "we will come back to this," "next time"). For now, the significance of the reference and the promise must be seen in light of the proclamation that "We must take desire literally."

The real of the universals in relation to the materiality and spirituality of Being, language, and desire begs to be realized within the reality of an understanding of Lacan's medievalism. At the core of this understanding is the subject's relationship to language as a material (but incorporeal) element within the world. In the excess of the dialectics of desire, the function of the desiring subject engages the real on a manifold level.

The Other of the Other only exists as a place. It finds its place even if we cannot find it anywhere in the real, even if all we can find to occupy this place in the real is simply valid insofar as it occupies this place, but cannot give it any other guarantee than that it is in its place.

It is in this way that another typology is established, the typology which institutes the relation to the real. And now we can define this relation to the real, and realize what the reality principle means. (*Seminar VII*, 66)

This new typology remains on the level of the interlinear analysis foundational to psychoanalysis. To find the real, we must recognize that the function of language speaks through the words that are articulated. Speaking *through* these words means to be perceived in the linguistic utterance but also to be perceived *beyond* that utterance. Language is material in the sense that it makes meaning in the world; it is spiritual in the sense that it reflects the impossibility of the wholeness of significance, and yet at any moment it conveys more and less than it intends.

Lacan's seminars on language and desire begin while he is reading Heidegger. The relationship between building and dwelling forged by Martin Heidegger comes down to the question of language. As Heidegger observes, *bauen*—to build—derives from "the Old High German word for building, *buan*, means to dwell" (*Écrits*, 324). Heidegger's etymology continues to state that the residue of the old term contains "the German word *Nachbar*, neighbor. The *Nachbar* is the *Nachgebur*, the *Nachgebauer*, the near-dweller, he who dwells nearby. The verbs *buri*, *büren*, *beuron*, all signify dwelling, the place of dwelling" (*Écrits*, 325). The immediate inclusion of the neighbor (he who dwells nearby) into the scene of being as dwelling invokes the other in relation to the self.[46] Heidegger's etymology continues:

The Old Saxon *wuon*, the Gothic *Wunian*, like the old word *bauen*, means to remain, to stay in a place. But the Gothic *wunian* says more distinctly how this remaining is experienced. *Wunian* means to be at peace, to be brought to peace, to remain in peace. The word for peace, *Friede*, means the free, das *Frye*; and *fry* means preserved from harm and danger, preserved from something, safeguarded. To free actually means to spare. The sparing itself consists not only in the fact that we do not harm the one whom we spare. Real sparing is something *positive* and takes place when we leave something beforehand in its own essence. *The Fundamental character of dwelling is this sparing.* It pervades dwelling in its whole range. That range reveals itself to us as soon as we recall that human being consists in dwelling and, indeed, dwelling in the sense of the stay of mortals on the earth. (*Écrits*, 327)

Dwelling, being in the world and in relation to others, is determined by a relationship to matter. It is the means by which we find peace, freedom, and one version of the sovereign good that Lacan struggled to achieve throughout his work.[47]

Recalling Lacan's consideration of the real of matter and his admission to his disciples that he cannot move this table, we turn to the desk, which speaks so eloquently in *Écrits*. When, in *Seminar II*, Lacan mentions that he knows what is real because he knows that he cannot lift the table in front of him and he then refers to the tables of presence, he gestures toward the discourse of the desk that is produced later in the same year under the title of "The Freudian Thing, or the Meaning of the Return to Freud in Psychoanalysis" and that is later collected in *Écrits*. The seminar in *Seminar II*, given in May 1955, clearly invites a further explication of the real and reality, and Lacan promptly addresses this complex in November 1955 in Vienna. The dedication of the lecture to his wife, Sylvia, foregrounds the "realism" of the matter at hand by bringing to light the love that is sublimated into a work that is explicitly engaged with the material elements of analytical discourse by comparing the ego with the desk so specifically that the discourses "coincide point by point" (*Écrits*, 132). Both are dependent upon the signifier, on the word, and this linguistic dependence binds the ego to materiality as much as the desk is bound to the self-same materiality.

> For this desk, no less than the ego, is dependent on the signifier, namely on the word, which bearing its function to the general, to the lectern of quarrelsome memory and to the Tronchin piece of noble pedigree, is responsible for the fact that it is not merely a piece of wood, worked in turn by the woodcutter, the joiner and the cabinet-maker, for reasons of commerce, combined with fashion, itself productive of needs that sustain its exchange value, providing it is not led too quickly to satisfy the least superfluous of those needs by the last use to which it will eventually be put, namely, as firewood. (*Écrits*, 132)

The obvious critique of capital, of the resources that travel among the hands of various laborers to produce and create the forms that the substance "wood" takes on in the realm of the material refers to the spiritual element of the immaterial substance once it has been used (and exploited). As "firewood" the final use of wood returns to the space of the illuminating production of knowledge and reenters the nonphysical realm. The implicit reference to the fire of knowledge, the production of a consideration of the proofs of God and subjectivity that Descartes constructs while sitting by his fire, should not be overlooked here. Additionally, Lacan pushes the materiality of the desk to a level of spirituality when he attributes it with the ability to convey ideas on par with the ego. "[T]he significations to which the desk refers are in no way less dignified than those of the ego, and the proof is that on occasion they envelop the ego itself" (*Écrits*, 132–33). The insertion of the ego into the desk eliminates the sense of alienation from labor that is dominant in Hegelian and Marxist views of materialist capital production. Pushing the metonymic relationship, Lacan further implies that the ego, invested in the thing itself, is therefore reflected by that thing. One cannot help but think of the cross on which Christ is crucified and which becomes a symbol of his ego as having been present and materialized in the world. Prosopopoeia takes the scene beyond one of personification and invests the wood of the desk with a projected voice, marking the very materiality of language and the spirituality of matter.

> I am prepared to lend my voice to the real desk so that it might speak
> of its existence, which, though utilitarian, is individual, of its history,
> which, however radically alienated it may seem, has left all the evidence
> that a historian might need: documents, texts, bills detailing its fate,
> which, though inert, is dramatic, since a desk is a perishable article,
> engendered in work, a fate subject to chance, to accident, to the ups and
> downs of fashion, of fatalities even, of which it becomes the intersign,
> and which is promised to an end of which there is no need to know
> anything for it to be one's own, since we all know what that end is.
> (*Écrits*, 133)

That "we all know what that end is" appears to be a rather eschatological view of being, illustrating Lacan's position within the Catholic system that he seeks to displace and revise within his work. He alters this by asserting a variation of the process of history à la Freud that accounts for a play with temporality within the preconscious and unconscious mind that signifies within the conscious realm.

> But the whole thing would become banal if, after this prosopopoeia,
> one of you dreams that he is this desk, possessed or not with the gift of
> speech, and since the interpretation of dreams has become a well known,
> if not everyday, practice, it could hardly come as a surprise if, in deciph-
> ering the use as a signifier that this desk will have assumed in the riddle
> in which the dreamer encloses his desire, and in analyzing the more or

less equivocal reference back that this use involves in the significations that the consciousness of this desk will have aroused in him, with or without its discourse, we touch on what might be called the preconscious of this desk. (*Écrits*, 133)

The conscious realm is the place and space wherein we make the desire of the unconscious literal (legible, literary, and physical). Consciousness is also the material realm in which we can, if only momentarily, take desire literally. This is not distinct from the unconscious; rather, the conscious and unconscious are bound precisely to each other and the spiritual, material, and phenomenological fields meet in the letter. To read the process of history as one that is embedded in the space of reality because it carries with it the historical traces of being in time, we also raise the level of matter to the spiritual plane (and simultaneously unite the two eliminating any hierarchy implied therein) when we project onto the desk what we might also find in the subject.

[W]e perceive the desk and give it its meaning, and as much trouble goes into doing so, perhaps, as into the making of the thing. But even if it had been a question of a more natural being, we should never inconsiderately swallow into the consciousness the high form which, however weak we may be in the universe, guarantees us an imprescriptible dignity in it — look up "reed" in the dictionary of spiritualist thought. (*Écrits*, 133)

The dignity found in the apparent banality of making matter speak is akin to the dignity of the troubadours who were able to put an elegant twist on the melancholy, trauma, and abject horror of the scene in which the subject recognizes the insatiability of desire and the impossibility of the sexual relationship. As both are bound to signification, the function of language fails in the face of the real. The desk, in this case, holds and enables the production of the text of the unconscious and produces its recognition as real. Thought becomes "real" as it is found to be circulating within the world. Recalling the real of the signifier we find that, rather than prohibiting the connection to the material or matter (and perhaps this is what is meant when we hear that psychoanalysis is *more* materialist than Marxism), the production of the subject, of the *human* subject, is called into relief as a subject who thinks, and whose thoughts are potentially reflective of the real of universals.

It isn't difficult to make what is called through emerge from the evolution of matter, when one identifies thought with consciousness. What is difficult to make emerge from the evolution of matter is quite simply *homo faber,* production and the producer.

Production is an original domain, a domain of creation *ex nihilo,* insofar as it introduces into the natural world the organization of the signifier. It is for this reason that we only, in effect, find thought — and not in an idealist sense, but thought in its actualization in the world — in the intervals introduced by the signifier. (*Seminar VII,* 213–14)

By way of the signifier, the reality of thought is asserted into the realm of the real that is also both materiality and spirituality.

The reconciliation of psychoanalysis and Marxism or materialism, when accomplished successfully, is dependent on an understanding of Lacan's adherence to the dialectical method. If we eliminate the ability to discuss the dialectical process of desire and the unconscious from a consideration of materiality in psychoanalysis, this does not necessarily remove the potential for an understanding of its materiality. In fact, by sidestepping the convoluted maneuvers required for a reconciliation of psychoanalysis and Marxism by way of dialectics, we open a door through which to understand the manifold of materiality, phenomenality, and spirituality evident in Lacan's realism. Although Lacan follows Freud in rejecting Marx, he outlines an alternate method for approaching the material when he calls forth the question of the balance between faith and reason as that which is produced in the world by way of language.

The place of God in this world is purely supplemented by the unconscious. As that which seeks to have an impossible relation with an unknowable other, the subject displaces desire onto the idea of God, created precisely to fill this position so that desire has a localized aim. David Tracy notes that, unlike most philosophers, theologians, and psychoanalysts, Lacan knows that "God, religiously construed, is not primarily the problem of consciousness but the question of the unconscious."[48] As a subject bound to language, the sublimation of this desire, having occurred once in the form of religious belief in God, doubles back on itself to believe in the possibility of the impossible word.

Notes

Introduction

1. Julia Kristeva's dissertation asserted her position as a medievalist. Her *Tales of Love,* trans. Leon Roudiez (New York: Columbia University Press, 1987) as well as her *In the Beginning was Love: Psychoanalysis and Faith,* trans. Arthur Goldhammer (New York: Columbia University Press, 1987) also have a profound effect on the study of medieval literature and psychoanalysis.

2. Hannah Arendt, *Love and Saint Augustine,* ed. Joanna Vecchiarelli Scott (Chicago: University of Chicago Press, 1996); Martin Heidegger, *Frühe Schriften,* ed. Friedrich-Wilhelm von Herrmann, *Gesamtausgabe,* Part 1, vol. 1 (Frankfurt: Vittorio Klostermann, 1978): Georges Bataille, "L'Ordene Chevalier" (diss., École des Chartres, 1922) and also see his later work, *The Trial of Gilles de Rais,* trans. Pierre Klossowski and Richard Robinson (Los Angeles: Amok, 1991). Bataille's oeuvre is permeated by his investment in the ideas, ideologies, and texts of the Middle Ages and important to Catholicism. The influence of Heidegger and Bataille on Lacan is enormous. Bruce Holsinger's "Medieval Studies, Postcolonial Studies, and the Genealogies of Critique," *Speculum 77* (2002): 1195–1227, was one of the first articles to address this important nexus of influence by way of methodological inquiry; also his *The Premodern Condition* (Chicago: University of Chicago Press, 2005), which appeared while *Lacan's Medievalism* was at the press.

3. For a useful intervention regarding medieval studies and Michel Foucault, see Karma Lochrie, "Desiring Foucault," *Journal of Medieval and Early Modern Studies* 27, no. 1 (Winter 1997): 3–16.

4. John Simons, "Medievalism as Cultural Process in Pre-industrial Popular Literature," in *Studies in Medievalism VII, Medievalism in England II,* ed. Leslie Workman (Cambridge: D. S. Brewer, 1995), 5. See also *From Medieval to Medievalism,* ed. John Simons (Houndmills: Macmillan, 1992). *Chaucer and the Challenges of Medievalism: Studies in Honor of H. A. Kelly,* ed. Donka Minkova and Theresa Tinkle (Frankfurt: Peter Lang, 2003) suggests that "medievalism" means establishing a "voice" of the Middle Ages that is "medieval." See also Peter L. Allen, "A Frame for

the Text? History, Literary Theory, Subjectivity, and the Study of Medieval Literature," *Exemplaria* 3, no. 1 (Spring 1991), 1–28. Allen sets up the problem of studying
the Middle Ages, thinking about and potentially understanding the past, and considering one's own subjectivity as one writes.

5. Norman F. Cantor's *Inventing the Middle Ages: The Lives, Words, and Ideas of
the Great Medievalists of the Twentieth Century* (New York: William Morrow, 1991)
demonstrates the difficulties in defining the Middle Ages. Anne Middleton's "Medieval Studies," in *Redrawing the Boundaries: The Transformation of English and
American Studies,* ed. Stephen Greenblatt and Giles Gunn (New York: Modern Language Association of America, 1992), 12–40, continues to dominate our understanding of difference between the medieval and the early modern periods. Her distinctions are important for various disciplinary and institutional (as well as practical)
reasons, but for the purposes of Lacan's work, it is necessary to alter our approach,
and her essay also supports that openness.

6. D. Vance Smith's *The Book of the Incipit: Beginnings in the Fourteenth Century*
(Minneapolis: University of Minnesota Press, 2001) presents an impressive argument about the complexity of beginnings in the Middle Ages and the desire for
origins, esp. 1–41. See also Allan Frantzen, *Desire for Origins: New Language, Old
English, and Teaching the Tradition* (New Brunswick, N.J.: Rutgers, 1990); Gayle
Margherita, in *The Romance of Origins* (Philadelphia: University of Pennsylvania
Press, 1994), rightly says that deconstruction and psychoanalysis are the "theoretical
systems most concerned with the problem of origins" (xii) and she shows this dis-
sembling by way of feminist and psychoanalytical studies of medieval texts. Roger
Dragonetti's *Le Mirage des Sources: L'Art du Faux dans le Roman Médiéval* (Paris:
Seuil, 1987) illustrates another insightful approach to this issue.

7. Josef Pieper, *Scholasticism: Personalities and Problems of Medieval Philosophy*
(New York: McGraw-Hill, 1964), 22–23.

8. Richard R. Glejzer, "Lacan with Scholasticism: Agencies of the Letter," *American Imago* 54, no. 2 (1997): 105–22.

9. Eugene Vance, *From Topic to Tale: Logic and Narrativity in the Middle Ages*
(Minneapolis: University of Minnesota Press, 1987).

10. This approach goes back to the Middle Ages when scholasticism is developed as a multidisciplinary enterprise. More recently, the nineteenth- and twentieth-
century development of medieval studies and comparative literature as simultaneous and overlapping enterprises may be seen in the foundational work of Erich
Auerbach, *Mimesis,* trans. Willard R. Trask (Princeton, N.J.: Princeton University
Press, 1953) and Ernst Robert Curtius, *European Literature and the Latin Middle
Ages* (Princeton, N.J.: Princeton University Press, 1953). Contemporary work in medieval studies reflects this continuing multifaceted approach to textuality. See espe-
cially *Medievalism and the Modernist Temper,* ed. R. Howard Bloch and Stephen G.
Nichols (Baltimore: Johns Hopkins University Press, 1996) and *The Postcolonial
Middle Ages,* ed. Jeffrey Jerome Cohen (New York: Palgrave, 2000).

11. For alternate approaches to the textuality of the Middle Ages, see Gabrielle M.
Spiegel, *The Past as Text: The Theory and Practice of Medieval Historiography* (Balti-
more: Johns Hopkins University Press, 1997), esp. xx–xxi and 57–80; see also Brian
Stock, *Listening for the Text: On the Uses of the Past* (Baltimore: Johns Hopkins Uni-
versity Press, 1990); and Peter W. Williams, "The Varieties of American Medievalism,"
Studies in Medievalism 1 (1982): 7–20.

12. Kristeva, *Tales of Love,* 183.

13. See Alexandre Leupin, "The Middle Ages, the Other," *Diacritics* 13, no. 3 (Fall 1983): 22–31.

14. Arthur Stephen McGrade provides a view of psychology within scholasticism in his "Enjoyment at Oxford after Ockham: Philosophy, Psychology, and the Love of God," in *From Ockham to Wyclif,* ed. Anne Hudson and Michael Wilks (Oxford: Basil Blackwell for the Ecclesiastical History Society, 1987), 63–88.

15. Paul Vincent Spade, *Five Texts on the Mediaeval Problem of Universals: Porphyry, Boethius, Abelard, Duns Scotus, Ockham* (Indianapolis: Hackett, 1994).

16. Boethius, *Second Commentary on Porphyry's Isagoge,* in Spade, *Five Texts,* 21.

17. Paul Zumthor, *Toward a Medieval Poetics,* trans. Philip Bennett (Minneapolis: University of Minnesota Press, 1992), xxiii. (Originally published as *Essai de poétique médiévale* [Paris: Seuil, 1972]).

18. To some extent my view of "medievalism" is always haunted and guided (or at least inflected) by the approaches taken in *The New Medievalism,* ed. Marina S. Brownlee, Kevin Brownlee, and Stephen G. Nichols (Baltimore: Johns Hopkins University Press, 1991), which I read during my first year of graduate school in the spring of 1994.

19. On the politics and poetics of sainthood, see Amy Hollywood, *Sensible Ecstasy: Mysticism, Sexual Difference, and the Demands of History* (Chicago: University of Chicago Press, 2002); Alexander Irwin, *Saints of the Impossible: Bataille, Weil, and the Politics of the Sacred* (Minneapolis: University of Minnesota Press, 2002).

20. Most notably, see Roger Dragonetti, *La Vie de la Lettre au Moyen Age* (Paris: Seuil, 1980); Jean-Charles Hûchet, *L'Amour Discourtois: La "Fin Amors" chex les premiers troubadours* (Toulouse: Bibliothèque historique Privat, 1987), *Littérature Médiévale et Psychanalyse* (Paris: Presses Universitaires de France, 1990), and *Le Roman Occitan Médiéval* (Paris: Presses Universitaires de France, 1991); Henri Rey-Flaud, *La Névrose Courtoise* (Paris: Navarin Éditeur; Diffusion, Seuil, 1983); Vance, *From Topic to Tale;* Sarah Kay, *Courtly Contradictions: The Emergence of the Literary Object in the Twelfth Century* (Stanford, Calif.: Stanford University Press, 2001), and *Subjectivity in Troubadour Poetry* (Cambridge: Cambridge University Press, 1990).

21. Dominick LaCapra, *Representing the Holocaust: History, Theory, Trauma* (Ithaca, N.Y.: Cornell University Press, 1994). Following trauma theory and the notion of displacement with regard to medievalism, see Kathleen Biddick, *The Shock of Medievalism* (Durham, N.C.: Duke University Press, 1998). For a different perspective on the uses of application, see David Aers, "Medievalists and Deconstruction," in *From Medieval to Medievalism,* ed. Simons, 24–40.

22. LaCapra works through the problem of analogy and repetition and refers the reader back to Freud's comment about the splitting of the psyche resembling the medieval theory of possession (*Representing the Holocaust,* 173–84).

23. For a broad discussion of "theory" within medieval studies, see Paul Strohm, *Theory and the Premodern Text* (Minneapolis: University of Minnesota Press, 2000).

24. Fruitful applications that also move to implication include but are not limited to Carolyn Dinshaw's queer historiography in *Getting Medieval* (Durham, N.C.: Duke University Press, 1999) and the brilliant speculations on the "medieval future" in *The Postcolonial Middle Ages,* ed. Cohen. See also *The Future of the Middle Ages: Medieval Literature in the 1990s,* ed. William D. Paden (Gainesville: University Press of Florida, 1994) where the connection between psychoanalysis and philology is

explained throughout the different essays collected. This movement is also prevalent in popular culture studies, and John Simons's broad characterization of "medievalism" is useful for an understanding of the dialogue between contemporary criticism and culture and premodern culture. See John Simons, "Medievalism as Cultural Process in Pre-industrial Popular Literature," *Studies in Medievalism* 7 (1995): 5–21. The series, which is edited by Leslie J. Workman, is especially prolific regarding medievalisms. Elizabeth Emery and Laura Morowitz present an approach from different disciplines that considers various elements of culture as textuality in their *Consuming the Past: The Medieval Revival in fin-de-siècle France* (Burlington, Vt.: Ashgate, 2003). See also Margherita, *Romance of Origins,* who addresses psychoanalysis and medieval literature in connection with feminist studies to promote a dissolution of the fetish of textual and bodily origins. Roger Dragonetti's *Le Mirage des Sources* established this problem by way of a unique discursive connection between Derridean and Lacanian language that is always medievalist.

25. See Roland Barthes's notion of "textual analysis" put forth in "The Death of the Author," in *Introduction to Modern Criticism and Theory,* ed. David Lodge (New York: Longman, 2000), 146–50; Barthes, "Textual Analysis: Poe's '*Valdemar,*'" in ibid., 151–72; Jacques Derrida, *Resistances of Psychoanalysis,* trans. Peggy Kamuf et al. (Stanford, Calif.: Stanford University Press, 1998); see also John Mowitt, *Text: A Genealogy of an Antidisciplinary Object* (Durham, N.C.: Duke University Press, 1992), esp. 95–98.

26. Shoshana Felman, "To Open the Question," in *Literature and Psychoanalysis,* ed. Shoshana Felman (Baltimore: Johns Hopkins University Press, 1982), 5–10. Initially published in *Yale French Studies* 55/56 (1977): 5–10. Paul Zumthor, *Speaking of the Middle Ages,* trans. Sarah White (Lincoln: University of Nebraska Press, 1986).

27. Jeffrey Jerome Cohen's introduction to *The Postcolonial Middle Ages,* 6, also points out this *extimate* relationship and he applies the structure of the Borromean knot to the study of the Middle Ages, which would then mean, in my view, that according to the logic of psychoanalysis, the Middle Ages are the symptom of the navel.

28. L. O. Aranye Fradenburg, "We Are Not Alone: Psychoanalytic Medievalism," *New Medieval Literatures* 2 (1998): 250.

29. Elizabeth Scala, "Historicists and Their Discontents: Reading Psychoanalytically in Medieval Studies," *Texas Studies in Literature and Language* 44, no. 1 (Spring 2002): 108–30; see also Elizabeth Scala, *Absent Narratives, Manuscript Textuality and Literary Structure in Late Medieval England* (New York: Palgrave, 2002).

30. Michael Uebel's view of perverse history and the "*fort/da*-like suspension" of medievalism assists in an understanding of this permanence of the unconscious in his "The Pathogenesis of Medieval History," *Texas Studies in Literature and Language* 44, no. 1 (Spring 2002): 54.

31. Throughout his work Baudrillard expresses a symptomatic nostalgia for the potential of universals. This is most evident in *The Spirit of Terrorism,* trans. Chris Turner (New York: Verso, 2002), esp. 28–29 and 71–76. A full explication of this point will have to be deferred for another occasion. Alain Badiou's concern with the event and the truth event also take the form of a participation in the quarrel about universals, and this is most evident in his *St. Paul: The Foundation of Universalism,* trans. Ray Brassier (Stanford, Calif.: Stanford University Press, 2003), where he shows

how St. Paul is an antiphilosopher to determine the debates over the relationship between words and things.

32. Jacques Lacan, *Écrits*, trans. Alan Sheridan (New York: W. W. Norton, 1977), 256–77. Brian Fink's translation of *Écrits, The First Complete Edition in English* (New York: W. W. Norton, 2006) appeared as *Lacan's Medievalism* was being copyedited and was not used as a reference for this book. References to *Écrits* are to the former translation by Alan Sheridan unless otherwise noted.

33. Bruce Fink also takes up this challenge in his *Lacan to the Letter* (Minneapolis: University of Minnesota Press, 2004). Fink's book, which appeared while the present project was in the process of revision, takes Lacan's work, "both literally and to the letter" and he sets up a "literality" of Lacan that accounts for a metaphorical understanding of language (vii). Fink's is a great introduction to the reading of Lacan that explains basic concepts without reducing them to cliché or oversimplifying to the point of killing the letter. Like Fink, I agree that "Lacan can be an extremely precise writer" and that some of the difficulties in understanding his work are due to problems with translation (viii). Still, this is not to say that Lacan's work is ever simple, and while I attempt to be clear throughout this text, *Lacan's Medievalism* is not an introductory primer to Lacanian psychoanalysis. Along with Fink's introduction, some other useful and informative introductions to Lacan that will assist the novice to psychoanalysis include Jean-Michel Rabaté, *Jacques Lacan* (New York: Palgrave, 2001); Catherine Clément, *The Lives and Legends of Jacques Lacan*, trans. A. Goldhammer (New York: Columbia University Press, 1983); Shoshana Felman, *Jacques Lacan and the Adventure of Insight* (Cambridge, Mass.: Harvard University Press, 1995); Jane Gallop, *Reading Lacan* (Ithaca, N.Y.: Cornell University Press, 1985); Elizabeth Grosz, *Jacques Lacan: A Feminist Introduction* (New York: Routledge, 1990); François Roustang, *The Lacanian Delusion*, trans. G. Sims (Oxford: Oxford University Press, 1990); Ellie Ragland Sullivan, *Jacques Lacan and the Philosophy of Psychoanalysis* (Urbana: University of Illinois Press, 1986). Of course, the *best* way to introduce oneself to Lacan is to read Lacan and then Freud and then Lacan again!

34. In *Read My Desire: Lacan against the Historicists* (Cambridge, Mass.: MIT Press, 1994), Joan Copjec addresses the literal quality of desire and the signifier. In *Imagine There's No Woman: Ethics and Sublimation* (Cambridge, Mass.: MIT Press, 2002), 4–5, Copjec then reformulates this position to contribute to the quarrel over universals and to claim that Lacan is a realist who believes in universals.

35. The concept of ex nihilo was extremely important to medieval thinkers, even (or especially) when they did not have a symbol for *zero*. See Michel de Certeau, "The Gaze of Nicholas of Cusa," trans. Catherine Porter, *Diacritics* 17, no. 3 (Autumn 1987): 2–38; J. Hillis Miller, "Zero," in *Glossalalia*, ed. Julian Wolfreys (New York: Routledge, 2003), 369–90; Brian Rotman, *Signifying Nothing: The Semiotics of Zero* (Stanford, Calif.: Stanford University Press, 1993); Charles Seife, *Zero: The Biography of a Dangerous Idea* (New York: Penguin, 2000).

36. Indeed, Copjec addresses this as Lacan's structuralism when she points out in *Read My Desire* Lacan's claim "that the structures he is diagramming are *real*" (11). She argues that "*it is the real that unites the psychic to the social*" by way of the death drive (39). Rather than focus on the debate regarding the extent to which Lacan is a strucuralist or a post-structuralist, the emphasis here is on the "real." Also see Slavoj Žižek, "Why Lacan is Not a 'Post-Structuralist,'" *Newsletter of the Freudian Field* 2, no. 2 (Fall 1987): 31–39.

37. Jacques Derrida, "Signature, Event, Context," in *Limited Inc* (Chicago: Northwestern University Press, 1988), 1–23.

38. Medieval studies tends to be more open to the discussion of Levinas and his medievalism than it has been to Lacan's medievalism. Ann W. Astell's work on this overlap has crucial implications for the dialogue between Levinas, Lacan, and medieval studies. See also the collection *Levinas and Lacan: The Missed Encounter*, ed. Sarah Harasym (Albany: SUNY Press, 1998).

39. Serge Leclaire, "Le réel dans le texte," *Littérature* 3 (1971). For the purposes of this introduction, I use the translation by Arthur Goldhammer "The Real in the Text," in *Literary Debate: Texts and Contexts, Postwar French Thought*, vol. 2, ed. Denis Hollier and Jeffrey Mehlman (New York: New Press, 1999), 320–23. Throughout this book, I refer to translations of Lacan that are available to readers of English so as to simplify cross-referencing and to avoid referring to too many texts that readers may not recognize. When necessary, I do refer to a few untranslated essays and original French formulations that I hope become clear in my formulations.

40. Kristeva, *Tales of Love*, 183.

41. The question of loving the neighbor has been an actively discussed problem. In addition to the work done by Freud, Lacan, Agamben, Derrida, and Levinas, see especially L. O. Aranye Fradenburg, "The Love of Thy Neighbor," in *Constructing Medieval Sexuality*, ed. Karma Lochrie, Peggy McCracken, and James A. Schultz, *Medieval Cultures* 11 (Minneapolis: University of Minnesota Press, 1997), 135–57; Julia Kristeva, *Strangers to Ourselves*, trans. Leon S. Roudiez (Columbia: Columbia University Press, 1991); Slavoj Žižek, Eric L. Santner, and Kenneth Reinhard, *The Neighbor: Three Inquiries in Political Theology* (Chicago: University of Chicago Press, 2006).

42. Etienne Gilson, *The Spirit of Mediaeval Philosophy*, trans. A. H. C. Downes (Notre Dame: University of Notre Dame Press, 1991) (originally published 1936), 86. This text and his *The Christian Philosophy of St. Thomas Aquinas*, trans. L. K. Shook (Notre Dame: University of Notre Dame Press, 1994) (originally published 1956), parallel Lacan's work in many ways such that I am led to believe that Lacan was in close contact with Gilson, his lectures, and his ideas throughout both of their careers. In the conclusion I speculate about the significance of this mirroring epistemology despite the differing topics and methods with regard to an understanding of the quarrel of the universals and the psyche.

43. Discussions of the significance of zero assist in a larger understanding of this process. See esp. Brian Rotman, *Signifying Nothing: The Semiotics of Zero* (Stanford, Calif.: Stanford University Press, 1987), and J. Hillis Miller's "Zero," in *Glossalalia*, ed. Julian Wolfreys (New York: Routledge, 2003), 369–90.

44. Luce Irigaray perceives and argues this throughout her work, especially in *Speculum of the Other Woman*, trans. Gillian C. Gill (Ithaca, N.Y.: Cornell University Press, 1985) and *This Sex Which Is Not One*, trans. Catherine Porter (Ithaca, N.Y.: Cornell University Press, 1985), and throughout her work approaches the female subject by way of this mimetic splitting, providing an alternate and equally alienated (excommunicated) approach to ontology as Lacan.

45. Slavoj Žižek, *The Metastases of Enjoyment* (New York: Verso, 1994).

46. The approach to (anti)periodicity and a concept of the premodern and the modern supports the title of Bruno Latour's insightful book, *We Have Never Been Modern*, trans. Catherine Porter (Cambridge, Mass.: Harvard University Press, 1993).

47. Alexandre Leupin, "What is Modernity? The Theory of Epistemological Cuts," Maxwell Cummings lecture, McGill University, Thursday, 4 October 2001. Leupin's work in general has been instrumental in creating insightful approaches to the mutual implications between medieval studies and psychoanalysis.

48. Sigmund Freud, "The Rat Man: Notes upon a Case of Obsessional Neurosis," in *Three Case Histories,* ed. Philip Rieff (New York: Collier Books, 1963), 36.

49. This is quite different from Louis Althusser's conception of the ideological forces that affect the unconscious set forth in his famous essay on "Ideological State Apparatuses," in *Lenin and Philosophy,* trans. Ben Brewster (New York: Monthly Review Press, 1971), 127–86. Beginning with this basic understanding of the unconscious as a real, it is important to outline first the way in which the unconscious is protected from the imposition or alteration of ideological forces and structures. Once this has been established, a more nuanced understanding of the effects of external stimuli on the unconscious will be addressed.

50. In "Towards a Semiology of Paragrams," in *The Tel Quel Reader,* ed. Patrick Ffrench and Roland-François Lack (New York: Routledge, 1998), 25–49, Julia Kristeva shows how "Poetic language is a dialogue between two discourses" (29).

51. Anicius Manlius Severinus Boethius, *The Theological Tractates,* trans. H. F. Steward, E. K. Rand, and S. J. Tester (Cambridge, Mass.: Harvard University Press, 1973), 16–17. All citations of Boethius are from this volume.

52. Isidore de Séville, *Etymologies,* trans. and ed. P. K. Marshall (Paris: "Les Belles Lettres," 1981–86).

53. Jacques Lacan, *The Seminar of Jacques Lacan, Book II: The Ego in Freud's Theory and in the Technique of Psychoanalysis,* ed. Jacques-Alain Miller, trans. Sylvana Tomaselli (New York: W. W. Norton, 1991).

54. Guy Durandin's most relevant text regarding this subject is *L'information, la désinformation et la réalité* (Paris: Presses Universitaires de France [coll. Le psychologue], 1993).

55. See Russell A. Peck, "Chaucer and the Nominalist Questions," *Speculum* 53 (1978): 745–60, esp. 757; see also Richard Paul Desharnais, "The History of the Distinction between God's Absolute and Ordained Power and its Influence on Martin Luther" (Ph.D. diss., Catholic University of America, 1966), 119.

56. Robert Myles, *Chaucerian Realism* (Cambridge: D. S. Brewer, 1994), 2.

57. Myles is not alone in this perception. In *Schools and Scholars in Fourteenth-Century England* (Princeton, N.J.: Princeton University Press, 1987), 173 n. 205. William J. Courtenay said that William of Ockham would not have called himself a nominalist since the term would likely have referred to Peter Abelard's language-theory. A. J. Minnis also notes this point in "Looking for a Sign: The Quest for Nominalism in Chaucer and Langland," in *Essays on Ricardian Literature in Honour of J. A. Burrow,* ed. A. J. Minnis, Charlotte C. Morse, and Thorlac Turville-Petre (Oxford: Clarendon Press, 1997), 144.

58. Myles, *Chaucerian Realism,* 1. The only main problem with these definitions is the qualification of "to some degree" that pervades the explanations of epistemological, semiotic or linguistic, and psychological realisms. I will assume that "to some degree" allows for various degrees and limits the nonrealist to one who simply does not believe in the potential for these forms of knowledge *at all.*

59. Jacques Lacan, "The Agency of the Letter in the Unconscious," in *Écrits,* 146–75.

60. Alexandre Leupin, *Lacan Today* (New York: Other Press, 2004), xxv.

61. I am paraphrasing from Jacques Lacan, "La logique du fantasm," and "De la psychanalyse dans ses rapports avec la réalité," in *Autres Écrits*, ed. Jacques-Alain Miller (Paris: Seuil, 2001), 327 and 351. Also see Leupin, *Lacan Today*, 112.

62. Jacques Lacan, *The Seminar of Jacques Lacan, Book XX: On Feminine Sexuality, the Limits of Love and Knowledge, Encore*, trans. Bruce Fink (New York: W. W. Norton, 1998), 126–27.

63. In *Lacan Today*, Leupin addresses the extent to which God is (a) real (105–23); for discussions of the impossibility of knowing God, also see Leupin's *Fiction and Incarnation* (Minneapolis: University of Minnesota Press, 2000); *God, the Gift, and Postmodernism*, ed. John D. Caputo and Michael J. Scanlon (Bloomington: Indiana University Press, 1999). On the relationship between psychoanalysis, theology, and literature, Françoise Meltzer's work is crucial and delightful; see *For Fear of the Fire: Joan of Arc and the Limits of Subjectivity* (Chicago: University of Chicago Press, 2001).

1. Singularity, Sovereignty, and the One

1. Chaucer the poet is also Chaucer the philosopher. Rodney Delasanta notes the origins of this perception in his "Nominalism and Typology in Chaucer," in *Typology and English Medieval Literature*, ed. Hugh T. Keenan (New York: AMS Press, 1992), 121–40. "When Sir Lewis Clifford returned from a diplomatic trip to France in 1386, he presented Geoffrey Chaucer with a ballade from Eustace Deschamps in which the French poet apostrophized his English counterpart as a 'Socrates plan de philosophie' and a 'Seneque en meurs.' At about the same time, while Thomas Usk was awaiting execution in Newgate and lucklessly importuning friends in high places with his *Testament of Love*, he saw fit to address Chaucer therein as 'the noble philosophical poete in Englissh' " (121).

"In concert with Aristotle he [Thomas Aquinas] insisted that human knowledge was generated from particulars apprehended by the senses, particulars from which universals *in re* could only be abstracted *post rem* by the active intellect. Although *ante-rem* universals remained exemplars in the mind of God, man knew reality, in the Thomistic synthesis, not by any illumination emanating therefrom but by a process of abstraction that proceeded from sense experience to image to idea: *nihil in intellecu quod prius in sensu*. Thus, to repeat the well-known Thomistic formula: essence precedes existence ontologically, but existence precedes essence psychologically" (124).

2. Jacques Lacan, *The Seminar of Jacques Lacan, Book VII: The Ethics of Psychoanalysis*, ed. Jacques-Alain Miller, trans. Dennis Porter (New York: W. W. Norton, 1992), 182.

3. In chapter 2 I will show how this fragility is also a signifier of animality.

4. Like Lacan, Slavoj Žižek uses the naked king as a refrain throughout his work.

5. A. J. Minnis, "Looking for a Sign: The Quest for Nominalism in Chaucer and Langland," in *Essays on Ricardian Literature in Honour of J. A. Burrow*, ed. A. J. Minnis, Charlotte C. Morse, and Thorlac Turville-Petre (Oxford: Clarendon Press, 1997), 141–78. Minnis questions the relationship between nominalism and classicism, which latter term he employs instead of "humanism." "[A]s far as Chaucer is concerned, there seems to be no necessity to allege the influence of radical, specifically Nomi-

nalist, ideas. And such influence should not be posited without necessity" (149). Robert Myles is obviously in agreement in his *Chaucerian Realism* (Cambridge: D. S. Brewer, 1994). Delasanta makes the argument a bit more complex by splitting Chaucer the Poet from Chaucer the Pilgrim. "At its philosophical/esthetic base, I contend that while Chaucer the *Pilgrim* serves as the spokesman for a *nominalist* epistemology that, by limiting its vision to the palpably empirical, unwittingly dramatizes the inadequacies of reason, Chaucer the *Poet* continues to uphold a more traditional epistemology that has abandoned neither those *ante-rem* ideas located 'perdurably in the devyne thought' (*Boece*, V, Prosa 4, 170) nor the *in-re* and *post-rem* universals whose *locus* is 'yplounged' and 'yhyd' deep in the 'rote of sothfastnesse' (*Boece*, III, Metrum 11)" (132).

6. See Seth Lerer, *Chaucer and His Readers* (Princeton, N.J.: Princeton University Press, 1993), 22–56.

7. This is, of course, not to say that all left-wing thinkers are intellectuals or that all right-wing adherents are ideologues; it is, rather, simply to follow Lacan's distinction of the fool from the knave and to begin to understand how this distinction participates in his contribution to the quarrel of universals.

8. *The Riverside Chaucer*, ed. Larry D. Benson, 3rd edition (New York: Houghton Mifflin, 1987). All Chaucer citations in this chapter are from this edition.

9. Drucilla Cornell, "Rethinking the Beyond of the Real," in *Levinas and Lacan: The Missed Encounter*, ed. Sarah Harasym (Albany: SUNY Press, 1998), 140.

10. Russell A. Peck, "Chaucer and the Nominalist Questions," *Speculum* 53 (1978): 746.

11. See also William J. Courtenay, "Nominalism and Late Medieval Religion," in *The Pursuit of Holiness in Late Medieval and Renaissance Religion: Papers from the University of Michigan Conference*, ed. Charles Trinkaus and Heiko A. Oberman (Leiden: Brill, 1974), 51–56, where we find a form of empiricism wherein knowing is bound to seeing in nominalism.

12. Jacques Lacan, *Télévision* (Paris: Seuil, 1974), and the translation *Television*, trans. Denis Hollier, *October* 40 (Spring 1987): 14.

13. Lacan already gives us a clear translation, but the history of the term στοιχεῖον, *stoicheion* or "element," contributes to an understanding of the significance of the *element* as a single body, or "one," within the history of knowledge and subjectivity. The element also has a role in change and genesis and it refers to the elements and principles in Pythagorean theory. It is also the "unnamed element" in Epicurean thought. See F. E. Peters, *Greek Philosophical Terms: A Historical Lexicon* (New York: New York University Press, 1967), 212.

14. Jacques Lacan, "The Mirror Stage as Formative of the Function of the I as Revealed in Psychoanalytic Experience," in *Écrits*, trans. Alan Sheridan (New York: W. W. Norton, 1977), 1–7.

15. In *Lacan Today* (New York: Other Press, 2004), Alexandre Leupin explains how Lacan's realism is not idealism.

16. This realism is strictly opposed to literary "realism," which presumes that one can fully represent the mind of a character or moment in time and space.

17. Anicius Manlius Severinus Boethius, *The Consolation of Philosophy*, trans. Richard Green (Indianapolis: Bobbs-Merrill, 1962).

18. Jacques Lacan, *The Seminar of Jacques Lacan, Book I: Freud's Papers on Technique*, ed. Jacques-Alain Miller, trans. John Forrester (New York: W. W. Norton, 1991).

19. Martha Nussbaum, *The Therapy of Desire* (Princeton, N.J.: Princeton University Press, 1994), 19.

20. St. Augustine, *Confessions*, trans. R. S. Pine-Coffin (New York: Penguin, 1961). Hannah Arendt's 1929 dissertation *Love and St. Augustine* (Chicago: University of Chicago Press, 1996) sets forth a brilliant intervention in discussion of Augustine's politics of desire.

21. Nussbaum, *Therapy of Desire*, 80–81, describes Aristotle's views on rational and irrational emotions as they equate the rational with truth and the irrational with falsity.

22. Aristotle, *Nichomachean Ethics*, in *The Basic Works of Aristotle*, ed. Richard McKeon (New York: Modern Library, 2001), 935–1126.

23. Jacques Lacan, *The Seminar of Jacques Lacan, Book XI: The Four Fundamental Concepts of Psychoanalysis*, ed. Jacques-Alain Miller, trans. Alan Sheridan (New York: W. W. Norton, 1977) (originally published 1973).

24. *Eudaimonia* means happiness.

25. Lacan's exploration into the game of even and odd, as well as his work on the purloined letter, addresses this element of "chance." I will return to a discussion of it in chapters 3 and 5.

26. As Edmund Reiss notes in his *Boethius* (Boston: Twayne, 1982), 53, Boethius had plans to translate Plato. In his commentaries on *On Interpretation* Boethius wrote: "Thus I may present, well ordered and illustrated with the light of comment, whatever subtlety of logic's art, whatever weight of moral experience, and whatever insight into natural truth, may be gathered from Aristotle. And I mean to translate all the dialogues of Plato, or deuce them in my commentary to a Latin form. Having accomplished this, I shall not have despised the opinions of Aristotle and Plato if I evoke a certain concord between them and show in how many things of importance for philosophy they agree" (*De Interpretatione vel periermenias translatio Boethii.*, *ed. secunda*, 2:2, trans. Henry O. Taylor, *The Mediaeval Mind* [Cambridge, Mass.: Harvard University Press, 1959], 1: 91–92). As Reiss reminds us, Boethius's Platonism was identified by Etienne Gilson who argues, "the logica of Boethius is a commentary on Aristotle's in which the desire to interpret it according to Plato's philosophy frequently shows through": *History of Christian Philosophy in the Middle Ages* (London: Sheed and Ward, 1955), 98, cited more frequently in the present text as *The Spirit of Mediaeval Philosophy*.

27. Etienne Gilson, *The Spirit of Mediaeval Philosophy*, trans. A. H. C. Downes (Notre Dame, Ind.: University of Notre Dame Press, 1991) (originally published 1936), 369.

28. L. O. Aranye Fradenburg, *Sacrifice Your Love: Psychoanalysis, Historicism, Chaucer* (Minneapolis: University of Minnesota Press, 2002), 107.

29. Shadia B. Drury's *Alexandre Kojève: The Roots of Postmodern Politics* (New York: St. Martin's Press, 1994) explores the debate between Kojève and Strauss in relation to the politics of modernity (esp. 143–60).

30. Much important work on sovereignty, politics, and free will has been done. For a good beginning that is relevant to this discussion, see Carl Schmitt, *Political Theology* (Cambridge, Mass.: MIT Press, 1985) (originally published 1922); see also *The Challenge of Carl Schmitt*, ed. Chantal Mouffe (New York: Verso, 1999).

31. I am grateful to Ann W. Astell for inviting me to discuss *The Clerk's Tale* at the Medieval Colloquium at Purdue University, and for assigning me the task of juxtaposing *The Clerk's Tale* with Lacan.

32. The fact that the Clerk cites Petrarch and follows his rendering of the tale instead of Boccaccio's suggests to me that Chaucer is representing the Clerk as one who addresses representation rather than investigating sources and origins. The play with citation and lack thereof calls attention to the lacks in the Clerk's education. The topic of intertextuality in the tale is a popular one, and this chapter seeks to participate in the debate in a way that opens intertextuality to include psychoanalysis. See J. Burke Severs, *The Literary Relationships of Chaucer's Clerk's Tale* (New Haven, Conn.: Yale University Press, 1942). Also see the essays in *"The Decameron" and the "Canterbury Tales": New Essays on an Old Question,* ed. Leonard Michael Koff and Brenda Deen Schildgen (Madison: Fairleigh Dickinson University Press; London: Associated University Presses, 2000); David Wallace, "'Whan She Translated Was': A Chaucerian Critique of the Petrarchan Academy," in *Literary Practice and Social Change in Britain, 1390–1530,* ed. Lee Patterson (Berkeley and Los Angeles: University of California Press, 1990), 156–215.

33. Much may be said about the father-daughter relationships in *The Clerk's Tale.* Because I am attempting to avoid the stereotypically pop-Freudian discussion of the Oedipus complex, and because Walter's substitution of his daughter for Griselda and Griselda's substitution of Walter for her father are quite obvious and directly express the process within the Oedipus complex, I will leave that to the reader to determine for herself. For a different approach that engages psychoanalysis, see Patricia Cramer, "Lordship, Bondage, and the Erotic: The Psychological Bases of Chaucer's *Clerk's Tale,*" *Journal of English and Germanic Philology* 89, no. 4 (October 1990): 491–511.

34. For a view that situates this obedience within a historical context, see Michael Hanrahan, "'A Straunge Successour Sholde Take Your Heritage': *The Clerk's Tale* and the Crisis of Ricardian Rule," *Chaucer Review* 35, no. 4 (2001): 335–50, esp. 338. On the power dynamics, see Donald C. Green, "The Semantics of Power: 'Maistrie' and 'Soveraynetee' in *The Canterbury Tales,*" *Modern Philology* 84, no. 1 (August 1986): 18–23, esp. 23 where he notes that the term "maistrie" does not occur in *The Clerk's Tale.*

35. Alain Badiou, *Ethics: An Essay on the Understanding of Evil,* trans. Peter Hallward (New York: Verso, 2001), 47.

36. In Sarah Stanbury's reading Walter's patriarchal masculine gaze denudes Griselda. See Sarah Stanbury, "Regimes of the Visual in Premodern England: Gaze, Body, and Chaucer's *Clerk's Tale,*" *New Literary History* 28, no. 2 (1997): 261–89; she draws on Michael Camille's analysis of the phallic gaze set forth in his *Gothic Idol: Ideology and Image-Making in Medieval Art* (Cambridge: Cambridge University Press, 1989), 304.

37. On Griselda, sexuality, and feminism, see Carolyn Dinshaw, *Chaucer's Sexual Poetics* (Madison: University of Wisconsin Press, 1989); Charlotte Morse, "The Exemplary Griselda," *Studies in the Ages of Chaucer* 7 (1985): 51–86; Emma Campbell, "Sexual Poetics and the Politics of Translation in the Tale of Griselda," *Comparative Literature* 55, no. 3 (Summer 2003): 191–216.

38. Warren Ginsberg notes in "Petrarch, Chaucer and the Clerk" the irony that the Clerk is an Aristotelian, and that he dismisses the prohemium, which provides evidence of Petrarch's shift from invective to moral philosophy, points to the gaps in the Clerk's hermeneutical skills as well as Chaucer's commentary on the limits of dialectics. Warren Ginsburg, *Chaucer's Italian Tradition* (Ann Arbor: University of Michigan Press, 2002), 240–69.

39. Jill Mann, *Chaucer and Medieval Estates Satire* (Cambridge: Cambridge University Press, 1973), 74.

40. Eugene Victor Wolfstein, *Psychoanalytic Marxism* (New York: Guilford Press, 1993).

41. Ann W. Astell, *Chaucer and the Universe of Learning* (Ithaca, N.Y.: Cornell University Press, 1996), 55. J. Burke Severs, "Chaucer's Clerks," in *Chaucer and Medieval English Studies,* ed. Beryl Rowland (London: George Allen and Unwin, 1974), 140–52.

42. Here Astell extends Donald Howard's argument that "The Idealized Clerk represents an estate other than the traditional three, but by Chaucer's time the universities were a world unto themselves" (56). See Donald Howard, *The Idea of the "Canterbury Tales"* (Berkeley and Los Angeles: University of California Press, 1967), 52.

43. Ann W. Astell, *Job, Boethius and Epic Truth* (New York: Cornell University Press, 1994), 73.

44. As Ann W. Astell shows in *Job, Boethius and Epic Truth,* the Book of Job becomes an epic central to the literature of the Middle Ages. To speak of the epic presumes the ability to speak of universals, however, and in order to understand these universals it is first crucial to find elements of realism, nominalism, and singularity within the potential order or disorder of categories. Despite the play with the categories of realism and nominalism that appears throughout Chaucer's oeuvre, he consistently produces texts that are structurally categorical. It may be said that the framed groupings of singular moments in *The Canterbury Tales, The Parliament of Fowls,* or *The Legend of Good Women* display monadic themes that seek to undo generalities; however, they still provide overarching narratives of group performance. Even the direct translations, *Boece, Troilus and Criseyde,* the *Romaunt of the Rose,* perform imitation in a manner that gestures to a realist adherence to linguistic universals.

45. Astell, *Job, Boethius, and Epic Truth,* esp. 104–5.

46. Drury, *Alexandre Kojève,* 143–60, explores the debate between Kojève and Strauss in relation to the politics of modernity.

47. Catherine Clément's *Syncope* (Minneapolis: University of Minnesota Press, 1994) thoroughly and brilliantly examines the manner in which ecstasy or rapture revises the history of philosophy.

48. Jacques Derrida, *Archive Fever,* trans. Eric Prenowitz (Chicago: University of Chicago Press, 1996), 77. Derrida also says that the One is violent: "As soon as there is the One, there is murder, wounding, traumatism. *L'Un se garde de l'autre.* The One guards against/keeps some of the other. It protects *itself* from the other, but, in the movement of this jealous violence, it comprises in itself, thus guarding it, the self-otherness or self-difference (the difference from within oneself) which makes it One.... The One makes itself violence. It violates and does violence to itself but it also institutes itself as violence. It becomes what it is, the very violence that it does to itself. Self-determination as violence" (78).

49. On this fragmentation, see Thomas Pepper, "The Story of I/i," in *Glossalalia,* ed. Julian Wolfreys (New York: Routledge, 2003), 129–56.

50. Repetition and repetition compulsion are significant to a process of analysis of the text and of the psyche.

51. Jacques Lacan, *The Seminar of Jacques Lacan, Book XX: On Feminine Sexuality, the Limits of Love and Knowledge, Encore,* trans. Bruce Fink (New York: W. W. Norton, 1998), 3.

52. Louise Olga (Aranye) Fradenburg, "Sovereign Love: The Wedding of Margaret Tudor and James IV of Scotland," in *Cosmos: The Yearbook of the Traditional Cosmology Society*, vol. 7, *Women and Sovereignty*, ed. Fradenburg (Edinburgh: Edinburgh University Press, 1992), 78–100. Reflecting the importance of group formation and hierarchy in the establishment of sovereignty, she also follows Pierre Bourdieu to argue that "Communitas is one of the means by which power makes love: it is the (ritual) refashioning of captivation as an experience of freedom, a remaking of the subject to enable identification with, and idealization of, an authority experienced as liberating and unifying rather than repressive and divisive; and it is a suspending of statuses or ranks to which the subject might aspire, of futures into which the subject might project his or her designs. As just such a redemption of the *difference* between sovereign and subject, communitas is essential to sovereign love: it captures productive desire *for* hierarchy" (80). For an insightful reading of sovereignty with relation to historicity and Arthuriana, see Patricia Ingham, *Sovereign Fantasies: Arthurian Romance and the Making of Britain* (Philadelphia: University of Pennsylvania Press, 2001); esp. relevant are 21–50.

53. Aristotle, *Organon*, in *Basic Works*, ed. McKeon, 1–217.

2. Duality, Ambivalence, and the Animality of Desire

1. Drucilla Cornell, "Rethinking the Beyond of the Real," in *Levinas and Lacan: The Missed Encounter*, ed. Sarah Harasym (Albany: SUNY Press, 1998), 171.

2. As Aristotle says in his explanation of priority, we must have two "ones" before we can have "two": "if 'two' exists, it follows directly that 'one' must exist, but if 'one' exists, it does not follow necessarily that 'two' exists" (*Categories*, 12, in *The Basic Works of Aristotle*, ed. Richard McKeon [New York: Modern Library, 2001], 34).

3. Renata Salečl's *(Per)versions of Love and Hate* (New York: Verso, 1998) is an excellent example of a text that walks the line between maintaining an awareness of ambivalence and accounting for the dialectical structure of binary interaction.

4. Eugene Vance's chapter by this title, "Si est homo, est animal," insightfully explores the realm of the animal in the human in Chrétien's *Yvain*, showing the ethical limitations of the "man-beast" and questioning, then, the implications for an understanding of ethics in more proper "men." See *From Topic to Tale: Logic and Narrativity in the Middle Ages* (Minneapolis: University of Minnesota Press, 1987), 53–79. This exploration continues in his subsequent chapter, "From Man-Beast to Lion-Knight: Difference, Kind, and Emblem" (80–108), where he shows the humanist ideal to be present in Chrétien, thus locating it earlier in history than the traditional placement in the "Renaissance."

5. Sigmund Freud, *Three Case Histories*, ed. Philip Rieff (New York: Collier Books, 1963).

6. Chris Powici, "A Wolf Sublime: Psychoanalysis and the Animal," *World Views: Environment, Culture, Religion* 6, no. 1 (March 2002): 1–11. Powici cites Alan Bleakley who in *The Animalizing Imagination* says that " 'what frightens us about animals — just as it simultaneously intrigues us — is not their irrationality, their bestiality, their primitiveness, but the depth, the sublimity, the sheer range and unpredictability of their aesthetic self-display' " (5). This furthers the notion that the unconscious process of desire is at stake in an accounting for the animality within the human as that which

is "uncontrollable" and "unpredictable"; in this sense, the speaking subject is constantly enacting an "aesthetic self-display."

7. The cutting open of the stomach refers to reproduction, the violence of birth and castration, and it reflects the fragility of the subject.

8. Plato, *Laws*, 8.843 and 11.933, in *The Collected Dialogues*, ed. Edith Hamilton and Huntington Cairns (Princeton, N.J.: Princeton University Press, 1961).

9. Plato, *Republic*, 8.564, especially the discussion of the drones in *Collected Dialogues*, ed. Hamilton and Cairns, 793. The potential for sovereignty in the Platonic case is one wherein the *human* is in control and the *animals*, the bees, are subject to the human. Of course, Aristophanes explores this in *The Bees*. Agamben shows how the captivation of the bees is represented as a distinguishing factor between the human and the animal; the process of desire at stake in this discussion, however, is uncannily similar to that portrayed by Lacan. The bees are also used as an example of the one and the many in the *Meno*.

10. Jacques Derrida, *Of Spirit: Heidegger and the Question*, trans. Geoffrey Bennington and Rachel Bowlby (Chicago: University of Chicago Press, 1989).

11. Giorgio Agamben, *The Open: Man and Animal*, trans. Kevin Attell (Stanford, Calif.: Stanford University Press, 2004). Agamben's early work on poetics asserts his voice as one that contributes to a conception of medieval poetics. See Giorgio Agamben, *Stanze: La parola e il fantasma nella cultura occidentale* (Turino: Einaudi, 1977).

12. Jacques Lacan, *The Seminar of Jacques Lacan, Book VII: The Ethics of Psychoanalysis*, ed. Jacques-Alain Miller, trans. Dennis Porter (New York: W. W. Norton, 1992), 19.

13. Heidegger in Agamben, *The Open*, 52–53.

14. Jacques Derrida, *Without Alibi*, trans. Peggy Kamuf (Stanford, Calif.: Stanford University Press, 2002). Like "For the Love of Lacan" (39–69) and the other essays (lectures) in *Resistances of Psychoanalysis*, trans. Peggy Kamuf et al. (Stanford, Calif.: Stanford University Press, 1998), as well as much of his other work, Derrida's *Without Alibi* sets forth what I see to be a commentary on and analysis of psychoanalysis especially with relation to sovereignty and ambivalence.

15. Jacques Lacan, *Television*, trans. Denis Hollier, *October* 40 (Spring 1987): 6–50.

16. Jane Gallop, *Thinking through the Body* (New York: Columbia University Press, 1988).

17. Heidegger quoted in Derrida, *Of Spirit*, 52–53.

18. In the final section of chapter 5 we will see how this transfers to Lacan's view of the Thing, for now the discussion is limited to the element of animality/humanity that is at stake in ambivalence.

19. The excised portion here says: "In being written or not all being written (for in crossing-through, Heidegger lets what he crosses through be read and he says in this very place that one 'ought' to cross through, but he doesn't, as if he were crossing-through the crossing-through, avoiding avoidance, avoiding without avoiding), it is as if, for the animal lacking access to the entity as such, the latter, i.e. the Being of the entity, were crossed out in advance, but with an absolute crossing-out, that of privation. . . . What is signaled by this animal crossing-through, if we can call it that? Or rather, what is signaled by the word 'crossing-through'; which we write a propos of the animal 'world' and which ought, in its logic, to overtake all words from the moment they say something about the world?" (Derrida, *Of Spirit*, 53–54).

20. Lacan adds that "This still leaves the category of *homme*-sick animals, thereby called domestics *(d'hommestiques)*, who for that reason are shaken, however briefly, by unconscious seismic tremors" *(Television,* 9). The consideration of domestic animals in the conception of the dissolution of anthropocentrism is a crucial one that has been undertaken by Donna Haraway, *The Companion Species Manifesto: Dogs, People, and Significant Otherness* (New York: Prickly Paradigm Press, 2003).

21. Agamben says in *The Open:* "The passage from animal to man, despite the emphasis placed on comparative anatomy and paleontological findings, was produced by subtracting an element that had nothing to do with either one, and that instead was presupposed as the identifying characteristic of the human: language. In identifying himself with language, the speaking man places his own muteness outside of himself, as already and not yet human" (34–35).

22. On becoming-animal and becoming-woman, see Gilles Deleuze and Felix Guattari, *A Thousand Plateaus: Capitalism and Schizophrenia,* trans. Brian Massumi (Minneapolis: University of Minnesota Press, 1987), 232–309.

23. R. Howard Bloch, *The Anonymous Marie de France* (Chicago: University of Chicago Press, 2003).

24. Agamben calls attention to the constructedness of this distinction, which Lacan also recognizes but cannot get beyond. For Agamben, the solution to the problem of the limit of language is a hybrid form of animalization of man or humanization of the animal: "What distinguishes man from animal is language, but this is not a natural given already inherent in the psychophysical structure of man; it is, rather, a historical production which, as such, can be properly assigned neither to man nor to animal. If this element is taken away, the difference between man and animal vanishes, unless we imagine a nonspeaking *man—Homo alalus,* precisely— who would function as a bridge that passes from the animal to the human. But all evidence suggests that this is only a shadow cast by language, a presupposition of speaking man, by which we always obtain only an animalization of man . . . or a humanization of the animal. . . . The animal-man and the man-animal are the two sides of a single fracture, which cannot be mended from either side" *(The Open,* 36).

25. This is in contrast to Boethius's notion of the werewolf. In *The Consolation of Philosophy* 4.3 (trans. Richard Green [Indianapolis: Bobbs-Merrill, 1962]) Boethius refers to the werewolf as a malevolent figure, revealing the animality of being that is not subject to reason, will, or "humanity."

26. Leslie Dunton-Downer, "Wolf Man," in *Becoming Male in the Middle Ages,* ed. Jeffrey Jerome Cohen and Bonnie Wheeler (New York: Garland, 1997), 203–18, esp. 204 and 205.

27. *The Lais of Marie de France,* trans. Robert Hanning and Joan Ferrante (Durham, N.C.: Labyrinth Press, 1982), lines 9–12. All citations are from this translation.

28. Alain Badiou, *Ethics: An Essay on the Understanding of Evil,* trans. Peter Hallward (New York: Verso, 2001), 47.

29. See R. Howard Bloch, *Medieval Misogyny and the Invention of Western Romantic Love* (Chicago: University of Chicago Press, 1991); E. Jane Burns explores the role of clothing and cross-dressing in courtly love in her essay "Courtly Love: Who Needs It? Recent Feminist Work in the Medieval French Tradition," *Signs* 27, no. 1 (Autumn 2001): 23–57.

30. Giorgio Agamben, *Homo Sacer: Sovereign Power and Bare Life* (Stanford, Calif.: Stanford University Press, 1998).

31. See Carl Schmitt, *Political Theology* (Cambridge, Mass.: MIT Press, 1985); George Schwab, *The Challenge of the Exception* (New York: Greenwood Press, 1970); Renato Cristi, *Carl Schmitt and Authoritarian Liberalism* (Cardiff: University of Wales Press, 1998); C. E. Merrian Jr., *History of the Theory of Sovereignty Since Rousseau* (New York: Columbia University Press, 1900; repr., AMS Press, 1968); Agamben, *Homo Sacer;* and *The Challenge of Carl Schmitt,* ed. Chantal Mouffe (New York: Verso, 1999).

32. On torture and the process of determining the "truth," see Page Du Bois, *Torture and Truth* (New York: Routledge, 1991) and Elaine Scarry, *The Body in Pain: The Making and Unmaking of the World* (New York: Oxford University Press, 1985).

33. This dualistic dynamic of attraction/repulsion takes on a specific discursive and scientific form as Eros/Thanatos in Sigmund Freud, *Beyond the Pleasure Principle,* trans. and ed. James Strachey (New York: W. W. Norton, 1961).

34. Sigmund Freud, *The Freud Reader,* ed. and trans. Peter Gay (New York: W. W. Norton, 1981), 431.

35. All of the fine essays in *Melusine of Lusignan: Founding Fiction in Late Medieval France,* ed. Donald Maddox and Sara Sturm-Maddox (Athens: University of Georgia Press, 1996) address this relationship between the composition and dissemination of *Mélusine* and the relationship between romance, history, maternal and paternal lines, as well as hybrid forms of monstrous-humans. Also see Jacques Le Goff and Emmanuel Le Roy Ladurie, "Mélusine maternelle et défricheuse," *Annales: Economies, Sociétés, Civilizations* 26 (1971): 587–622.

36. Jean d'Arras, *Mélusine: Roman du XIV Siècle,* ed. Louis Stouff (Dijon: Publication de l'Université, 1932; rpt. Geneva: Slatkine Reprints, 1974); Jean d'Arras, *Le Roman de Mélusine ou l'histoire des Lusignan,* trans. into modern French by Michèle Perret (Paris: Stock Plus, 1979); and the mimetic appropriation of the text by Coudrette, *Le Roman de Mélusine ou Histoire de Lusignan,* ed. Eleanor Roach (Paris: Klincksiek, 1982); Coudrette, *Le Roman de Mélusine,* trans. into modern French by Laurence Harf-Lancner (Paris: Garnier-Flammarion, 1993). Unless otherwise noted I am referring to the Old French Jean d'Arras edited by Stouff as cited above.

37. For Douglas Kelly, this means that she "never attains humanity" ("The Domestication of the Marvelous in the Melusine Romances," 33), for Stephen Nicols this signifies ambivalence ("Melusine Between Myth and History," 139), and Gabrielle M. Spiegel notes the maternal and the phallic in her form ("Maternity and Monstrosity," 107), all in *Melusine of Lusignan,* ed. Maddox and Sturm-Maddox.

38. Derrida discusses the problematic connection between the gift and the punishment in *Dissemination,* trans. Barbara Johnson (Chicago: University of Chicago Press, 1983) as well as *The Gift of Death,* trans. David Wills (Chicago: University of Chicago Press, 1995).

39. Especially nineteenth-century historians as "mére Lusigne" or mother of the Lusignan family sometimes read "Mé-lusine."

40. Jules Baudot, *Les Princesses Yolande et Les Ducs de Bar de la Famille des Valois* (Paris: Alphonse Picard et Fils, 1900).

41. Ibid., 330. See the *Chroniques de Froissart,* ed. and trans. John Jolliffe (London: Harvill Press, 1967). Baudot's text covers the different forms of histories that in some way rely on Mélusine. These include Histories of Kings, Histories of Places, particular genealogical histories, Chronicles of France, histories of literature between the fourteenth and sixteenth centuries.

42. It is likely that Jean d'Arras composed the prose tale under the patronage of the duke of Berry as a gift for Marie de France. This would place it in appropriate juxtaposition, enabling ease of comparison by way of Seth Lerer's argument about the anthologization of texts in manuscript collections and patronage histories: "Medieval English Literature and the Idea of the Anthology," *PMLA* 118, no. 5 (October 2003): 1251–67.

43. *The Romans of Partenay*, ed. Walter W. Skeat, EETS o.s. 22 (London: Early English Text Society, 1866; New York: Kraus Reprint, 1987), xv.

44. Coudrette's Old French reads, "Le philozophe fut moult sage / Qui dist en la premiere page / De sa noble Methaphisique / Que humain entendement s'aplique / Naturelment a concevoir / Et a aprendre et a savoir. / Ce fut bien dit et sagement, / Car tout humain entendement / Desire venir a ce point / De savoir ce qu'il ne sect point, / Ou soit d'amour ou de reproche / Et mesmement quant il lui touche" (*Roman de Mélusine*, ed. Roach, 1–12).

45. In her insightful contemporary analysis of Mélusine, *La Fée Mélusine au Moyen Age* (Paris: Le Léopard d'or, 1991), Françoise Clier-Colombani employs a transferential mode of writing about Mélusine, exhibiting a strong desire to protect Mélusine from being associated with prostitution (a danger implied by her imagistic proximity to Bathsheba and the Whore of Babylon). Her transferential defense of Mélusine's virtue is evidence of a medievalism that persists in the sublimation of desire in literary history. The crime of prostitution is that it promises pleasure without reproduction. This accusation is directly contrary to what emerges from the histories to be Mélusine's role as the supernatural matriarch of a broad lineage.

46. See Lionel Gossman, *Medievalism and Ideologies of the Enlightenment* (Baltimore: Johns Hopkins University Press, 1968).

47. Much has been written about Julia Kristeva's notion of the abject and woman as monstrous put forth in *Powers of Horror*, trans. Leon S. Roudiez (New York: Columbia University Press, 1982). See especially Jeffrey Jerome Cohen, *Of Giants: Sex, Monsters, and the Middle Ages* (Minneapolis: University of Minnesota Press, 1999); as well as *Monster Theory*, ed. Jeffrey Jerome Cohen (Minneapolis: University of Minnesota Press, 1996); see also David Williams, *Deformed Discourse: The Function of the Monster in Mediaeval Thought and Literature* (Montreal: McGill-Queen's University Press, 1996).

48. Kathleen Biddick takes off from the notion of traumatic shock making sense retroactively to forward her reading of the "shock" of medievalism: *The Shock of Medievalism* (Durham, N.C.: Duke University Press, 1998).

49. Coudrette describes the vision of Mélusine as "l'horrible vraiment" (*Roman de Mélusine*, ed. Roach, 3074).

50. Sarah Stanbury, "Feminist Film Theory Seeing Chrétien's Enide," *Literature and Psychology* 36 (1990): 47–66, esp. 49, 56, and 59. For Stanbury, Enide is an example of the woman who both is looked at and reflects that look, and then performs the right to look when she critically examines Erec's naked, sleeping body (59). Her general project is also exciting and instructive in its approach to film theory and medieval texts. See also A. C. Spearing, *The Medieval Poet as Voyeur: Looking and Listening in Medieval Love-Narratives* (Cambridge: Cambridge University Press, 1993).

51. Belsey, *Desire*, 88.

52. This differs from Marie de France's *Lanval* where we find a real love for a fictional ideal categorical woman.

53. Lacan's original French *Écrits* (Paris: Seuil, 1966) opens with the seminar on "The Purloined Letter," "Le séminaire sur *La Lettre Volée*" (19–75).

54. Jacques Lacan, *The Seminar of Jacques Lacan, Book XI: The Four Fundamental Concepts of Psychoanalysis*, ed. Jacques-Alain Miller, trans. Alan Sheridan (New York: W. W. Norton, 1977), 84–85.

55. Lacan's claim that there is no sexual relationship is the outcome of his research on courtly love and his attempt to respond to accusations of antifeminism.

56. Of course, the most insightful text on the abject remains Julia Kristeva's *Powers of Horror*.

57. Perhaps the most famous example of synesthesia and excess is found in the speech made by Bottom Weaver in Shakepeare's *A Midsummer Nights' Dream*.

58. Notably, even this scatological view of Lady Ena is a part of the cultural history of desire and language. Consider Dominique Laporte's *The History of Shit*, trans. Nadia Benabid and Rodolphe el-Khoury (Cambridge, Mass.: MIT Press, 2000), esp. the first chapter entitled "The Gold of Language, the Luster of Scybala" (2–25).

59. Norbert Elias, *The Court Society*, trans. Edmund Jephcott (New York: Pantheon, 1983) provides an important analysis of the ideological history of courtly culture.

60. Overt misogyny notwithstanding, the scatological elements cause this poem to differ from other courtly love poems. See Bloch, *Medieval Misogyny*.

61. E. Jane Burns's *Bodytalk: When Women Speak in Old French Literature* (Philadelphia: University of Pennsylvania Press, 1993) foregrounds the problems of this conflation of orifices in Old French fabliau. She analyzes the poem *Berangier au long cul* in which a woman cross-dresses in armor to challenge her husband, who is unaware of her identity. The wife offers an alternate challenge to fighting. She suggests that the husband kiss her ass. Thinking that he is fighting a man, and having chosen the second option (the kiss), the husband responds with horror stating that "he'd seen no ass that long before" (157). Marshall Leicester has also addressed the question of orifices and signification; see H. Marshall Leicester, *The Disenchanted Self: Representing the Subject in the Canterbury Tales* (Berkeley and Los Angeles: University of California Press, 1990).

62. Jacques Lacan, *The Seminar of Jacques Lacan, Book XX: On Feminine Sexuality, the Limits of Love and Knowledge, Encore*, trans. Bruce Fink (New York: W. W. Norton, 1998), 72.

63. Elizabeth Roudinesco, *Jacques Lacan*, trans. Barbara Bray (New York: Columbia University Press, 1997), 363.

64. In addition to E. Jane Burn's *Bodytalk*, cited above, see Joseph Bédier, *Les Fabliaux: Études de literature populaire et d'historie littéraire du moyen age*, 2nd ed. (Paris: Librairie Emile Boullion, 1895); R. Howard Bloch, *The Scandal of the Fabliaux* (Chicago: University of Chicago Press, 1986); Kathryn Gravdal, *Vilain and Courtois: Transgressive Parody in French Literature of the Twelfth and Thirteenth Centuries* (Lincoln: University of Nebraska Press, 1989), esp. 55–80. In the case of Arnaut Daniel's scatological poem one might see the female body as abject, along the lines of Julia Kristeva's theory articulated in *Powers of Horror*. However, I do not see Lady Ena as abject; rather, she is the embodiment of the obstacle presented by "reality" in the scene of the "proper" fantasy of courtly love.

65. Aristotle, *Nichomachean Ethics*, in *Basic Works*, ed. McKeon, 256–58.

66. Aristotle's continued analysis of the obstacle of pleasure prefigures Freud's discussion of the Eros-Thanatos conflict in *Beyond the Pleasure Principle*. His supposition that pleasure and a joy for life are interrelated will lead to the corollary thought that if we perform actions that harm us we are resisting the life instinct.

67. Aristotle, *Nichomachean Ethics*, in *Basic Works*, ed. McKeon, 258.

68. See *The Wolf Man*, ed. Muriel Gardiner and including Sigmund Freud, "The Case of the Wolf-Man," and forward by Anna Freud (New York: Basic Books, 1971), 135.

69. A nice transition between the animality and the courtly model is to consider Richard Fournival's *Le Bestiaire d'Amour*, ed. C. Hippeau (Paris, 1860; repr., Geneva: Slatkine Reprints, 1969), which accounts for the animal quality of courtly love and plays with universal categories. Jeanette Beer's *Beasts of Love* (Toronto: University of Toronto Press, 2003) shows how the characterization of humans as rational is threatened and alternately reinforced by courtly poetics.

70. Jacques Lacan, "Of Structure as an Inmixing of an Otherness Prerequisite to Any Subject Whatever," in *The Structuralist Controversy: The Languages of Criticism and Sciences of Man*, ed. Richard Macksey and Eugenio Donato (Baltimore: Johns Hopkins University Press, 1972), 186–200.

71. Ibid., 191.

72. This is further supported by the Rat Man's imagined wish/fear that his parents can read his thoughts: Freud, *Three Case Histories*, 23.

3. Dialectics, Courtly Love, and the Trinity

1. William D. Paden, "The Troubadour's Lady as Seen through Thick History," *Exemplaria* 11, no. 2 (Fall 1999): 221–44.

2. Don A. Monson, "The Troubadour's Lady Reconsidered Again," *Speculum* 70 (1999): 255–74.

3. Don A. Monson, "The Troubadour's Lady, Yet Again," *Exemplaria* 14, no. 2 (Fall 2002): 485–97.

4. William D. Paden, "The Troubadour's Lady, One More Time," *Exemplaria* 14, no. 2 (Fall 2002): 498–513. William D. Paden, "The Troubadour's Lady, A Summing Up," *Exemplaria* 14, no. 2 (Fall 2002): 514–17.

5. Paden, "Troubadour's Lady, One More Time," 499.

6. Paden, "Troubadour's Lady as Seen through Thick History," 224.

7. This argument follows that of Jacques Derrida, but it is also made clear by Jean-Charles Hûchet, *Littérature Médiévale et Psychanalyse* (Paris: Presses Universitaires de France, 1990), 7, 9. As well as Roger Dragonetti, *La Vie de la Lettre au Moyen Age* (Paris: Seuil, 1980), and Alexandre Leupin who questions the category of difference in reading in "The Middle Ages, the Other," *Diacritics* 13, no. 3 (Fall 1983), 28–29; and see L. O. Aranye Fradenburg, *Sacrifice Your Love: Psychoanalysis, Historicism, Chaucer* (Minneapolis: University of Minnesota Press, 2002), 64–65.

8. Annoyance also stands out as an allergic reaction, an irritant that can cause great damage to one's system, as Avital Ronell says about the process of writing in *Stupidity* (Urbana: University of Illinois Press, 2002), 25–29.

9. For general introductions to the troubadours, see Robert S. Briffault, *The Troubadours* (Bloomington: Indiana University Press, 1965); Linda M. Paterson, *Troubadours and Eloquence* (Oxford: Clarendon Press, 1975); Linda M. Paterson, *The World*

of the Troubadours (Cambridge: Cambridge University Press, 1993); L. T. Topsfield, *Troubadours and Love* (Cambridge: Cambridge University Press, 1975); *A Handbook of the Troubadours*, ed. F. R. Akehurst and Judith Davis (Berkeley and Los Angeles: University of California Press, 1995); and *The Troubadours, an Introduction*, ed. Simon Gaunt and Sarah Kay (Cambridge: Cambridge University Press, 1999).

10. Sarah Kay, *Courtly Contradictions: The Emergence of the Literary Object in the Twelfth Century* (Stanford, Calif.: Stanford University Press, 2001), esp. 18–19.

11. In addition to Kay and Hûchet, other readings of courtly love and psychoanalysis include those by Rouben C. Cholakian, *The Troubadour Lyric: A Psychocritical Reading* (Manchester: Manchester University Press, 1990) and Henri Rey-Flaud, *La Névrose Courtoise* (Paris: Navarin Éditeur; Diffusion, Seuil, 1983).

12. See Slavoj Žižek, *The Metastases of Enjoyment* (New York: Verso, 1994), 89–112.

13. A *tenson* is a debate poem. The genre was common to the troubadours.

14. Jacques Lacan, "Subversion of the Subject and the Dialectic of Desire in the Freudian Unconscious," in *Écrits*, trans. Alan Sheridan (New York: W. W. Norton, 1977), 292–325.

15. I would like to thank my former student Tristan Blease for reproducing these graphs for display in this volume.

16. See Ferdinand de Saussure, *Course in General Linguistics*, trans. Roy Harris (LaSalle, Ill.: Open Court Classics, 1983). When I characterize Lacan's work for people unfamiliar with psychoanalysis at all (in my undergraduate introduction to theory, for instance), I explain *reductively* that his theory is a combination of ideas put forth by Sigmund Freud, Martin Heidegger, Ferdinand de Saussure, and Roman Jakobson, and that it is grounded in literature by way of his interest in the Middle Ages.

17. Notably, the troubadours already anticipated this form of future anterior syntax in their poetics. Jaufré Rudel's lines regarding the infinite regression of the object of his desire will be addressed later in this chapter.

18. Slavoj Žižek employs this notion of the rear view to argue that ideology has historicity and is revealed by the return of the repressed in *The Sublime Object of Ideology* (New York: Verso, 1989), 55–62. It is also now famously understood by way of Hitchock's *Rear Window*.

19. As Lacan notes in "The Mirror Stage as Formative of the Function of the I as Revealed in Psychoanalytic Experience," in *Écrits*, 1–7, the actual encounter with the mirror reveals that *méconnaissance* is the only detour by way of which one will come to know the impossibility of knowing oneself as anything other than a fragmented subject.

20. In *Lacan Today* (New York: Other Press, 2004), xx, Alexandre Leupin shows that the translation of "demand" as "demand" asserts a dogmatic and patriarchal force into Lacan's language that is not there if we use the proper translation of the term, "request."

21. The resemblance of this aspect of Lacan's theory to the problems of castration anxiety raises a crucial question regarding the centrality of the phallus to the notion of the cut.

22. In identification the subject and object relate to each other in response to the imaginary desires that each expects the other has. This is most clearly articulated in Lacan's "Seminar on the Purloined Letter": Jacques Lacan, *Écrits* (Paris: Seuil, 1966), 19–75; *The Purloined Poe: Lacan, Derrida and Psychoanalytic Reading*, ed. John P.

Muller and William J. Richardson (Baltimore: Johns Hopkins University Press, 1988), 28–54; and *Écrits*, trans. Bruce Fink (New York: W. W. Norton, 2006), 6–50.

23. Citations from G. W. F. Hegel's *The Phenomenology of Spirit* may be found in *Hegel: The Essential Writings*, ed. Frederick G. Weiss (New York: Harper, 1974), here 75; for a more complete dual edition, see *Hegel's Phenomenology of Spirit*, trans. Howard P. Kainz (University Park: Pennsylvania State University Press, 1994).

24. See Alexandre Leupin's *Barabolexis: Medieval Writing and Sexuality*, trans. Kate M. Cooper (Cambridge, Mass.: Harvard University Press, 1989), where rhetorical tropes such as euphemism and antiphrasis play a crucial role in the political and poetic display of the literary construct of desire.

25. Jacques Lacan, *The Seminar of Jacques Lacan, Book XX: On Feminine Sexuality, the Limits of Love and Knowledge, Encore*, trans. Bruce Fink (New York: W. W. Norton, 1998), 86.

26. Theodor Adorno, *Negative Dialectics*, trans. E. B. Ashton (New York: Seabury Press, 1973), 56. Originally published as *Negative Dialektik* (Frankfurt am Main: Suhrkamp Verlag, 1966).

27. Judith Butler discusses this problem in *Subjects of Desire: Hegelian Reflections in Twentieth-Century France* (New York: Columbia University Press, 1987), 63–78.

28. Butler, *Subjects of Desire*, 47.

29. Jacques Lacan, *The Seminar of Jacques Lacan, Book VII: The Ethics of Psychoanalysis*, ed. Jacques-Alain Miller, trans. Dennis Porter (New York: W. W. Norton, 1992), 163.

30. Cited in *Desiring Discourse: The Literature of Love, Ovid through Chaucer*, ed. James J. Paxson and Cynthia A. Gravlee (Selinsgrove: Susquehanna University Press, 1998), 45. And *Handbook of the Troubadours*, ed. Akehurst and Davis, 68. See also Thomas Pepper, "The Story of I/I", in *Glossalalia*, ed. Julian Wolfreys (New York: Routledge, 2003), 129–56.

31. According to Sarah Kay, "The emergence of courtly love is identified by Lacan as a significant factor historically because its entire framework is secular. Instead of being subject to religious law, the lover subjects himself to a rule which is ascribed to a woman" (*Courtly Contradictions*, 26).

32. Cited and translated in *Lyrics of the Troubadours and Trouvères: An Anthology and a History*, trans. and introduced by Frederick Goldin (New York: Anchor Press/Doubleday, 1973).

33. Another way of understanding this would be to return to the oedipal struggle with the Law of the Father that must be obeyed and overcome simultaneously. In the interest of moving the argument in this book away from "application" and any assumptions that psychoanalysis can be broken down to sexuality and the Oedipus complex, I resist this approach here. Further, such explorations would necessitate a discussion of Deleuze and Guattari's two volumes *Anti-Oedipus: Capitalism and Schizophrenia* (Minneapolis: University of Minnesota Press, 1983), and *A Thousand Plateaus: Capitalism and Schizophrenia*, trans. Brian Massumi (Minneapolis: University of Minnesota Press, 1987). Both texts rebel against the Father of psychoanalysis by refusing the validity of the oedipal triangle. But, as Paul Strohm perceives, their approach is a "refinement, rather than a refutation, of Lacan's structuration of desire": *Theory and the Premodern Text* (Minneapolis: University of Minnesota Press, 2000), 195. Slavoj Žižek also addresses this resistance in *Organs without Bodies*

(New York: Routledge, 2002). And the argument is implicit in the mode of Freudian analysis of repression and resistance that pervades psychoanalytical thinking as well as Elizabeth Scala's work in *Absent Narratives, Manuscript Textuality and Literary Structure in Late Medieval England* (New York: Palgrave, 2002).

34. Alain Badiou, "The Scene of Two," *Lacanian Ink* 21 (Spring 2003): 42–55. Badiou thoroughly explores the function of the "event" in *Ethics: An Essay on the Understanding of Evil*, trans. Peter Hallward (New York: Verso, 2001).

35. Jacques Lacan, *The Seminar of Jacques Lacan, Book III: The Psychoses* (New York: W. W. Norton, 1993), 116.

36. For Freud, discourse regarding sexuality was best accomplished using proper terminology for the genitals. In *Dora* Freud claims that it is appropriate to call a vagina a vagina rather than employ euphemistic or metaphorical terms.

37. Isidorus Hispalensis, *Etymologiae*, ed. P. K. Marshall (Paris: Belle Lettres, 1981–86).

38. Ibid., II 25.1.

39. Roger Dragonetti also uses this term when he discusses subjectivity in trou-badour poetics in *La Vie de la Lettre au Moyen Age*, esp. 21, 32, 71.

40. Dragonetti, *La Vie de la Lettre au Moyen Age*, 64–65. Dragonetti also plays with homonyms, esp. 78.

41. Dante Aligheri, *Purgatorio*, trans. Allen Mandelbaum (New York: Bantam, 1982). Roger Dragonetti's "The Double Play of Arnaut Daniel's *Sestina* and Dante's *Divina Commedia*," in *Literature and Psychoanalysis: The Question of Reading Otherwise*, ed. Shoshana Felman (Baltimore: Johns Hopkins University Press, 1982), 227–52, makes a convincing and admirable argument regarding Dante's engagement with Arnaut.

42. Jacques Lacan, *Télévision* (Paris: Seuil, 1974), and the translation *Television*, trans. Denis Hollier, *October* 40 (Spring 1987), 27.

43. For a truly original and insightful reading that responds to Lacan's request for attention to this issue of divinity and matter, see Alexandre Leupin, *Phallophanies: La chair et le sacré* (Paris: Editions du Regard, 2000).

44. Jacques Lacan, *The Seminar of Jacques Lacan, Book II: The Ego in Freud's Theory and in the Technique of Psychoanalysis*, ed. Jacques-Alain Miller, trans. Sylvana Tomaselli (New York: W. W. Norton, 1991), 220.

45. Laura Kendrick's *The Game of Love* (Berkeley and Los Angeles: University of California Press, 1988), shows how the linguistic games of the poetics engage the prominence of game playing in troubadour poetics.

46. In Ross Arthur, *Medieval Sign Theory and Sir Gawain and the Green Knight* (Toronto: University of Toronto Press, 1987), 37.

47. Ibid., 37–38.

48. In "*Unitrinum Seu Triuum:* Nicholas of Cusa's Trinitarian Mysticism," in *Mystics: Presence and Aporia*, ed. Michael Kessler and Christian Sheppard (Chicago: University of Chicago Press, 2003), 90–117, esp. 92–95, Bernard McGinn situates the importance of mathematics in the history of attempts to understand the universe in a manner that is useful for contextualizing Lacan's investment in Cusa as more than a passing fancy.

49. Michel de Certeau notes this slippage in the work of Nicholas of Cusa and he links it to his linguistic praxis and to his gaze. De Certeau also develops Lacan's

argument about the gaze by way of Cusa. See Michel de Certeau, "The Gaze of Nicholas of Cusa," *Diacritics* 17, no. 3 (Autumn 1987): 2–38.

50. Peter Abelard, "The Glosses on Porphyry," in *Five Texts on the Medieval Problem of Universals*, trans. and ed. Paul Vincent Spade (Indianapolis: Hackett, 1994), 50–51.

51. R. Howard Bloch argues in *Medieval French Literature and Law* (Berkeley and Los Angeles: University of California Press, 1977) that the shift from physical combat to inquest in medieval law conflates the search for truth with the creation of linguistic fictions. In Marie de France's *Lanval*, the medieval trope in which a queen attempts to seduce a vassal is represented as enabling a space for language that transgresses the boundaries of courtly law and the language of the feudal hierarchy/ patriarchy. Although the queen is ultimately punished for her seductive act, the seduction itself is the catalyst for a legal and authoritative inquest that seeks to achieve the truth of the act.

In Marie de France's *Lanval*, we witness the court desiring to "know what really happened." Further, this epistemophilia is manifested in a conflation of language and action, rendering a conception of language as performative that already begins to blend the difference between justice as physical revenge and justice as legal narrative. The transition from pure faith to epistemological concerns—concerns that are, nevertheless, closely linked to a search for the knowledge of God—signifies a move within medieval texts from an inflated concern with ritual, as it is instituted and enacted before God, to a form of justice that relies on language as a narrative of a more secular form of truth.

52. I call the supernatuaral Queen in *Lanval* Queen A because she signifies the *objet a*.

53. Slavoj Žižek, *The Fragile Absolute: Or, Why is the Christian Legacy Worth Fighting For?* (New York: Verso, 2000), 38. Also central here is Alexandre Leupin's *Fiction and Incarnation*, trans. David Laatsch (Minneapolis: University of Minnesota Press, 2003).

54. Elizabeth Roudinesco, *Jacques Lacan*, trans. Barbara Bray (New York: Columbia University Press, 1997).

4. The Quadrangle, the Hard Sciences, and Nonclassical Thinking

1. Jacques Derrida, *Resistances of Psychoanalysis*, trans. Peggy Kamuf et al. (Stanford, Calif.: Stanford University Press, 1998), esp. 1–9.

2. Freud's concept of the dream navel, the omphalos, as that place where the proper incision will reveal the significance of signs is thus taken up by Lacan as the locus of meaning, the *objet a*, the thing *(das Ding)*, and the *point-de-capiton*, simultaneously, and is therefore reflective of the opening into the Real. Sigmund Freud, *Interpretation of Dreams*, in *The Standard Edition of the Complete Psychological Works of Sigmund Freud*, trans. James Strachey (London: Hogarth Press and the Institute of Psychoanalysis, 1974), 5:525. In Paul Strohm's reading, this is characterized by a "blind spot" that is at the "center of every text." Paul Strohm, *Theory and the Premodern Text* (Minneapolis: University of Minnesota Press, 2000), 213. The difference between Strohm's view and Lacan's is one that accounts for a lack of

"center" in a properly Derridean fashion, resulting in a knot that cannot be localized or, therefore, properly untied; therein lies Lacan's struggle to find the proper and impossible cut in the knot of the unconscious and of desire.

3. In *The New Medievalism* (Baltimore: Johns Hopkins University Press, 1991), 3–5, Stephen G. Nichols discusses the multidisciplinary aspect of the astrolabe as an aesthetic and scientific object that participates in the growing concern with boundaries.

4. Jacques Lacan, *The Seminar of Jacques Lacan, Book XX: On Feminine Sexuality, the Limits of Love and Knowledge, Encore,* trans. Bruce Fink (New York: W. W. Norton, 1998), 16.

5. Jacques Lacan, *The Seminar of Jacques Lacan, Book II: The Ego in Freud's Theory and in the Technique of Psychoanalysis,* ed. Jacques-Alain Miller, trans. Sylvana Tomaselli (New York: W. W. Norton, 1991), 4.

6. *Meno* part 96, in *The Collected Dialogues,* ed. Edith Hamilton and Huntington Cairns (Princeton, N.J.: Princeton University Press, 1961), 380.

7. Arkady Plotnitsky, "Difference," in *Glossalalia,* ed. Julian Wolfreys (New York: Routledge, 2003), 66.

8. Ibid.

9. Jean-Claude Milner, "Lacan and the Ideal of Science," in *Lacan and the Human Sciences,* ed. Alexandre Leupin (Lincoln: University of Nebraska Press, 1991), 28. Milner notes that for Kojève "antique" means pagan and "modern" means Christian.

10. Milner cites Foucault, Marx, Hegel, as well as Kojève and Koyré as he leads to his description of Lacan's theory of the cut, esp. ibid., 30–31.

11. Milner writes: "In the philosophical tradition, condition (2) has something to do with contingence and also with the contrast between synthetic and analytical statements. Lacan connected it with the *manqué:* that is, with the most essential part of Freudian doctrine. Hence the thesis: *Psychoanalysis is possible only in a universe where a mathematicized science deals with what could fail to be where it is or what could fail to be as it is.* Indeed, Koyré always insisted on the radical novelty of the fact that mathematics could be connected with empricity rather than eternity" (ibid., 35).

12. François Regnault, "Lacan and Experience," in *Lacan and the Human Sciences,* ed. Leupin, 47.

13. Cf. Arkady Plotnitsky, *Complementarity* (Durham, N.C.: Duke University Press, 1994), *The Knowable and the Unknowable* (Ann Arbor: University of Michigan Press, 2002), *On Lacan and Mathematics* (New York: Other Press, 2000); *Mathematics, Science and Postclassical Theory,* ed. Barbara Herrnstein Smith and Arkady Plotnitsky, *South Atlantic Quarterly* 94, no. 2 (1995), 371–88. In one of the most amusing and telling moments in this narrative of science, Otto Neugebauer entitles an essay "The Study of Wretched Subjects," in *Astronomy and History, Selected Essays* (New York: Springer-Verlag, 1983), 3–4. See also Thomas Kuhn, *The Copernican Revolution: Planetary Astronomy in the Development of Western Thought* (New York: Vintage Books, 1957); Paul Feyerabend, *Against Method* (New York: Verso, 1988); Larry Laudan, *Science and Values: The Aims of Science and Their Role in Scientific Debate* (Berkeley and Los Angeles: University of California Press, 1984), esp. 131–37, as well as his *Beyond Positivism and Relativism: Theory, Method, and Evidence* (New York: Westview Press, 1996), esp. 69–85.

14. Texts on the subject abound. See Marijane Osborn, *Time and the Astrolabe in the "Canterbury Tales"* (Norman: University of Oklahoma Press, 2002); Owen Gingrich, *The Eye of Heaven* (New York: American Institute of Physics, 1993), as well as the texts cited below in note 26.

15. Georges Bataille, "The Critique of the Foundations of the Hegelian Dialectic," trans. Allan Stoekl, *Visions of Excess,* ed. Stoekl (Minneapolis: University of Minnesota Press, 1985), 105–15.

16. See Kurt Gödel, *On Formally Undecidable Propositions of Principia Mathematica and Related Systems,* trans. B. Meltzer (New York: Basic Books, 1962). Lacan's writings on language and its lack are extensive.

17. Alexandre Leupin states that "The scientificity of psychoanalysis is one of Lacan's earliest preoccupations and claims" (*Lacan and the Human Sciences,* ed. Leupin [Lincoln: University of Nebraska Press, 1991], 1).

18. Jacques Lacan, *Écrits* (Paris: Seuil, 1966), 724. Translation from Alexandre Leupin, "Introduction: Voids and Knots in Knowledge and Truth," in *Lacan and the Human Sciences,* ed. Leupin (Lincoln: University of Nebraska Press, 1991), 7–8.

19. Elizabeth Roudinesco, *Jacques Lacan,* trans. Barbara Bray (New York: Columbia University Press, 1997), 363.

20. As Roudinesco points out, Lacan was an active heterosexual, in fact, falling toward the extreme of "womanizing" or "wanting to possess women." He also, however, was one of the few working psychoanalysts who did not perceive homosexuality to be a perversion, and who was more than willing and happy to engage in the transferential relationship of analyst/analysand with many queer intellectuals.

21. The Nietzschean resonance here is striking (Truth is a woman).

22. Dominick LaCapra, *Representing the Holocaust: History, Theory, Trauma* (Ithaca, N.Y.: Cornell University Press, 1994).

23. The role of cultural aesthetics within philosophical terrain is addressed by the play with strings, knots, and their metaphorical supplementation for the process of linguistic articulation of desire. The study of knots brings together the desire for a scientific discourse in psychoanalysis and the way in which textuality resists that discourse. Like psychoanalysis, the discipline of medieval studies also has a long history of attempting to remain within the realm of scientific discourse. The visual use of knots, graphs, and textual illuminations aids in an empirical display of textual performance.

24. I cannot overestimate the importance of Roustang's work for any reader of Lacan.

25. François Roustang, *The Lacanian Delusion,* trans. G. Sims (Oxford: Oxford University Press, 1990), 22. Citing Lacan's *Écrits,* 91.

26. See J. C. Eade, *The Forgotten Sky: A Guide to Astrology in English Literature* (Oxford: Clarendon Press, 1984); Sigmund Eisner "Chaucer's Use of Nicholas of Lynn's Calendar," *Essays and Studies* 29 (1976): 1–22; Theodore Otto Wedel, *The Medieval Attitude toward Astrology* (New Haven, Conn.: Yale University Press, 1920); Chauncey Wood, *Chaucer and the Country of the Stars* (Princeton, N.J.: Princeton University Press, 1970).

27. See J. D. North, *Chaucer's Universe* (Oxford: Clarendon Press, 1988); Joseph Priestly, *Man and Time* (Garden City: Doubleday, 1964); Wayne Shumaker, *The Occult Sciences in the Renaissance* (Berkeley and Los Angeles: University of California

Press, 1972); *Astrology, Science and Society,* ed. Patrick Curry (Woodbridge: Boydell Press, 1987), esp. 24–26.

28. Larry D. Benson states that this self trickery is the "most interesting" feature of the tale since the subject is attempting to practice a science that he does not understand (*The Riverside Chaucer,* 3rd ed. [New York: Houghton Mifflin, 1987], 20).

29. Ibid.

30. Otto Neugebauer, "On the Planetary Theory of Copernicus" (1968), reprinted in *Astronomy and History,* 491–506.

31. Ibid., 491.

32. Especially Plotnitsky, *Complementarity, The Knowable and the Unknowable,* and *Mathematics, Science and Postclassical Thinking,* ed. Smith and Plotnitsky.

33. *A Treatise on the Astrolabe; addressed to his son Lowys by Geoffrey Chaucer,* ed. Walter W. Skeat, Early English Text Society (Oxford: Oxford University Press, 1968), xxxi.

34. For an insightful reading of the placement of Chaucer's *Treatise* in a post-colonial context, see Jenna Mead, "Reading by Said's Lantern: Orientalism and Chaucer's *Treatise on the Astrolabe,*" *Al Masaq: Islam and the Medieval Mediterranean* 15, no. 1 (March 2003): 77–82.

35. For various reasons I am not going to engage the concept of "envy" in relation to Freudian texts here. Such an exploration occurs in the next section of this chapter with reference to pedagogy and the master's discourse. However, I want to avoid a comparison of Lacanian desire with Freudian envy that would convolute both theories and misrepresent what I perceive to be an expression of *desire* in Chaucer's text. It is not appropriate, in my mind, to think about Chaucer's reference to envy in the context of Freud's discussion because the topics and their goals and outcomes are quite distinct.

36. Nicholas of Lynn, *The Kalendarium of Nicholas of Lynn,* ed. Sigmund Eisner (Athens: University of Georgia Press, 1980), 58.

37. Elsewhere, we might think through these questions by placing Chaucer's text in the context of Faustian and Promethean legends and myths copiously written and rewritten in the history of literature. Juxtaposing Marlowe's *Dr. Faustus* or Spencer's *Faerie Queene* with Chaucer's *A Treatise on the Astrolabe* provides insight into the way that astronomical sciences are represented as mitigating and motivating envy.

38. Derek Brewer, "Arithmetic and the Mentality of Chaucer," in *Literature in Fourteenth-Century England,* ed. Piero Boitani and Anna Torti, The J. A. W. Bennet Memorial Lectures, Prugia, 1981–1982 (Tübingen: Gunter Narr Verlag; Cambridge: D. S. Brewer, 1983), 155–64.

39. Alain Badiou, "The Scene of Two," *Lacanian Ink* 21 (Spring 2003): 43.

40. Many historians of science report this phenomenon, but Thomas Kuhn gives the clearest description in *Copernican Revolution,* esp. 59–64.

41. Neugebauer continues: "Contemporary with the haphazard steps of an elementary astronomy and the mathematical geography are the most brilliant achievements of Greek abstract mathematical thought. The theory of irrational quantities by Theaetetus and Eudoxus, Aristotelian logic, Euclid, Archimedes' integrations, and Apollonius's conic sections are examples of mathematical structures whose significance was fully recovered only in modern times" ("On Some Aspects of Early Greek Astronomy," in *Astronomy and History: Selected Essays* [New York: Springer-

Verlag, 1983], 369). This suggests that the premodern and the postmodern are more alike than the time in between the two.

42. Teresa Brennan, *History after Lacan* (New York: Routledge, 1993), 8. Alain Badiou asserts a complex notion of history that derives from his psychoanalytical investment when he discusses the "truth-event" in his *Ethics: An Essay on the Understanding of Evil,* trans. Peter Hallward (New York: Verso, 2001).

43. Joan Copjec, *Read My Desire: Lacan against the Historicists* (Cambridge, Mass.: MIT Press, 1994).

44. For Nietzsche, Monumental History is an absolutist view of history. It is the aspect of his three categories of history set forth in Friedrich Nietzsche, "The Utility and Liability of History for Life," in *Unfashionable Observations,* trans. Richard T. Gray (Stanford, Calif.: Stanford University Press, 1995), 85–167, esp. 96–102.

45. See Gabrielle M. Spiegel, *The Past as Text: The Theory and Practice of Medieval Historiography* (Baltimore: Johns Hopkins University Press, 1997); see also Brian Stock, *Listening for the Text: On the Uses of the Past* (Baltimore: Johns Hopkins University Press, 1990).

46. Contemporary studies of *Antigone* forward and alter the assertions put forth by Hegel and Lacan on tragedy, history, and desire. For the most part they center on the political implications and ethics of subjectivity in the play. See Judith Butler, *Antigone's Claim: Kinship between Life and Death* (New York: Columbia University Press, 2000); Joan Copjec, *Imagine There's No Woman: Ethics and Sublimation* (Cambridge, Mass.: MIT Press, 2002), 15–16, 32, 40–45; Sarah Kay, *Courtly Contradictions: The Emergence of the Literary Object in the Twelfth Century* (Stanford, Calif.: Stanford University Press, 2001), 217–19, 256; Alenka Zupančič, *The Ethics of the Real* (New York: Verso, 2000).

47. Jacques Lacan, *The Seminar of Jacques Lacan, Book VII: The Ethics of Psychoanalysis,* ed. Jacques-Alain Miller, trans. Dennis Porter (New York: W. W. Norton, 1992), 243.

48. For a reading of the Cathars in relation to courtly love, see Denis de Rougemont, *Love in the Western World,* trans. Montgomery Belgion (Princeton, N.J.: Princeton University Press, 1983) (originally published in 1940).

49. Lacan moves quickly from a discussion of the fear of punishment, "that of being buried alive in a tomb" (*Seminar VII,* 248), to her aesthetic effect on the tragedy itself.

50. In addition to recalling the language of his essay on the mirror stage, Lacan's rhetoric here imitates that employed by Aquinas in his discussion of optics and the divine.

51. The most overt example of this is found in Derrida's reading of *Hamlet* and Marxism, *Spectres of Marx,* trans. Peggy Kamuf (New York: Routledge, 1994).

52. Lawrence Rickels has examined the potential for psychoanalytical tools in an analysis of the Dracula phenomenon in popular culture and literary history in *The Vampire Lectures* (Minneapolis: University of Minnesota Press, 1999), esp. 1–13.

53. Although the uncanny is an element of the "zone" between the two deaths, it remains distinct from it. When Lacan discusses Antigone's fear of being buried alive, he implicitly invokes the uncanny. This remains, however, a foundational aspect of between the two deaths and not its equivalent.

54. As if he is overcompensating for his early foray into the classical that involved a back-and-forth movement between antiquity and the Middle Ages, here Lacan

provides a vast array of classical plays, some of which were important to Freud and some of which remained unmentioned by him.

55. Gilles Deleuze, *The Fold* (Minneapolis: University of Minnesota Press, 1993).

5. The Pentangle and the Resistant Knot

1. Jacques Derrida's *Resistances of Psychoanalysis*, trans. Peggy Kamuf et al. (Stanford, Calif.: Stanford University Press, 1998), 1–38, makes the point that analysis itself is a form of resistance.

2. Elizabeth Scala, "Historicists and Their Discontents: Reading Psychoanalytically in Medieval Studies," *Texas Studies in Literature and Language* 44, no. 1 (Spring 2002): 108–30; and Elizabeth Scala, *Absent Narratives, Manuscript Textuality and Literary Structure in Late Medieval England* (New York: Palgrave, 2002). "In" here is a reference to L. O. Aranye Fradenburg's "We Are Not Alone: Psychoanalytic Medievalism," *New Medieval Literatures* 2 (1998): 250.

3. Avital Ronell, "On the Misery of Theory without Poetry: Heidegger's Reading of Hölderlin's 'Andenken,'" *PMLA* 120, no. 1 (January 2005): 17.

4. Roger Dragonetti foregrounds this connection throughout his work, but most explicitly in "Propos sur l'étymologie," in *La Musique et les Lettres: Etudes de Littérature Médiévale* (Geneva: Droz, 1986), 59–107.

5. See Jeffrey Jerome Cohen, *Of Giants: Sex, Monsters, and the Middle Ages* (Minneapolis: University of Minnesota Press, 1999), 144–52; and Jeffrey Jerome Cohen, "Decapitation and Coming of Age: Constructing Masculinity and the Monstrous," *Arthurian Yearbook* 3 (1993): 203–13.

6. One of the most interesting aspects of Elizabeth Scala's approach to history in "The Wanting Words of Sir Gawain and the Green Knight: Narrative Past, Present and Absent," *Exemplaria* 6, no. 2 (Fall 1994): 305–38, is the comparison of the first reader of *Sir Gawain and the Green Knight* who inscribes the famous line "honi soit qui mal y pense" at the close of the narrative with the contemporary twentieth-century reader, paralleling textual strategies and modes of nostalgia for an always already lost ideal past (306).

7. Amy Hollywood, "Mysticism and Catastrophe in Georges Bataille's *Atheological Summa*," in *Mystics: Presence and Aporia*, ed. Michael Kessler and Christian Sheppard (Chicago: University of Chicago Press, 2003), 182, n. 13.

8. Jacques Lacan, *The Seminar of Jacques Lacan, Book III: The Psychoses* (New York: W. W. Norton, 1993), 3.

9. Jacques Lacan, *Télévision* (Paris: Seuil, 1974), and the translation *Television*, trans. Denis Hollier, *October* 40 (Spring 1987), 23.

10. Shoshana Felman in *Writing and Madness*, trans. Martha Noel Evans, Shoshana Felman, and Brian Massumi (Ithaca, N.Y.: Cornell University Press, 1985), esp. 119–40, addresses this problem of fiction and science with regard to writing and hysteria.

11. Even more than the essays that are often taught as an introduction to Lacan's thinking, "The Mirror Stage" and "The Signification of the Phallus," Lacan's "Seminar on the Purloined Letter" characterizes his approach to language, desire, the drives, and it relates to the traces of the letter in history. Jacques Lacan, "Le séminaire sur *La Letter volée*," in *Écrits* (Paris: Seuil, 1966), 19–75. The seminar is repro-

duced in translation and with the critical debate surrounding it in *The Purloined Poe: Lacan, Derrida and Psychoanalytic Reading*, ed. John P. Muller and William J. Richardson (Baltimore: Johns Hopkins University Press, 1988), 28–54.

12. On *Sir Gawain and the Green Knight* as a text that foregrounds the constructed nature of masculinity, see Cohen, "Decapitation and Coming of Age."

13. *Sir Gawain and the Green Knight*, ed. J. R. R. Tolkien and E. V. Gordon, rev. Norma Davis (Oxford: Clarendon Press, 1967), 1.629.

14. Ross Arthur, *Medieval Sign Theory and Sir Gawain and the Green Knight* (Toronto: University of Toronto Press, 1987), 34.

15. David Baker, "The Gödel in *Gawain:* Paradoxes of Self-Reference and the Problematics of Language in *Sir Gawain and the Green Knight*," *Cambridge Quarterly* 32, no. 4 (2003): 349–66.

16. Boethius, *De Arithmetica*, in Arthur, *Medieval Sign Theory*, 34.

17. See also R. A. Shoaf, *The Poem as Green Girdle: Commercium in Sir Gawain and the Green Knight* (Gainesville: University Presses of Florida, 1984). Shoaf works through the problem of beheading as it is related to circumcision and shows how the text itself intertwines these issues.

18. Helen Cooper, "Notes," in *Sir Gawain and the Green Knight*, trans. Keith Harrison (Oxford: Oxford University Press, 1998), 91. Translations throughout are from this volume.

19. See Scala, "Wanting Words"; Geraldine Heng, "A Woman Wants: The Lady, *Gawain*, and the Forms of Seduction," *Yale Journal of Criticism* 5, no. 3 (1992): 101–34. Stephen Manning, "A Psychological Interpretation of *Sir Gawain and the Green Knight*," *Criticism* 6 (1964): 165–77.

20. Carolyn Dinshaw, "A Kiss Is Just a Kiss: Heterosexuality and Its Consolations in *Sir Gawain and the Green Knight*," *Diacritics* 24, nos. 2–3 (Summer–Fall 1994): 205–26. Also see *Constructing Medieval Sexuality*, ed. Karma Lochrie, Peggy McCracken, and James A. Schultz (Minneapolis: University of Minnesota Press, 1997) and Patricia Ingham, *Sovereign Fantasies: Arthurian Romance and the Making of Britain* (Philadelphia: University of Pennsylvania Press, 2001), 107–36.

21. L. O. Aranye Fradenburg reminds us that in *The Ethics of Psychoanalysis* Lacan points to shame as the limit on the horizon of desire. Fradenburg says, "Like its obverse, beauty, shame marks the limit of the ideal image and points, comically or punitively, to what lies beyond it": *Sacrifice Your Love: Psychoanalysis, Historicism, Chaucer* (Minneapolis: University of Minnesota Press, 2002), 289, n. 32.

22. Sigmund Freud, *Three Case Histories*, ed. Philip Rieff (New York: Collier Books, 1963), 166.

23. A crucial text on this issue as well as the problem of language in Schreber's text is Michel de Certeau "The Institution of Rot," in *Psychosis and Sexual Identity: Toward a Post-Analytic View of the Schreber Case*, ed. David B. Allison, Prado de Oliveira, Mark S. Roberts, and Allen S. Weiss (New York: SUNY Press, 1988), 88–100.

24. See also Allen Frantzen, *Before the Closet* (Chicago: University of Chicago Press, 1998); John Boswell, *Christianity, Social Tolerance, and Homosexuality* (Chicago: University of Chicago Press, 1980); David M. Halperin, *One Hundred Years of Homosexuality* (New York: Routledge, 1990); Mark D. Jordan, *The Invention of Sodomy in Christian Theology* (Chicago: University of Chicago Press, 1997); and *Pre-modern Sexualities*, ed. Louise O. Fradenburg and Carla Freccero (New York: Routledge, 1996).

25. Scala, *Absent Narratives,* 44. Scala does much to forward the argument that psychoanalysis is always already present in literary and critical, as well as historiographical, texts.

26. Jean-Louis Baudry, "Freud and 'Literary Creation,'" trans. Roland-François Lack, in *The Tel Quel Reader,* ed. Patrick Ffrench and Roland-François Lack (New York: Routledge, 1998), 70.

27. Georges Bataille, *The Unfinished System of Non-knowledge,* trans. Michelle Kendall and Stuart Kendall (Minneapolis: University of Minnesota Press, 2001).

28. Georges Bataille, *On Nietzsche,* trans. Bruce Boone (New York: Paragon House, 1992).

29. Jacques Lacan, "Subversion of the Subject and the Dialectic of Desire in the Freudian Unconscious," in *Écrits,* trans. Alan Sheridan (New York: W. W. Norton, 1977), 292–325. Although Lacan is not listed as having participated in the seminar, he is no doubt influenced by his conversations with Bataille, by others who were present, and by his own reading of *On Nietzsche* as well as Bataille's other work including his medievalist thesis, "L'Ordre de Chevalerie."

30. Fradenburg, *Sacrifice Your Love;* de Certeau "Institution of Rot."

31. Of course, Lacan also addresses mysticism and *jouissance* in his Rome seminars on feminine sexuality: *The Seminar of Jacques Lacan, Book XX: On Feminine Sexuality, the Limits of Love and Knowledge, Encore,* trans. Bruce Fink (New York: W. W. Norton, 1998).

32. Both Gawain and Schreber experience the dissonance between "earthly time" and "Christian eternity" noted about *Sir Gawain and the Green Knight* by J. A. Burrow, *A Reading of Sir Gawain and the Green Knight* (London: Routledge & Kegan Paul, 1965).

33. In this sense, Gawain prefigures the ambivalence, procrastination, and repetition compulsion also at stake in another obvious psychoanalytical case, Shakespeare's Hamlet.

34. Jacques Lacan, *The Seminar of Jacques Lacan, Book XI: The Four Fundamental Concepts of Psychoanalysis,* ed. Jacques-Alain Miller, trans. Alan Sheridan (New York: W. W. Norton, 1977), 53–54.

35. Elizabeth Grosz in Eluned Bremner, "Margery Kempe and the Critics: Disempowerment and Deconstruction," in *Margery Kempe: A Book of Essays,* ed. Sandra J. McEntire (New York: Garland, 1992), 133.

36. *Hali Meiðheð in Medieval English Prose for Women,* ed. Bella Millet and Jocelyn Wogan-Browne (Oxford: Clarendon Press, 1990), 10. *Hali Maidenhead, an Alliterative Homily of the Thirteenth Century,* ed. Oswald Cockayne (London: Early English Text Society, 1866) (orig. ca. 1200–30?).

37. Schreber is tormented by the scatological terms by which God attempts to seduce him.

38. Daniel Paul Schreber, *Memoirs of My Nervous Illness,* trans. and ed. Ida Macalpine and Richard A. Hunter (Cambridge, Mass.: Harvard University Press, 1988 [1955]), 63.

39. Freud, *Three Case Histories,* 112.

40. Francis Barker, *The Tremulous Private Body* (Ann Arbor: University of Michigan Press, 1995), 51.

41. See Sigmund Freud, *The Ego and the Id* (New York: W. W. Norton, 1966). I would also like to forward Deleuze and Guattari's connection between weapons

and projection put forth in *A Thousand Plateaus: Capitalism and Schizophrenia*, trans. Brian Massumi (Minneapolis: University of Minnesota Press, 1987): "Weapons have a privileged relation with projection. Anything that throws or is thrown is fundamentally a weapon, and propulsion is its essential moment. The weapon is ballistic; the very notion of the 'problem' is related to the war machine. The more mechanisms of projection a tool has, the more it behaves like a weapon, potentially or simply metaphorically" (395). I must add, however, that I would critique the phrase "simply metaphorical"; metaphor is never simple.

42. In his analysis of the armor-subject, Klaus Theweleit points out that the liminal space, in which Schreber first expresses his desire to be a woman and which is also the place of syncope, "unites the 'masculine' body armor with the repressed 'feminine' interior": *Male Fantasies* (Minneapolis: University of Minnesota Press, 1987), 166. Schreber literally transforms his "masculine" body armor into a feminine one, blending interior with exterior, and completing his armored subjectivity. In the scene of Schreber's transvestitism, sexuality itself becomes a form of armor, a construct that is put on as one goes to battle with the symbolic world.

43. The externalization of Schreber's image of his "trunk" recalls Tausk's discussion of Nataljia A and demonstrates the technologization of the dispossessed body. In the case of Nataljia A the female trunk becomes externalized as a coffin and a mechanical apparatus. See Victor Tausk, *Sexuality, War, and Schizophrenia*, trans. Eric Mosbacher et al. (New Brunswick, N.J.: Transaction Publishers, 1991), 194.

44. Also see Eric L. Santer, *My Own Private Germany: Daniel Paul Schreber's Secret History of Modernity* (Princeton, N.J.: Princeton University Press, 1996).

45. Jacques Lacan, *The Seminar of Jacques Lacan, Book I: Freud's Papers on Technique*, ed. Jacques-Alain Miller, trans. John Forrester (New York: W. W. Norton, 1991), 245.

46. Three important analyses of the role of the neighbor with regard to psychoanalysis and Marxism may be found in Slavoj Žižek, Eric L. Santner, and Kenneth Reinhard, *The Neighbor: Three Inquiries into Political Theology* (Chicago: University of Chicago Press, 2006).

47. In "Stealing Material: The Materiality of Language According to Freud and Lacan," in *Lacan and the Human Sciences*, ed. Alexandre Leupin (Lincoln: University of Nebraska Press, 1991), 59–105, Ellie Ragland Sullivan marks a clear distinction between the materialism evident in Lacan's approach to language and that found in Heidegger. It is not my intention to elide this important difference here, but rather to mark the thick history of Lacan's materialism and to foreground the element of dwelling as dimensionality as well as the element of spirituality in the material.

48. David Tracy, "Mystics, Prophets, Rhetorics: Religion and Psychoanalysis," in *The Trials of Psychoanalysis*, ed. Françoise Meltzer (Chicago: University of Chicago Press, 1987), 260.

Index

Abelard, Peter, 33, 67, 142
abjection, 85, 88–89, 94, 124–25, 129, 221;
    and woman, 95, 97, 239n47
Adorno, Theodor, 119
Agamben, Giorgio, 1, 69–78, 80–84,
    236n11, 237n21, 237n24, 237n30
Alain de Lille, 171
alchemy, 154, 165, 167
alienation, 115
alterity, 4, 117, 164, 210
ambivalence, 105–7, 127; and animality,
    32, 66–85; and courtly love, 90–92,
    98–99; and desire to see, 90, 102–3;
    and real, 88; and troubadours, 111
amor de longh, 111, 129
anagrams, 5
analysis, 7, 31, 99. *See also* textual
    analysis
analytic ideals, 41
anamorphosis, 92, 111, 130, 144;
    anamorphotic, 125, 143
Antigone, 147, 180–88, 249n46
anti-intellectualism, 37
antiquity, 3, 43, 134, 152, 164, 166
anxiety-hysteria, 68. *See also* hysteria
Aquinas, Thomas, 16–18, 34, 44, 57, 112,
    145. *See also* Thomism
Arendt, Hannah, 1, 232n20
Aristotle, 42–46, 72, 170–71; Aris-
    totelian, 32, 106; and Boethius, 20,

23; dialectics, 102; and element,
    39; ethics, 62; and homonyms, 4;
    and love, 138; and sovereign good,
    40, 100–101; and universals, 32,
    64, 67
Arnaut Daniel, 32, 91–99, 124, 129, 135–
    36, 143, 240n64
astrolabe, 33; history of, 161, 175–76; and
    indeterminacy, 188; and uncertainty,
    167–69, 171–72
astrology, 154, 164–67, 170–71
astronomy, 154, 164–66, 170–71
authenticity, 41
automaton, 45, 78, 207, 211, 214
autre. *See* Other, the

Badiou, Alain, 50, 128–29, 173–74,
    226n31
bare life, 80–84
baroque, 111, 141, 144, 188, 198
Barthes, Roland, 1, 7, 226n25
Baruzi, Jean, 18
Bataille, Georges, 1, 155, 205–6, 223n2,
    252n29
Bataille, Sylvia, 143, 219
Baudrillard, Jean, 10, 226n31
Baudry, Jean-Louis, 203–4
becoming-woman, 211. *See also*
    Schreber, Daniel Paul
bees, 69–73, 236n9

being, 73, 217; categories of, 31; as copula, 105; crossing out of, 67; and dwelling, 104; as an ideal, 41; of language, 11; moments of, 9; of objects, 11; as real, 127; as reality, 31; state of, 186; of the subject, 104; and the thing, 102; in time, 221; in the world, 22, 40, 67, 75, 219. *See also* Heidegger, Martin

Bentham, Jeremy, 62

between the two deaths, 180–82, 184–87, 191, 214

Boccaccio, Giovanni, 50, 57

Boethius, Anicius Manlius Severinus: Boethian, 44; causality, 11, 17–18; and Chaucer, 38, 47–48, 165; and happiness, 35; and Isidore, 132; and mathematics, 171, 195, 197; as moderate realist, 21; Neoplatonism of, 46; platonism of, 32; quarrel of universals, 2, 4–5, 20–23, 42, 66–67; and werewolf, 237n25

Borromeos arms, 157

Brennan, Teresa, 178

Canterbury Tales, The, 14, 36, 57. *See also* Chaucer, Geoffrey

caritas, 106

castration, 84, 117; castrate, 206; as resistance, 207

Cathars, 184, 249n48

catharsis, 61, 184. *See also* syncope

causality, 83, 171; absence of, 46, 88, 111, 144; of desire, 127, 179; universal, 153; woman's, 158

chain of signification, 11, 29. *See also* signifying chain

chance, 45–46, 57. *See also* tuché

chastity, 208–9

Chaucer, Geoffrey, 9, 165, 230n1, 234n44, 248n37; as Boethian, 38; as father of the fool, 32–37; and nominalism, 38; quarrel of universals, 154, as a realist, 14; and realism, 28, 51, 175; and translation, 165

Chaucer, Geoffrey, works of: *Boece,* 47–48; *The Canterbury Tales,* 56, 168–69, 175; *Canon's Yeoman's Tale,* 165;

Clerk's Tale, 36–38, 50–52, 56–66; *General Prologue,* 51–52; *Miller's Tale,* 164; *Second Nun's Tale,* 165; *Treatise on the Astrolabe,* 33, 147, 153–54, 164–65, 167–76; *Wife of Bath's Tale,* 55, 58

Che vuoi?, 104, 112, 114–16, 176

Christ, 133–34, 170, 195; and cross, 200; and *jouissance,* 137; and lack, 137; proof of God, 17; suffering of, 91

Christine de Pizan, 87

Cicero, 171

Clerk's Tale, 36–38, 50–52, 56–66, 233; clerk as fool, 37, 57. *See also* Chaucer, Geoffrey

consciousness of self, 115, 120. *See also* Hegel, Martin; self: self-consciousness

consistency, 50–51, 80

Copernican revolution, 2, 19

Copernicus, 165–66

Copjec, Joan, 178–79, 227

Cornell, Drucilla, 38, 67

Coudrette, 86–88

Courbet, Gustav, 143–44

courtly love, 6, 32, 37, 91, 93–101, 128–31, 162, 217; as anamorphosis, 92, 130; and Christianity, 111, 133, 137–38, 179; and *Clerk's Tale,* 63–64; dynamic(s), 191, 192; expectations of, 194; history of, 188; and desire, 15, 39, 70, 118; and knowing the subject, 31; Lombarda, 123–25; master/slave in, 100; (non)dialectics of, 111–12, 118–19, 125, 144, 146; obstacles within, 191, 206; poetics, 1, 122; refusal of, 206; resistance to, 191; triangulation of, 106, 107–8; as universal category, 111

cult of the virgin, 137

cut, 115–17, 152–53, 207; and bees, 71; and knot, 33, 192–93

Dante, Aligheri, 107, 110, 135–36, 184, 244n41

Das Ding, 75–76. *See also* thing, the

death drive, 206, 208

decency, 32, 67, 88

de Certeau, Michel, 206, 244–45n49

Deleuze, Gilles: and Félix Guattari, 152, 252–53n41

de Rougemont, Denis, 138
Derrida, Jacques, 1, 7, 12, 35, 60, 69–77;
  on being, 236n19; and the gift, 238n38;
  on One, 234n48
Descartes, René, 140, 210, 220; Cartesian
  logic, 212
desire, 25, 39, 41–43, 70–72, 89–91, 111–
  24, 134–38, 143–45, 208, 217; absence
  of, 132; and absent cause, 111, 133; as
  ambivalent, 68, 84, 92; animality of,
  32, 66, 97; articulation of, 177; and
  Badiou, 50–51; and Bataille, 205; to
  become woman, 210; of bees, 70–71;
  cause of, 143, 179; chart of, 113; and
  Chaucer, 170; and courtly love, 6, 15,
  95–99; 111, 128, 138; dialectics of, 64,
  108, 110, 142, 146; of disciple, 164 (see
  also transference); discourses of, 179;
  and envy, 169; erotic, 12; facts of, 163;
  gaps in, 186; Gawain's, 199, 202; and
  goodness, 203; graph(s) of, 113–20;
  historiography of, 187; and ideal,
  40–41; insatiability of, 221; knot of,
  130, 146, 156, 194; to know, 172; for
  knowledge, 62, 100 (see also epistemophilia); Lacan's, 160–62;
  Lacan's seminars on, 218; Lacan's
  theory of, 32, 63, 93, 175–76, 180–81,
  185; and language, 145; limits of, 206;
  mathematized, 112; notation for, 163;
  object of, 57, 103, 109, 111, 127, 143,
  180; obstacle of, 100, 109, 112; for
  origins, 224n6; of the Other, 11, 144;
  of the other/Other, 11, 39, 94, 104,
  115, 144 (see also Che vuoi?); persecutory, 206; and phantasm, 204; and
  politics, 180; process of, 152, 222;
  realism of, 174; real of, 12, 35, 103,
  126, 181; to resist desire, 191; retrograde effect of, 175–78; sacrificing,
  204; scene of, 204; Schreber's, 207;
  scientificity of, 163, 164; to see, 102;
  state of, 120; sublimated, 200; and
  sublimation, 131; taken literally, 10–
  12, 14, 132, 177, 179, 217; topography
  of, 112; and tragedy, 180, 185, 188;
  triangulation of, 107; and truth,
  48; uncontainability of, 33; unconscious, 141, 198–200, 221; as universal, 92, 112
dialectical: and history, 178; method,
  222; play, 186; process, 33, 107, 111;
  resistance to, 32; sublimation, 99;
  system 124, 152. See also dialectic(s);
  Hegel, G. W. F.; master-slave
  dialectic
dialectic(s), 64, 119–21, 140, 195; and
  ambivalence, 67, 106; Aristotelian,
  102; and Chaucer, 50–51; of courtly
  love, 108, 144; and desire, 64, 101, 108,
  110–13, 142, 146; excess of, 108; and
  logic, 3; mathematical structure of,
  107; postdialectical, 67; universality
  of, 155. See also dialectical; Hegel,
  G. W. F.
difference, 7, 41, 210
différance, 210
Dinshaw, Carolyn, 198, 200
disciplinarity, 1, 3, 7; disciplinary lines,
  169, 175
discourse(s): academic, 182; of analysis,
  192; of analyst, 146–49; of desire, 179;
  four, 146–49, 207; of hysteric, 146–49,
  192–93; of master, 25, 146–49, 164; of
  obsessional, 24; of psychotic, 193; and
  reality, 102; scientific, 193; of university, 146–49
dit, 133
Dragonetti, Roger, 5, 133, 224n6, 225–
  26n24
drive, 134
dualism, 62. See also duality
duality, 32, 62, 66, 67, 69, 80, 105, 107; of
  ambivalence, 111; animal/human, 71–
  83, 103
duke of Berry, 87, 239n42
Durandin, Guy, 23–25
duty, 41, 58, 207
dwelling, 218–19

element (stoicheion), 39
Elizabethan theatre, 35
Empedocles, 39
enunciation, 42
envy, 110, 169–72, 188, 248n35
Epicurus, 9, 19, 42–44, 46–47, 48

epistemological cuts/break, 2, 9, 19, 176–77. *See also* periodicity
epistemophilia, 4, 52, 84, 87, 122, 172
epochal difference, 147
epochal distinctions, 1, 4, 19, 177
epochal shifts, 153
epochs, 175; play with, 117
Eros and Thanatos, 67
error, 43
ethics, 183; and desire, 72–73; of pleasure, 101; of psychoanalysis, 35, 182
Eudoxus, 176
euphemism, 118, 124, 140
excess, 92–95, 118, 124–25, 129, 214; of dialectics, 108, 217. *See also* surplus
excommunication, 5
existentialism, 50
ex nihilo, 11, 17–18, 29, 123, 126, 196, 222, 227n35
extimacy, 8, 93, 226n27

fabliau(x), 92, 96, 99, 124, 240n61
faith: Gawain's, 201; lack of, 58, 82; in order of cosmos, 140, 165; in real, 192; and reason, 4, 16–17, 153, 222; in self and other, 85; unconscious, 29, 34; in universals, 57
fantasy, 127, 131, 133; as singular, 115; of womanhood, 211
Felman, Shoshana, 7–8
femininity: Schreber's performance of, 210
feminism, 97, 224n6; anti-feminism, 101–2. *See also* ideology
fetish, 207, 210
fidelity, 51, 79, 100
fin amor, 136
Fink, Bruce, 227n33
fool, 35–36, 50–53; clerk as, 57; and knave, 52; and medieval–early modern transition, 36
formalism, 154
Fort/Da, 20, 103, 130, 194, 226n30
Foucault, Michel, 1, 179
four discourses, 146–49, 207
Fradenburg, L. O. Aranye, 9, 47–48, 63, 206, 235n52, 251n21

fragility, 84, 201, 212; of sovereign and power, 36, 62; of subjectivity, 90
freedom, 48
free will, 45, 48, 57, 69, 80–81; and knowledge, 38
Frege, Gottlob, 105
Freud, Sigmund, 3–9, 29, 96, 164, 183; debt to, 181; and desire, 11, 144, 204; exegesis of, 18; and fantasy, 106; Freudian, 99, 112, 124; and history, 220; literary, 12, 14; and Marx, 222; *Mélusine*, 86; and omphalos, 245n2; on paranoia, 200–201; Rat Man, 32, 68, 91, 106; and the real, 204; return to, 163; Schreber, 200, 210, 215; and scientificity, 156, 163; and treatment, 182; and unconscious, 19, 44–45, 49, 192, 202; Wolf Man, 32, 68–69, 85, 90–92, 103, 106; and woman, 55

Galileo, 152
Gawain, 33, 191–92, 194–204, 206–8, 213, 215. *See also Sir Gawain and the Green Knight*
gaze, 110, 136, 137
Gilson, Etienne, 17–18, 138, 228n42, 232n26
Glejzer, Richard, 3
God, 17, 19–20, 29; absence of, 110; as causality, 18; courting, 205, 207; and Dante, 107; death of, 93; as desire, 30; desire for, 204, 208–11, 214; dread of, 208; and Gawain, 206; impossibility of, 102; and infinity, 195; and *jouissance*, 138; Lady as, 200; and love, 30, 179; as Other, 30; proofs of, 220; as a real, 33; and Schreber, 206, 209; as singularity, 58; unconscious, 30, 32, 34, 136–39, 143, 222; union with, 110, 208; will of, 201
Gödel, Kurt, 156, 195–96
good: and evil, 58, 64; vs. bad, 38. *See also* sovereign: good
graph(s) of desire, 104, 113–18, 153–54, 158, 175
Grosz, Elizabeth, 207–8

Guilbaud, Georges-Th., 157–58
Guillaume IX, 111, 125–26, 129, 139. *See also* courtly love

Hali Meiðheð, 208
happiness, 35, 232n24
hard sciences, 33, 146–47, 155, 162–64, 177; idealization of, 33, 147, 151, 154
Hegel, G. W. F., 120–23, 140, 144, 155, 178, 183. *See also* Hegelian
Hegelian, 17, 106, 220; dialectic(s), 52–53, 58–59, 94, 112, 114, 118–23, 178; historiography, 177–78; history, 179–80; State Law, 112. *See also* master/slave dialectics; self: self-consciousness
Heidegger, Martin, 1, 3, 69–77, 102, 218
Herrnstein Smith, Barbara, 166
historiography, 86, 160, 178–79; of desire, 187; as excess, 180; Hegelian, 177–78
history, 87, 175, 177–79, 186, 217, 221; Catholic, 216; of desire, 118; ends of, 48; and Freud, 220; of language, 132; of the letter, 132; as a real, 180; thick, 108–110
Hobbes, Thomas, 54
Hollywood, Amy, 192
homonym(s), 4–5, 104, 133, 145, 184
Hûchet, Jean Charles, 5, 7
humanism, 77
hybrid: human-animal, 32, 66–67, 75, 80, 82–85, 88, 98, 103–4; woman-animal, 88
hysteria (hysterical subject), 33, 159, 192, 194, 207; anxiety-, 68; discourse of, 193; hysteric, 146, 149, 215

identification, 114, 242n22; and alterity, 4, 164; dialectical; 118; and narcissism, 124; and projection, 131; and *tenson*, 112
ideological power, 36;
ideological state apparatuses, 143
ideological systems, 7, 182
ideology, 36–37, 242n18; feminist, 97
imaginary, 13, 41, 65, 129, 141

imago, 211, 213
infinite: circle, 140, 197; infinity, 141, 191, 195–96
Irigaray, Luce, 228n44
Isidore of Seville, 23, 57, 132

Jaufré Rudel, 91, 100, 111, 129
Jean D'Arras, 32, 86, 239n42
Jerome, 57
Job, 57
jouissance, 134–38, 147, 149, 181–82; and Cathars, 184; and courtly love, 111; and Dante, 107, 110; and the drives, 134; and ethics, 62; feminine, 137; graph of desire, 117; and mystics, 136; and reality, 102; woman's, 138
Jung, Karl, 31, 202

Kant, Emmanuel, 3, 41, 163
Kierkegaard, Søren, 174
king: as sovereign, 36. *See also* naked king
kinship, 180
knot(s), 152–62; analytical, 130, 192; and Boethius, 22, 57, 64; Borromean, 158–59; in chain of signification, 122; of desire, 10, 33, 57, 111, 130, 146, 160, 189, 191; and dialectics, 122–23, 144, 195; endless (endeles), 195; of girdle, 201; of historiography, 89; of history, 178; of holiness, 191; (im)perfection of, 198; Lacan's play with, 142, 162, 188; of language, 17, 189, 190; linguistic, 6; mathematical, 196, 201; of paradox, 196; and pentangle, 190–91, 196; perfect, 191; resistant, 33, 190, 192; and science, 247n23; sexual, 196; as symptom, 145, 207; theological, 196; theory, 154, 164; of unconscious, 6, 10, 33, 111, 130, 146, 156, 161, 189, 192–94, 196–97, 245–46n2
Kojève, Alexandre, 3, 48, 152–53, 164, 246
Koyré, Alexandre, 152–53, 164–66, 246
Kristeva, Julia, 1, 4, 16–17, 63, 215, 223n1, 239n47
Kuhn, Thomas, 176

LaCapra, Dominick, 7, 160, 225
lack, 91, 128–30, 137; and *Clerk's Tale,* 60; and cut, 116; of desire, 112; disavowal of, 85; and excess, 118, 125, 128; female, 99; as fullness, 40; in language, 114, 156; of other, 123; sexual, 99; of sexual difference, 170; in subjectivity, 104; of wholeness, 115; woman as, 124
la femme (the woman), 32, 55–56, 59; impossibility of writing, 86
language: as a universal, 164. *See also* mathematical language; *matheme(s)*
law, 55, 62, 112, 180; and bed, 62, 66; and pleasure, 38; sovereign, 191. *See also* ideology
Law of the Father, 54, 112, 243n33
Leclaire, Serge, 14–15
Lefèbvre-Pontalis, Jean-Bertrand, 23–26
letter, the, 15, 34, 49, 132; arrival of, 194
Leupin, Alexandre, 19, 29, 156–57, 230n63, 231n15, 242n20, 247n17
Levinas, Emmanuel, 1, 228n38
literal, 10, 15–17, 34, 66; analysis, 16
logic, 3, 22, 43, 52, 121. *See also* reason
Lombarda, 123–24
love, 25, 126–29, 200; and *Bisclavret,* 82, 84; and *Clerk's Tale,* 60; demand for, 11; and desire, 178; and God, 142; ideal, 41; and knowledge, 161; mathematization of, 173–74; *Mélusine,* 89; object of, 6; for Other, 92; scene of, 94; and sexuality, 188; as a sign, 147, 149; sublimated, 219; for unity, 16. *See also* courtly love
lovesickness, 194

Macrobius, 171
Maimonedes, Moses, 215–17
Many and One, 53–54, 112, 123
Marchande, Valérie, 157–58
Marie de France, 32, 66, 87, 239n42; *Bisclavret,* 66, 78–85, 90, 103, 106; *Guigemar,* 196; *Lanval,* 143, 239n52, 245n51
Marx, Karl, 17, 178
Marxism, 3, 155, 220, 221. *See also* materiality
Massahalla, 169

Masson, André, 143–44
master-slave dialectic, 8, 59–60, 63, 104, 111, 118, 178; master/servant, 118
materiality, 15, 34, 73, 99, 215, 217; material, 24, 142, 196, 207; language as, 218, 220 materialist(s), 100; and the desk, 219; psychoanalysis as, 215
mathematical language, 163–64, 172–73, 193; vs. poetry, 190–91
mathematics, 152, 154–56, 170, 173–74, 180
matheme(s), 33, 146–47, 153–54, 156–57, 163–64, 173–75; and desire, 159
méconnaissance, 114, 242n19
Medea, 50
Mélusine, 32, 85–91, 102–3, 106, 239
Meno, 33, 43, 147, 149–52
metamorphosis, 80–81, 83, 85
metaphor, 5, 10, 12, 117; metaphorical, 15–16, 93
metonymy, 5, 12; metonymical, 145
Milner, Jean-Claude, 152–53, 246
modern(ity), 2–3, 18–19, 152, 164, 166, 182
moral law, 42
mourning, 91, 186
multiplicity, 5, 12, 122; and Unity, 39; and signification, 115, 117
Myles, Robert, 28–32
mystic(s), 136–37, 206; mysticism, 137, 192; mystical, 210, 212

naked king, 36, 39, 53, 59, 61–62, 66, 83
name (naming), 76, 78, 104, 126
narcissism, 91, 123–24
negation, 122
neighbor, 218, 228n41, 253n46
neologism(s), 5, 132, 135–36
Neugebauer, Otto, 165–66, 177, 248n41
neurosis, 68, 103, 207; neurotic, 215
Nicholas of Cusa, 140–41, 195
Nicholas of Lynn, 164, 169–71
Nietzsche, Friedrich, 29, 205, 249n4
nominalism, 6, 17, 24, 67, 126, 154; of Boethius, 4, 14–15; and Chaucer, 38, 52–53, 56; and knowledge, 28; and Lacan, 29, 41, 49, 102; limits of, 36; and singularity, 151

nominalist, 12, 14–16, 26–28, 150, 161;
    Baudrillard as, 10; Chaucer, 58;
    Ockham as, 38; and real, 123
nonclassical, 33, 152, 176, 180, 189;
    thinking, 33, 147, 175, 177
nothing, 124–27
Nussbaum, Martha, 43–44

objet a, 96, 127, 179–80
obscene, 85, 89, 129, 134; and courtly
    love, 124; and divine, 92, 136; and
    sublimation, 96–99
obscenity, 93–95; and decency, 67; and
    divinity, 142; of proximity, 32
Oedipus Complex, 5, 243n33
Oedipus, 5
One, 31–32, 39, 62; as "I", 60; and the
    many, 53–54, 112, 123; oneness, 47, 51;
    and signifier, 92; and two, 105; and
    woman, 102; unknowable, 41
Other, the, 62, 111–12, 115, 122, 180;
    demand of, 39; desire of, 39, 114–15;
    God, 136, 138; of the Other, 218; and
    self, 91, 210; as symptom of, 193;
    voice of, 44; want of, 199

paranoia (paranoid subject), 33, 192,
    200–201, 202, 204; union with, 110
Parmenides, 19, 62
past and future, 117
patience, 58–61
pentangle, 33, 190–91, 195, 197; and per-
    fect circle, 34, 190
performative utterance, 73
periodicity, 3, 175–76, 228n46; periodi-
    zation, 166, 177, 182, 184. See also
    epistemological cuts/break; epochal
    distinctions
Petrarch, 50
phallic-mother, 86, 89
phallus, 103, 137; absent, 89; absence of,
    90, 102–3; signification of, 101; as
    signifier, 86
philology, 4
Plato, 19, 39, 46, 170, 176; Platonism, 32;
    Platonists, 43; Platonic, 47, 92, 96;
    Laws, 69; Meno, 33, 43, 147, 149–152;
    Timeaus, 140

pleasure, 43, 100
pleasure principle, 41, 45, 207
Plotnitzsky, Arkady, 151, 154, 166
Poe, Edgar Allan, 89
poetic(s), 3–7, 93–99, 116; and Boethius,
    20; and Chaucer, 57; and desire, 33,
    106; importance of, 190–91; medieval,
    9, 102; and other, 111; repetition in,
    110; and sacred, 205; and theory, 132;
    troubadour, 111. See also courtly love
Porphyry, 4–5, 19–20, 42, 132
postclassical era, 24, 166. See also
    nonclassical
postmodernity, 2, 10, 19, 89, 182;
    medievalism, 129
poststructuralist world, 67
premodernity, 3, 19, 164, 166, 180, 182
projection, 118, 131, 210–11; of evil onto
    woman, 203
prosopopoeia, 220
Provence, 10, 217
proximity, 99, 113
psyche, 5–7, 9, 19, 31, 154, 190, 199, 225;
    literary element of, 14; textuality
    of, 193
psychosis, 194, 207, 215
psychotic, 215; discourse, 192; speech,
    193
Ptolomy, 170–71

quadrangle, 33, 146, 151
quarrel of the universals, 42, 57, 106,
    154, 169, 226n31, 231n7. See also
    nominalism; real (Real); realism;
    universals

Raimbaut, 126
Rat Man, 32
real, the 69; encounter with, 44–45
real (Real), 6, 9–13, 15–16, 20, 23–27, 31,
    34, 41, 63–65, 71, 74, 76, 89, 99, 141–43,
    161, 215–17; animal as, 76; arrival at,
    207; and automaton, 207; categories
    of, 27, 38, 67, 86; of desire, 123, 181;
    desk as, 221; and Hegel, 120; of
    history, 180; of hysteria, 192; impos-
    sible, 51; impossibility of writing,
    179; and language, 49, 193, 221;

real (Real) *(continued)*, of mysticism, 192; paradox of, 192; possibility of, 194; of psychoanalysis, 44; and reality, 194; sacred, 205; of signified, 113; of signifier, 127, 221; unconscious as, 4, 103, 105, 123, 146, 176, 189, 190, 192, 196, 207, 214; unanalyzable element of, 192; universal, 2, of universals, 139, 161, 177, 216, 221; of virtue, 189

realism, 6, 12, 14–15, 17, 24–25, 28–32, 38, 40–41, 64, 102, 143, 151, 154, 159, 161, 175, 203; classical, 33; of desire, 174; linguistic, 31; literary, 13; moderate, 4, 38; psychological, 31; semiotic, 31

realist, 6, 12–14, 30, 34, 39, 49, 150, 215; and Chaucer, 165; epistemological, 31; ethical, 31; foundational, 28, 30; intentional, 28, 30

reality, 12, 13, 110; and *jouissance*, 102; and real, 194

reality principle, 41–42, 218

reason, 4, 16, 17, 22, 153, 222; and drives, 165; limits of, 34

recognition, 113, 161; mutual, 111; self-, 114; of subject, 111

Regnault, François, 153

repetition, 61, 105, 108–9, 161, 186, 191, 203, 225; Gawain's, 207

repression, 65, 69, 90, 134; repressed, 110, 114

resistance, 9–10, 98, 139, 149, 153–54, 207; to courtly love, 191; to dialectical system, 32; Gawain's, 191; to psychoanalysis, 35, 190; to the sovereign law, 191

retrograde effect, 114, 175–76, 181, 189

romance, 3, 85, 106

Ronell, Avital, 190–91, 241n8

Roudinesco, Elizabeth, 143, 157–60, 247n20

Roustang, François, 162–64

sacrifice, 206

Sartre, Jean-Paul, 90, 205

Saussure, Ferdinand de, 3, 114

Scala, Elizabeth, 9, 190, 203

scatology, 32, 93, 96, 98, 128–29, 131, 143

scene of two, 32–33, 105, 127–28, 173–74

scholasticism, 3, 19, 48, 51

scholastic(s), 2–6, 14, 19, 23, 29, 37, 39–40, 43, 48, 51–52, 64, 105, 196, 215, 224; debates, 19, 93, 95. *See also* quarrel of the universals

Schreber, Daniel Paul, 33, 192, 200, 204–15

scoptophilia, 85; scoptophilic drive, 84. *See also* voyeurism; seeing

seeing: traumatic, 88

self: as other, 210; as psychic, 208; self-consciousness, 114, 118, 121; self-mutilation, 207

sex: and death, 208

sexual difference, 62, 70, 110, 128, 130, 136, 170, 192

sexual encounter, 112, 204

sexual rapport, relation(ship), 62, 111, 119, 128, 140, 173–74, 240n55; absence of, 100, 129; impossibility of, 91, 93–99, 124, 127–28, 159, 221; and lack, 30; mathematization of, 118, 161

shame, 199–203

sign, 10, 30, 49; impossibility of, 102

signification, 113, 115, 178, 186, 221; chain(s) of, 117, 122; and desire, 117; limits of, 98; scene of, 99

signified, 10, 17; 93; real of, 113

signifier(s), 6, 92–93, 109, 193; being of, 138; and desire, 10–11, 113, 115, 117; emptiness of, 125; and ideal, 39; master, 147, 149; as mediator, 130; perfect, 154; and phallus, 101; as real 12; and realism, 17; and subject, 176; treasure of, 115

signifying chain, 113

Sir Gawain and the Green Knight, 33, 194–201, 203–4, 207; between the two deaths, 191; and uncanny, 186. *See also* Gawain

Skeat, Walter, 167–68

Socrates (Socratic) 4, 19, 31, 43, 150, 189. *See also* Meno

Solomon, 203

Sophocles. See *Antigone*

Soury, Pierre, 158

sovereign, 36, 56, 62–63; ethics of, 38; good, 31–32, 38–42, 46–47, 62, 66, 219; and language, 39, 50; law, 191; master, 112; power, 36, 82–84; tyranny, 36, 63; unity, 38, 39, 43

sovereignty, 31–32, 35, 40; and *Bisclavret,* 78, 80; and *Clerk's Tale,* 51, 53–55, 59, 61–65; fragility of, 50, 66; as goodness, 70; phantasmatic, 39; as singularity, 32, 35–36; of the subject, 90

speech act, 54. *See also* performative utterance

sphere, 141

Spinoza, Baruch, 216

spirituality, 34, 74, 215, 217; language as, 218; of matter, 220; spiritual, 142, 196, 207

split consciousness, 191. *See also* subject: fragmented

square root of negative one, 104, 118, 128, 174

St. Augustine, 2, 43, 48–49

stoicheion, 39. *See also* Empedocles

stoics, 46–47; stoicism, 59, 62, 65; stoic, 60–61

Strauss, Leo, 42–43, 48–49, 217

subject, 104, 114–15, 147, 149, 176, 221; absolute, 152; as automaton, 214; desire of, 110, 122; desiring, 68, 217; fragmented, 11, 40, 90; paranoid, 192; and recognition, 111; and signifier, 131; sovereign, 39; speaking, 11, 15, 99, 104, 112. *See also* subjective fragmentation

subjective fragmentation, 67, 91

sublation, 108, 114, 115, 121; of being, 186

sublimation, 98–100, 103, 108; and courtly love, 111, 128–31, 138, 188; of desire, 200; and dialectics, 32–33, 122; obstacles to, 206; and the real, 69; sublimated, 106, 110, 112, 134

sublime, 78–79, 185

supplement: language as, 110

surplus, 92; bodily, 94, 99; of desire, 93, 102; of the letter, 180; universals as, 32. *See also* excess

symbolic, 13, 41, 65, 141, 189; limitation of, 33

symptom/symptomatic, 6–7, 82, 144–45, 160, 191; and ambivalence, 90, 99; of desire, 207; Lacan's, 26–27; projection of, 193; somatic, 72; and transference, 157–58; of writing, 109

syncope, 60–61

Tausk, Victor, 214, 253n43

technē, 211

tenson(s), 109, 111–12, 123, 242n13

Teresa of Avila, 2, 9, 206

textual analysis, 7, 226n25

Theweleit, Klaus, 253n42

thing, the, 8, 10, 74, 102, 125; dialectics of, 64; itself, 4, 194; in the world, 75. *See also* Das Ding

the woman. See woman, the

Thomism, 4; Thomist, 4, 34, 215; Thomistic, 16–18

topology, 157

transference, 31, 131, 156–57, 159–61, 163, 216; transferential, 149

translatio, 135

translation theory, 134. See also *translatio*

transvestitism. *See* Schreber, Daniel Paul

trauma, 103, 225; and representation of desire, 33; and the One, 60

triangle, 107, 140–41; as wholeness, 107

trieb, 134

trinity, 107, 110, 140–42

troubadour(s). *See* courtly love

tuché, 44–46, 62

tyranny, 50

Uexküll, 71–72

uncanny, 78, 82, 185–86, 191, 249n53

uncertainty, 33, 167–68

unconscious, 1–6, 65, 68, 77, 205; articulation of, 193, 196; and Boethius, 47; and Christianity, 138; concealed, 33; desire of, 141, 197; "discovery of," 43–44, 188; drives, 12; Gawain's, 194–99; and God, 46–47, 136, 222; knot of, 130, 146, 189, 192, 197; and law, 62; like a language, 9, 12, 31, 43–44, 48, 145; medieval, 188;

unconscious *(continued)*, in the Middle Ages, 194, 197; navel of, 146, 191, 207; as a real, 8–9, 11, 15, 19, 45–46, 51, 74, 103, 105, 112, 126, 153, 192, 196, 202–4; repressed, 203, 207; riddle of, 194, 207; structure of, 33; as transhistorical, 7, 9, 109, 151; as a universal, 9, 31, 112, 146; universality of, 151
unity, 129, 140, 177; and goodness, 47
universal, 13, 41, 55, 58, 63–64, 142, 151, 154; category, 4, 12–13, 16, 31–32, 101, 103, 147, 176, 196; cause, 153; crossed out, 75; forms, 214; and human, 78; language, 162; (non)knowledge, 205; universalism, 12; universalizing, 19; vs. particular, 154, 167, 172
universals, 2, 6, 10, 19, 21–22, 33, 40, 48, 64, 67, 102, 215; existence of, 10; quarrel of, 2–6, 12–15, 23, 26–27, 32, 34–36, 50–51, 63–64; real of, 32, 36, 55, 58, 75, 102, 216, 221
unknowability: 168; of unconscious, 202
unknowable, 33, 115, 138

Valabrega, Jean-Paul, 141
Vance, Eugene, 3, 235n4
virtue, 149–51
voyeurism, 88–89; as ambivalent, 90

William of Ockham: and free will, 22; and nominalism, 27, 38
Wolf Man, 32, 90, 103
woman, 143; as category, 51, 56; as cause of desire, 143; as impossible, 65; and *jouissance*; Schreber's desire to be, 208–10
woman, the, 98, 101–2, 109, 131; as category, 102; vs. lack, 101
woman, the, 32, 50–51, 56, 66–67, 74–75, 101–2, 138; as being, 75; as universal real, 88
wordplay, 4–5. See homonymn(s); neologism(s)

Zeno's paradox, 108
Žižek, Slavoj, 1, 18, 36, 210, 242n18
Zumthor, Paul, 5, 7, 146

Erin Felicia Labbie is assistant professor of English at Bowling Green State University in Ohio, where she teaches medieval studies and critical theory and has affiliate status with the Program in American Culture Studies. She has published articles on medieval literature and psychoanalysis.